The Nikon Guide

The Nikon Guide

A Modern Camera Guide Series
(Revised Edition)

JOHN C. WOLF

AMPHOTO
American Photographic Book Publishing
An Imprint of Watson-Guptill Publications
New York, New York 10036

To my parents, who bore with me, and still do.

 Published in New York, New York by Amphoto: an imprint of Watson-Guptill Publications, a division of Billboard Publications, Inc.

Library of Congress Cataloging in Publication Data
Wolf, John C.
The Nikon guide.

(A Modern camera guide series)
Includes bibliographical references and index.
1. Nikon camera. 2. Photography—Handbooks, manuals, etc. I. Title. II. Series: Modern camera guide series.
TR263.N5W64 1981 771.3'1 80-28143

ISBN 0-8174-5046-7
ISBN 0-8174-5045-9 (pbk.)

Manufactured in the United States of America

Acknowledgments

The author wishes to thank a number of people by name, in addition to many others who helped to make this book possible.

Mr. Richard LoPinto of Ehrenreich Photo-Optical Industries, Inc., Nikon's U.S. distributor, who provided me with information about the latest Nikon equipment and photos of the hardware.

Mr. Frank Diamond and Ms. Barbara Schwartz, of Gilbert, Felix, & Scharf, Inc., and Mr. Gene Hosansky of AC & R, Inc., who gave me last-minute updates on technical specifications.

The staff at Amphoto, especially Mark Iocolano, Lynn Burrasca, and Richard Liu, who shepherded the book through editing and production.

Modernage Custom Darkrooms, Inc., one of New York's finest photographic laboratories, who made almost all the black-and-white prints in this book, to my very exacting specifications.

My wife, Susan, who kept the author going while he kept the book going, and typed the manuscript as well; and my kids, Alexandra and Benjamin, who kept the author entertained when he was supposed to be working.

All equipment photos are courtesy of Nikon, Inc. All other photographs are by the author, unless otherwise credited.

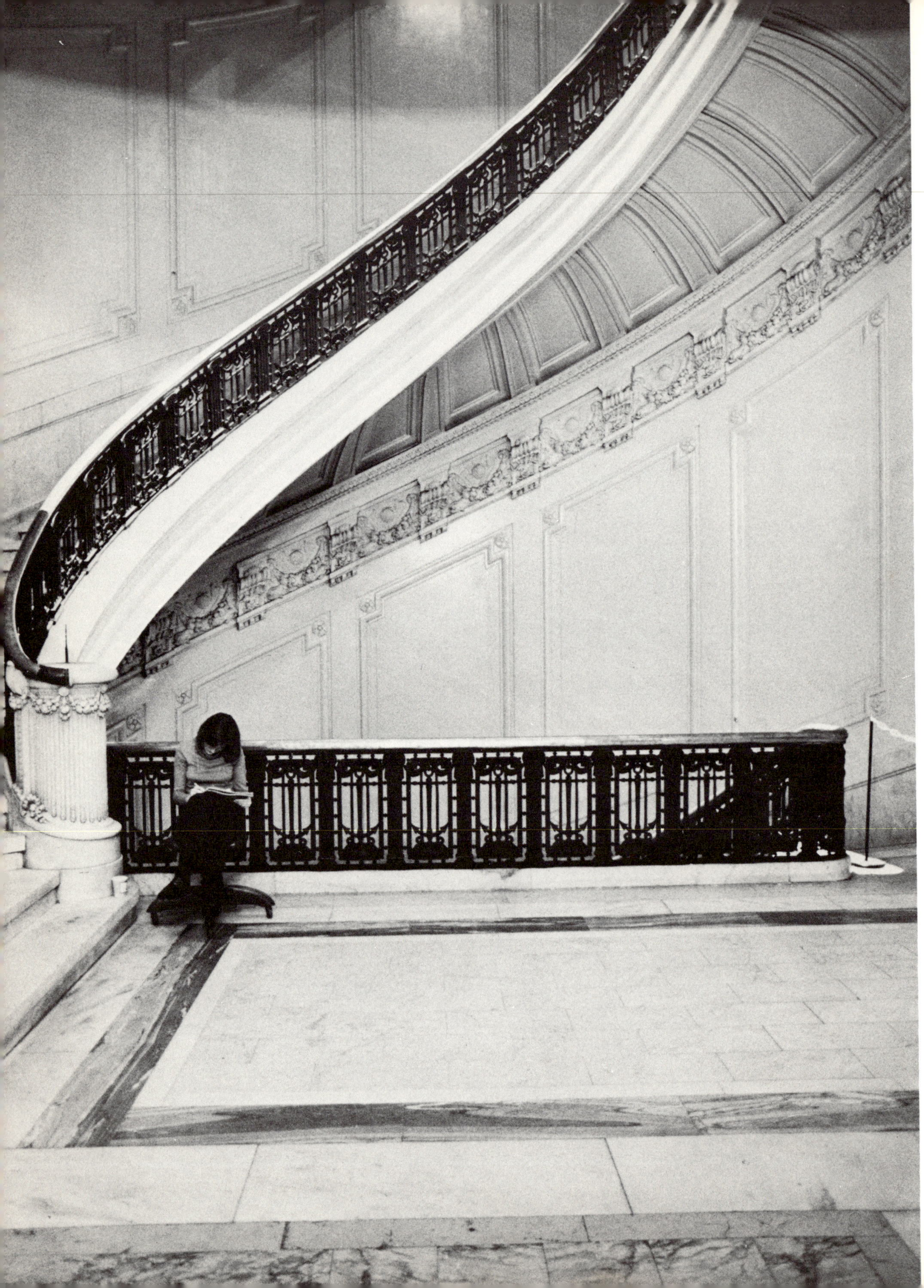

Table of Contents

Introduction

Since 1959, Nikon single-lens reflexes have revolutionized 35 mm photography. They have also paved the way for hundreds of thousands of amateur and professional photographers to revolutionize their own photographic work. By combining optical and mechanical excellence with ruggedness and convenience, Nikon cameras permit the casual snapshooter to get pictures of professional quality quickly and easily. The more serious amateur can add to his equipment to advance and explore ever more sophisticated realms of photographic excellence. For the professional, the virtually unlimited capabilities of the Nikon system provide the means of taking every kind of photograph known, under every circumstance imaginable.

The purpose of this book is to help you get the most out of *your* Nikon. It will describe the various Nikon cameras, viewfinders, lenses, and other accessories—both current and older models—and then discuss in simple terms how to use them. But this is intended to be more than a simple how-to guide to hardware. By explaining certain basic photographic principles, by describing and illustrating various picture-making options, by suggesting new areas of photography to explore, we hope to stimulate your visual imagination.

The Nikon Guide is designed to show you *why* certain things are done, as well as how. For as good as Nikon equipment is, *it* doesn't "make good pictures"; *you* do. The more you understand of the photographic process, the more able you are to apply your precision equipment intelligently. The fewer "rules" you obey blindly, and the more choices you see in almost every picture-taking situation, the more likely it is that your photographs will be unusual and memorable, or to use that over-used and abused term, "creative."

Whatever your present level of skill in photography, good equipment will help you to better it. Nikon equipment is among the best there is, and this book will assist you in determining what additional items you will want to acquire to expand your own system. But most of all, we hope to help you to think photographically, so that your choice of equipment, and its use, will lead to the most satisfying photographic results: better pictures.

When you get right down to it, that is the only reason to own a Nikon in the first place.

CHAPTER 1

The Nikon Single-Lens Reflex Cameras

All current Nikon (and Nikkormat) cameras are 35 mm single-lens reflex cameras manufactured by Nippon Kogaku K.K. (Japan Optical Company, Ltd.), of Tokyo, Japan. They are imported into the United States, where they are distributed by Nikon, Inc., a subsidiary of Ehrenreich Photo-Optical Industries, Inc. (EPOI), of 623 Stewart Ave., Garden City, New York 11530. The cameras share many common characteristics: their "family" similarities make them one of the most respected lines of precision instruments ever produced, and their uniformity of performance, from one model to another, is best expressed by the slogan "progress which defies obsolescence."

THE NIKON COMPANY

Nippon Kogaku K.K. was founded in 1917, principally as a manufacturer of optical instruments. The firm began making its own lens components in 1923 and complete lenses, for aerial photography, in 1929. Its first lenses for standard cameras were brought out in 1935. In its early years nearly all of the company's output was purchased by the Japanese government, but this output had expanded to include microscopes, telescopes, and binoculars, as well as lenses for other makes of 35 mm cameras.

In 1948, Nippon Kogaku brought out its own first 35 mm camera—the Nikon Model I, a rangefinder model—and accompanying Nikkor lenses. This innovation led to the famous "S" series of rangefinder Nikons which were produced through 1959. The firm's reputation was established internationally in 1950, when U.S. photographers covering the Korean War brought home several of the Nikkor lenses they had purchased in Japan and used in combat. These lenses, and the Nikon S cameras which followed them, were of such high quality that they completely revised world opinion about Japanese manufacturing standards. By the time the Nikon F—the company's first single-lens reflex (SLR)—was introduced, in 1959, "Nikon" had become synonymous with optical and mechanical excellence. The cameras were well on their way to becoming the most popular professional cameras in the world.

The basic Nikon F of 1959 incorporated many of the principles that keep Nikon the dominant force in 35 mm SLR photography. This camera, manufactured with various improved viewfinders through 1972, was entirely modular in concept. Lenses, viewfinders, backs, and other accessories were removable and interchangeable from one camera or model to another; the basic camera body remained the same. In fact, although the current generation of Nikons is substantially improved over that first model, most Nikon products are fully compatible from the earliest to the latest camera. This compatibility is the crux of "systems" photography.

Since earlier Nikon reflexes, as well as the latest models, are alike in so many ways, their identical features will be discussed first, leaving their individual aspects for later. Those of the newest cameras which differ significantly, as in automatic exposure determination, will be covered in separate sections of this chapter and the one following.

EVOLUTION OF THE CAMERAS

The term "35 mm" refers to the use in the camera of 35-mm-wide film, or the type used for professional cinema. The film is loaded into special 20- or 36-exposure cartridges. The actual size of the negative or transparency made by the Nikon is 24 × 36 mm, or about 1" × 1½". This small picture led to the term "miniature camera" in former times, but advances in phototechnology in the past 50 years have made that term obsolete: Nikon slides and negatives are now capable of truly enormous enlargement, while retaining all their original sharpness, clarity, and texture. Thirty-five millimetre photography, as exemplified by the current Nikon cameras, dominates the photographic world today.

The concept of the single-lens reflex is not new, but has been carried to new lengths by Nikon cameras. It is simply a means whereby the photographer can see through the lens of the camera itself, rather than through an auxiliary viewing system. This is accomplished through a mirror-and-prism arrangement (thus, the term "reflex") that directs light from the lens to a ground-glass screen visible in the eyepiece. When the camera is fired, the mirror swings out of the path of the light, which then strikes the film. Once the exposure is made the mirror returns instantly to the viewing position.

The advantages of the mirror-and-prism arrangement are manifold. The most important convenience is that the photographer sees *exactly* what the camera will photograph and thereby avoids such mistakes as photographing chopped-off heads, feet, and edges that ruin so many family snapshots. A second advantage is that since the image entering the camera is cast upon a visible surface—the screen—focusing is reduced to a certainty, simply because the photographer sees directly what is (and what is not) in focus. Moreover, the Nikon viewing systems may be augmented by special attachments that facilitate viewing under unusual circumstances—magnifiers, corrections lenses, and the like. These special features will be discussed in Chapter 4, "Nikon Accessories." The third advantage is that because of their reflex construction, the Nikons can be built to measure light as it falls on the focusing screen, thus making possible through-the-lens metering and exposure determination.

In fact, the major changes in the Nikon F, through the years, have concerned light measurement. The *Photomic* finder of 1962 combined an eye-level viewfinder with a cross-coupled cadmium sulfide (Cds) exposure meter. The meter, however, was of the external, direct-reading type, and therefore might not have measured exactly what the lens "saw," especially if a filter or some other device were in front of or behind the lens. The *Nikon F Photomic T* was then introduced in 1964. This was the same Nikon F, but with a *through-the-lens* finder/meter. Light from the lens was bounced off the mirror and measured at the focusing screen; the information was then transmitted to a meter needle visible in the viewfinder, so the photographer could establish his exposure and set the camera controls without ever taking the camera from his eye. The Photomic T finder set the pattern for all subsequent Nikon viewfinder metering systems; the *Photomic TN*, of 1967, and the *Photomic FTN*, of 1969, both incorporated additional improvements, but retained the through-the-lens, modular characteristics of the earlier models.

Simultaneously, Nikon sought to accommodate those photographers who wanted to use Nikon's superb lenses (now numbering over 50) and other accessories, but who felt that a Nikon camera was beyond their means. In 1962 they brought out the *Nikkorex F* camera, which was discontinued in 1964. The next year the first *Nikkormat* camera appeared, and it, too, has evolved to the present day as an inexpensive line of cameras compatible with most Nikon lenses and accessories. A discussion of both these cameras is, how-

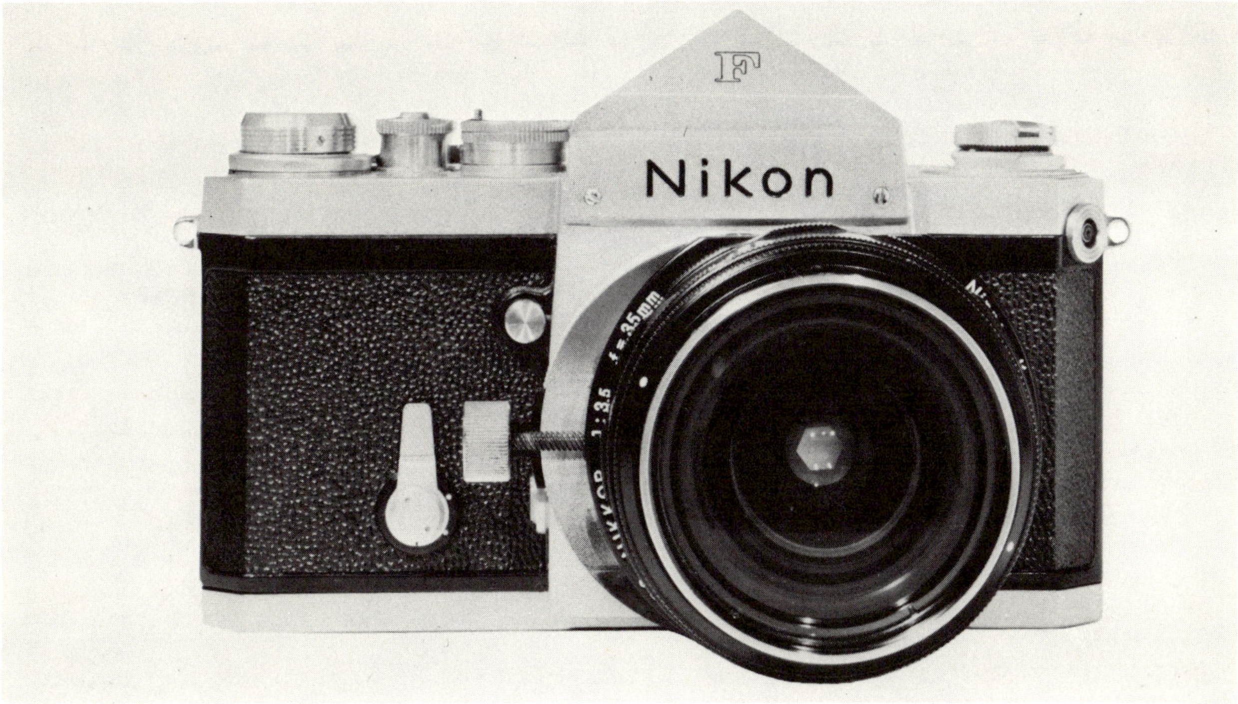

Original Nikon F, of 1959 (above), with pentaprism finder and PC Nikkor lens. Basic Nikon F3, of 1980 (below), also with eye-level pentaprism, no lens.

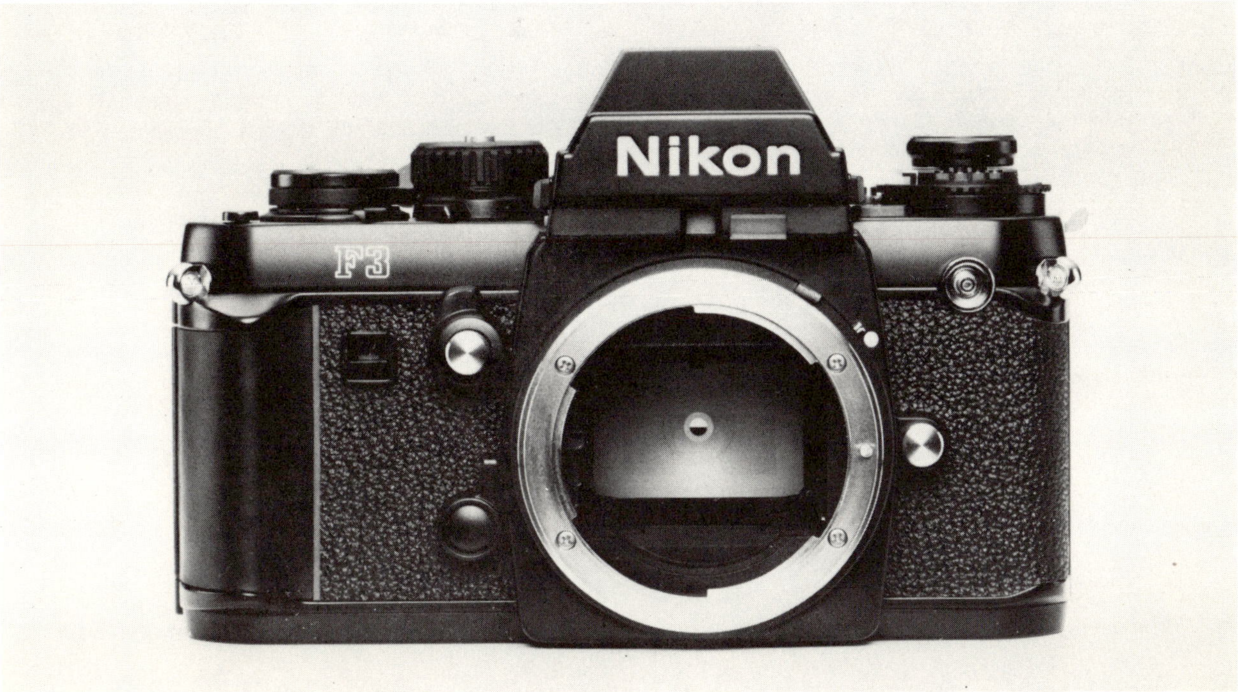

ever, beyond the scope of this book.

Durable and flexible as the Nikon F was—about 200,000 of them are still currently in use—by the early 1970's Nippon Kogaku felt they had taken the camera as far as it could go. An all-new camera, the Nikon F2, was unveiled in 1972.

Evolutionary rather than revolutionary in nature, the changes incorporated into the original F2 were such that they continued much of the compatibility with the earlier cameras (all the lenses and most of the accessories fit from one camera to the other), yet looked forward to a new generation of equipment. The Nikon F2 was to become the "basic" camera—much like the Nikon F of 1959—around which improvements could be made that would reflect the state of the art of photography, until the F3 of 1980.

In fact, the first modifications, the *Nikon F2 Photomic* and the *Nikon F2S Photomic*, both introduced in 1972, were, like the first Photomics, new finder/meters joined to the same camera body. The F2 Photomic finder turned the Nikon F2 into a through-the-lens metering camera, and the F2S Photomic finder added extra light sensitivity and light-emitting diodes (LED's) to replace the standard meter needle. These glowing lights permit the camera to be used in light so poor that ordinary meter needles cannot be read! Moreover, the F2S model could be combined with the EE Aperture Control Attachment (Model DS-1) to turn the camera into a shutter-priority, fully automatic camera.

Shortly thereafter, the *F2Sb Photomic* finder added silicon photocells to Nikon's formidable light-measuring equipment. Silicon is quicker to respond, freer of "memory" defects, and less subject to misinterpretation of colors than cadmium sulfide. An improved over/underexposure set of LED's, an eyepiece shutter, and an illuminator for the shutter-speed and aperture indexes were other features of the new finder. But these improvements only set the stage for Nikon's major news of the decade: an entire new generation of cameras, incorporating five new models introduced simultaneously, two of which were complete departures from the history of the Nikon nameplate.

In mid-1977, Nippon Kogaku brought out the cameras (and lenses) that revolutionized Nikon photography. The groundwork was laid by the introduction of the *AI-Nikkor* lenses. These automatic aperture-indexing (AI) lenses automatically program the meters of the new cameras, without special adjustments, while continuing to work with older models in precisely the same way as the older Auto-Nikkors. They also provide aperture direct reading (ADR), or the ability to *see* the aperture at which the lens is set directly through the viewfinder of any of the new cameras.

The *Nikon F2A Photomic* and *F2AS Photomic* were improved versions of the F2 and F2Sb finders, on the same reliable Nikon F2 body. Owners of the previous models were assured that their cameras could be brought up to date by merely replacing the finders. Better still, they could be certain that all the newer equipment—especially the lenses—would work with the older cameras. The principal departure in the new finders was the inclusion of a meter-coupling lever, which replaced the familiar Nikon coupling pin. This allows the corresponding meter-coupling flange (or "ridge") on the AI-Nikkors to make contact, thus assuring automatic alignment ("indexing") of the maximum apertures of the new lenses as each is mounted on the camera.

The *Nikon FM* was Nikon's first entry into the growing compact-camera field. Smaller by far than any Nikon SLR to that date, the FM has the advantage of all of Nikon's previous experience in 35 mm camera-making, and takes its best features from other Nikons. For example, the FM uses the same AI-Nikkors (or older Auto-Nikkors) as any other Nikon. It uses the same LED meter display as the F2AS Photomic, and even surpasses the big Nikon in that its meter system uses newly developed gallium photodiodes (GPD's), the latest improvement in meter sensitivity and responsiveness. This small marvel even has its own relatively inexpensive motor-drive unit (MD-12), which converts it into a fully integrated motorized camera capable of taking 3.5 frames per second (fps).

The *Nikon EL2* was Nikon's first fully electronic camera. It not only provides automatic exposure control, but also programs the electronic shutter to *any* speed required for absolutely precise exposure, even if that speed is 1/465 sec. or 1/19 sec. Like the other Nikons, the EL2 takes all Nikkor

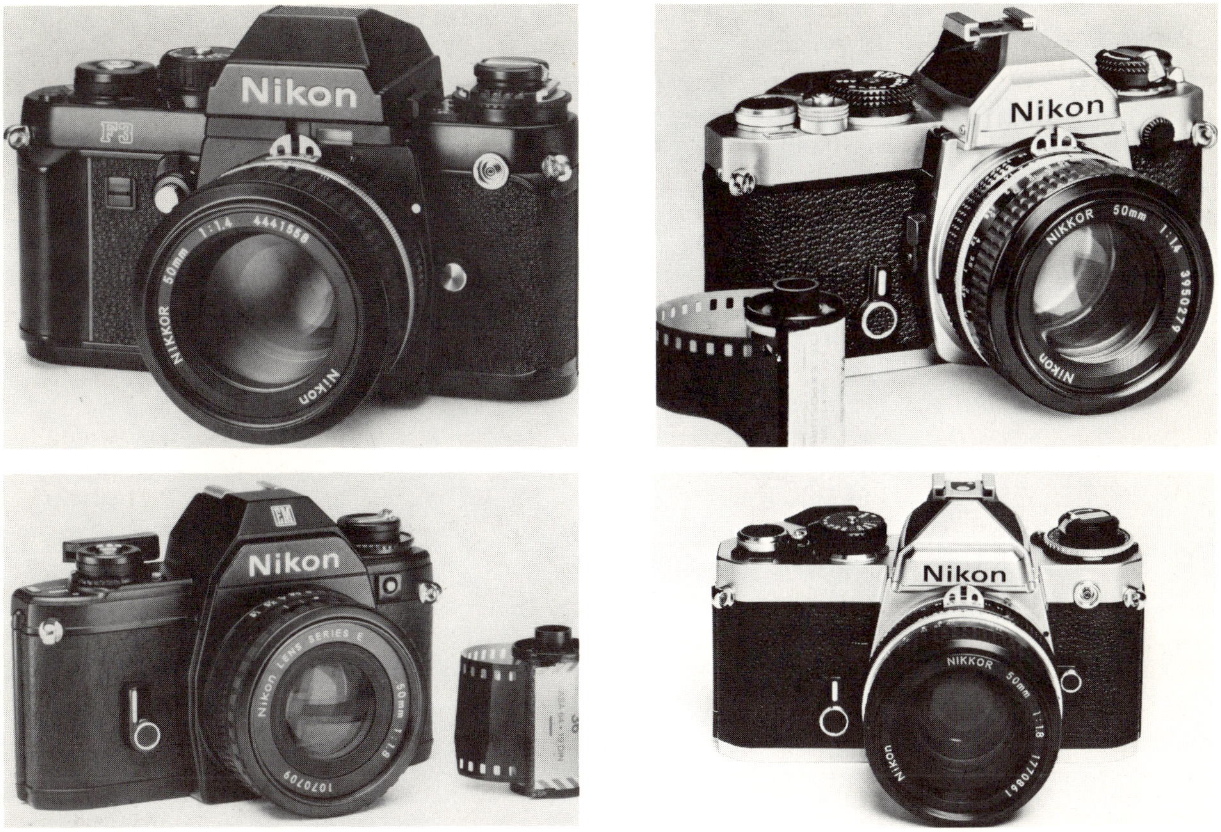

Current Nikon reflex cameras: Nikon F3 (top left); compact, metered-manual Nikon FM (top right); ultra-simplified automatic Nikon EM (bottom left); and compact/automatic Nikon FE (bottom right).

lenses and nearly all Nikon accessories.

The *Nikon FE* (1978), a still later entry, combines the fully automatic features of the EL2 with the compact size of the FM. It is Nikon's second electronic camera, with precise shutter programming for unerring aperture-priority automatic exposures. It uses all Nikkor lenses and accessories and adds interchangeable screens and automatic flash synchronization as well.

The *Nikon EM* (1979) carries the trend toward simplification and miniaturization a giant step further. An all-automatic camera with its own lens system, "dedicated" electronic flash, and flyweight motor-drive unit, the EM is the easiest Nikon to use. It is, however, as precise a photographic instrument as any previous Nikon, and uses most Nikon accessories. The EM is budget-priced, aiming for a large market of amateur photographers.

In 1980, Nikon brought together all the developments in electronics, metering, automatic exposure, size reduction, and mechanical improvement, added a few brand-new twists, and brought out their third basic professional model, the *Nikon F3*. Destined to be in the 1980's what the F and F2 were to the 60's and 70's, the F3 is a fully automatic electronic camera, with its metering and auto-exposure provisions (including auto-flash) built into the body, not the finder. Yet, the camera has interchangeable finders, backs, lenses (AI and ADR), and an enormous list of accessories.

We will examine the F and F2 first, then get to the F3.

CONSTRUCTION OF THE NIKON F AND F2 CAMERAS

The bodies of the two basic Nikon models are essentially similar: The F2 is distinguished by softer, more rounded contours and the word "Nikon" alone imprinted on its various finders; the Nikon F has an additional large engraved "F" on its finder. The two cameras are about the same size and weight and have fully interchangeable finders, screens, lenses, and backs. (The back and bottom plates of the Nikon F come off in one piece when the camera is opened; the back swings open on the Nikon F2, but may also be removed.) Both cameras have the same instant-return mirror; the same lensmount; the same film loading and unloading mechanism (although the rewind release is in different positions) and provisions for film flatness; and a self-timer in the same position. Many other features of the two cameras, which will be discussed, are nearly identical but are located in different places. Consult the accompanying illustrations to see where each feature is located on your camera.

SHUTTER

The shutters of both cameras are of the horizontal focal-plane type, with curtains made of titanium foil. Their speeds are one second, 1/2, 1/4, 1/8, 1/15, 1/30, 1/60, 1/125, 1/250, 1/500, 1/1000, and (on the F2) 1/2000 sec., plus B ("bulb": the shutter stays open as long as the shutter-release button is pressed) and T ("time": the shutter remains open until the dial is reset) on the Nikon F. The shutter of the F2 is also capable of timed, longer speeds of 2, 4, 6, 8, and 10 seconds, in conjunction with the self-timer. On the shutter-speed dial, next to the film-advance lever, the upper part of the fraction is omitted. The numbers inscribed on the dial (when there is no Photomic finder mounted over it) are: 1, 2, 4, 8, 15, 30, 60, 125, 250, 500, 1000, 2000 (on the F2), B, and T (on the F). On the Nikon F, the "60" is red, indicating that 1/60 sec. is the "X," or electronic-flash synchronization speed. On the Nikon F2, a red line between 60 and 125 indicates 1/80 sec., the X-synch speed for that camera. Numbers below this point are white; above, green. The F2 is capable of any intermediate speed between settings that are above 1/80 sec.

When any of the Photomic finders is mounted on either camera, the dial is covered by the finder, which has its own dial that also doubles as an ASA film-speed dial. A second set of shutter-speed numbers, which appears on the column of the dial, is visible from behind the camera, except for the "T" setting on the Nikon F. The shutter-release button is on the top plate of both cameras, next to the film-advance lever. It is surrounded by a finger-guard, which on the Nikon F also serves as an advance-rewind (A-R) switch, and on the Nikon F2 as a timer-locking (T-L) switch. The traverse (the time it takes the shutter curtain to travel across the film plane) is 14.5 milliseconds for the Nikon F. A 10-millisecond traverse for the F2 makes possible the higher, 1/2000 sec. top speed and the 1/80 sec. X-synch speed.

THE NORMAL LENS

The Nikon reflexes are currently supplied with a choice of three standard lenses: the 50 mm *f*/2 AI-Nikkor, the 50 mm *f*/1.4 AI-Nikkor, or the 55 mm *f*/1.2 AI-Nikkor. Before the "AI" designation, these lenses were called "Auto-Nikkors," or just "Nikkors." The AI versions, designed for automatic aperture indexing and direct aperture readout on the latest F2 Photomic finders, are easily distinguished from the older versions by their meter-coupling "ridge" on the aperture ring, the *slotted* meter-coupling prong sticking up in front of the aperture scale, and the second aperture scale—in smaller numbers—behind the prong. Later versions of the Auto-Nikkors and the AI-Nikkors also

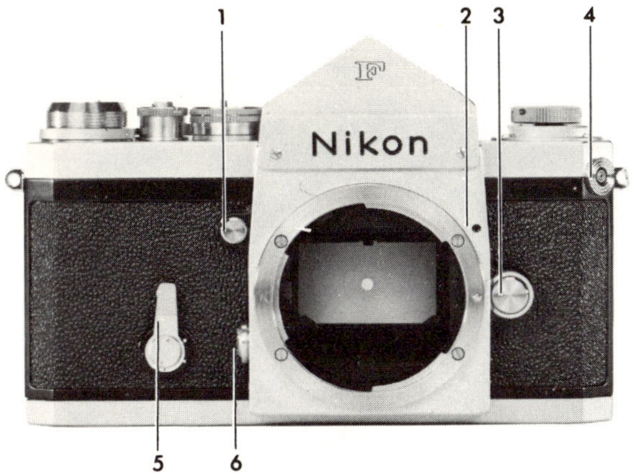

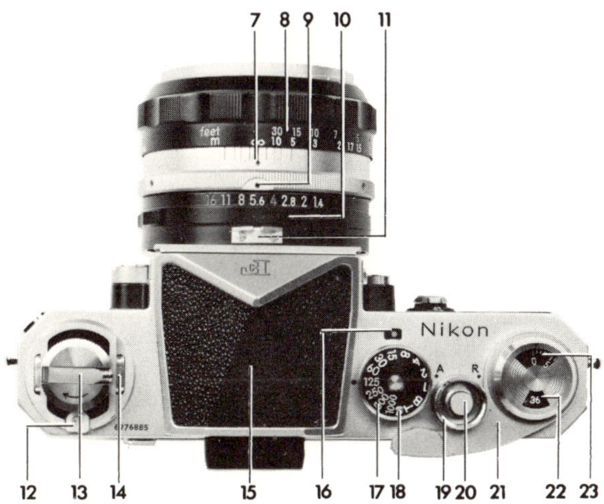

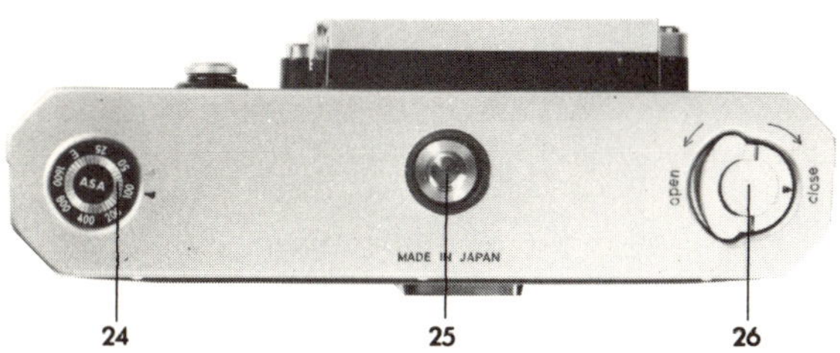

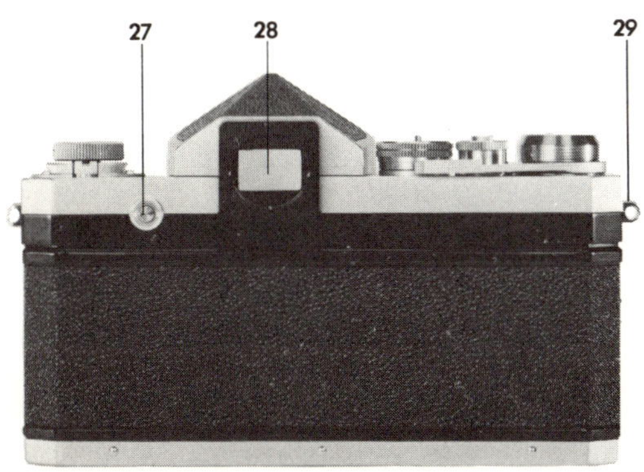

Parts for Nikon Photomic F

1. Depth-of-field preview button: press to preview how much background or foreground is in or out of focus
2. Black dot: for alignment with the black dot on the lens barrel when removing the lens.
3. Lens-release button: unlocks the lens for removing or changing lenses
4. Flash terminal: accepts synchro cord for electronic flash or flash units other than Nikon BC-7
5. Self-timer: can be set for picture-taking delay up to 10 seconds
6. Mirror-lock knob
7. Distance indicator with depth-of-field scale: arrow points to the focused distance on the distance scale. Color-coded markings give depth of field for different apertures
8. Focusing ring with distance scale: easy-to-grip, knurled ring for quick accurate focusing. Distance scale shows focused distance or can be used to prefocus to a measured or estimated distance
9. Aperture-indicator dot: when lined up with the f/numbers engraved on the aperture ring, indicates the aperture set
10. Lens-aperture ring: rotates to set the lens diaphragm at the desired f/stop
11. Slotted coupling prong: for coupling diaphragm to exposure meter
12. Flash contact: for cordless Flash Unit BC-7.
13. Film-rewind crank: handle folds out for smooth, effortless film rewinding
14. Accessory shoe: accepts the Nikon Flash Unit BC-7 or Flash Unit Adapter
15. Eye-level pentaprism viewer: for comfortable, easy viewing, composing, and focusing.
16. Synch selector window: has color-coded markings
17. Shutter-speed dial: for setting shutter speed from 1/1000 to 1 second plus B and T
18. Synch-selector ring: for flash synchronization control. Sets the camera's synchronization mechanism to match the type unit or bulb in use
19. A-R ring: sets for film advance (A) and rewind (R)
20. Shutter-release button: with screw thread for cable release
21. Film-advance lever: advances the film, cocks the shutter, and operates the frame counter
22. Film-load reminder: can be set at 20 or 36
23. Frame counter: indicates the number of frames exposed
24. Film-speed reminder dial: can be set for color or black-and-white and for ASA ratings from 25 to 1600
25. Tripod socket: threaded to accept standard tripod screw
26. O/C lock: for removing camera back
27. Finder-release button: for removing interchangeable finder and viewing screen
28. Finder eyepiece: permits comfortable viewing of the entire screen
29. Neckstrap eyelet

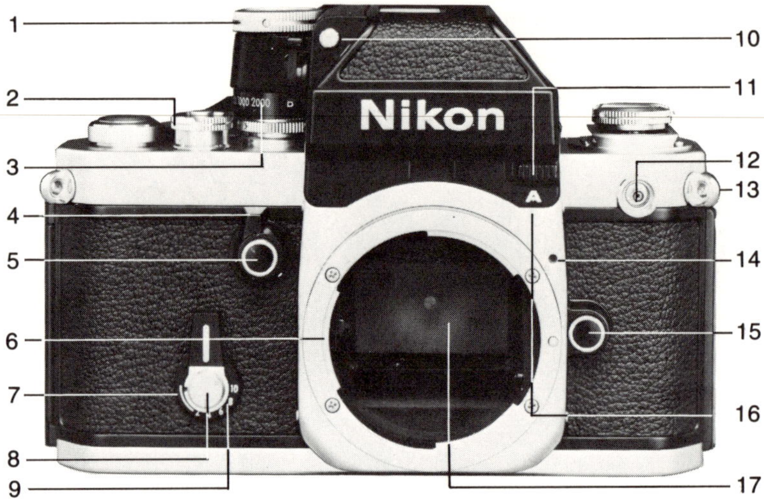
1
2
3
4
5
6
7
8
9
10
11
12
13
14
15
16
17
Nikon
A

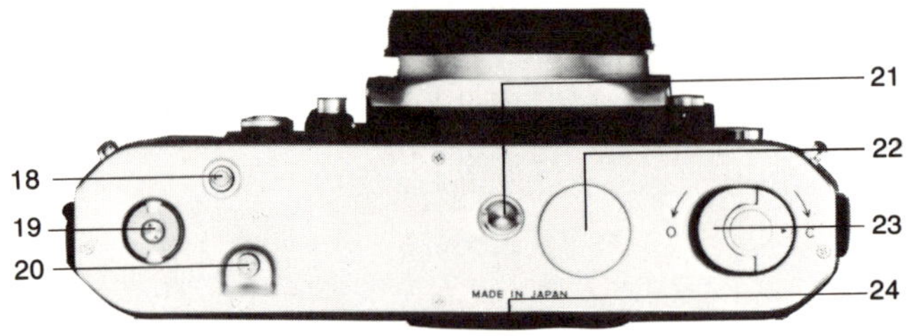
18
19
20
21
22
23
24
MADE IN JAPAN

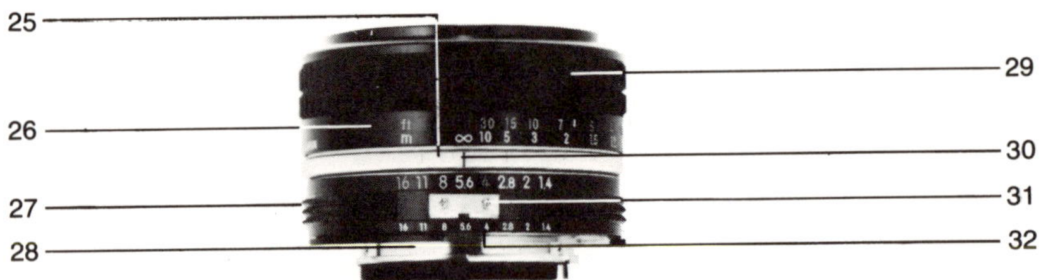
25
26
27
28
29
30
31
32

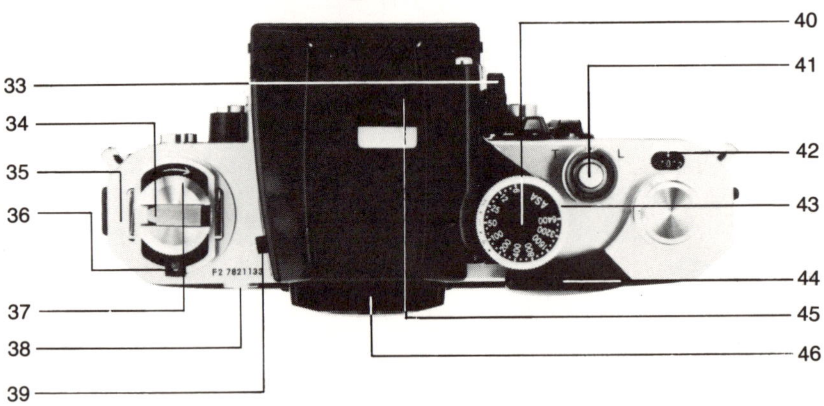
33
34
35
36
37
38
39
40
41
42
43
44
45
46
ASA
F2 7821133

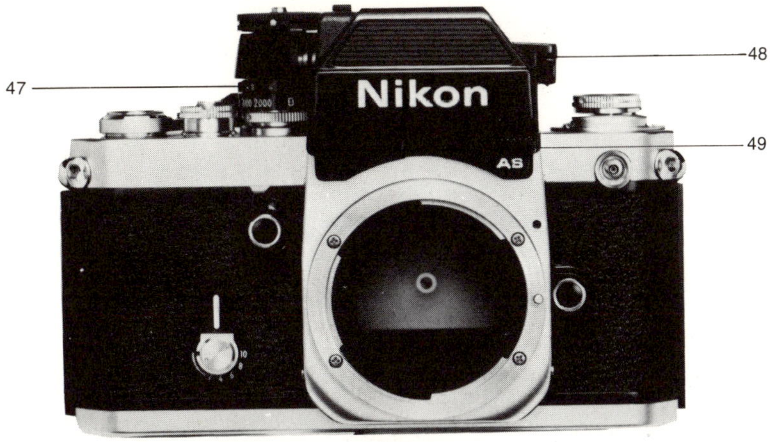

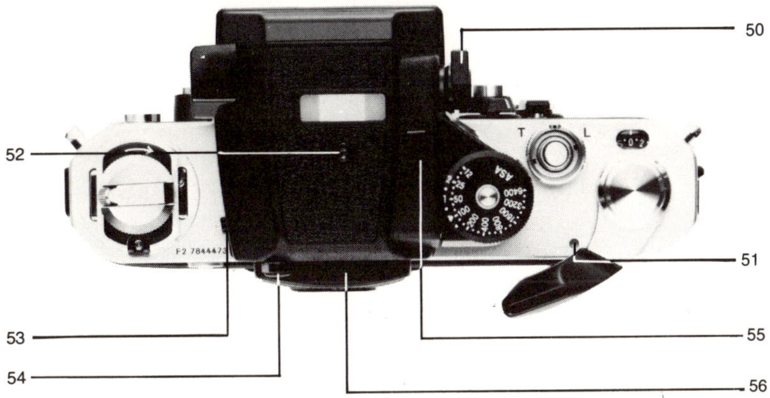

Parts Nomenclature for Nikon F2A Photomic, With Additional Parts for Nikon F2AS Photomic (right side)

1. Shutter-speed dial
2. T-L fingerguard
3. Shutter-speed scale
4. Mirror-lockup lever
5. Depth-of-field preview button
6. Lens-mounting flange
7. Timer index
8. Self-timer
9. Timer scale
10. Power-check button
11. Coupling lever release
12. Threaded sync terminal
13. Neckstrap eyelet
14. Lens-mounting index
15. Lens-release button
16. Meter-coupling lever
17. Reflex mirror
18. Motor drive shutter-release coupling
19. Motor drive film-advance coupling
20. Film-rewind button
21. Tripod socket
22. Battery chamber
23. O/C key
24. Memo holder
25. Depth-of-field indicators
26. Distance scale
27. Aperture ring
28. Meter coupling ridge
29. Focusing ring
30. Aperture/Distance-scale index
31. Meter-coupling shoe
32. Aperture-direct-readout scale
33. Finder-release lever
34. Film-rewind crank
35. Accessory shoe
36. Hot-shoe contact
37. Film-rewind knob
38. Finder-release button
39. Ready-light contact
40. ASA film-speed scale
41. Shutter-release button
42. Frame counter
43. ASA film-speed index ring
44. Film-advance lever
45. Meter window
46. Viewfinder eyepiece (w/ready-light)
47. Extra-long exposure scale
48. EE aperture control contacts
49. Coupling lever release
50. Finder-release lever
51. Meter ON index
52. External "correct exposure" indicator
53. Ready-light contact
54. Eyepiece shutter control
55. Illuminator switch
56. Viewfinder eyepiece (w/ready-light)

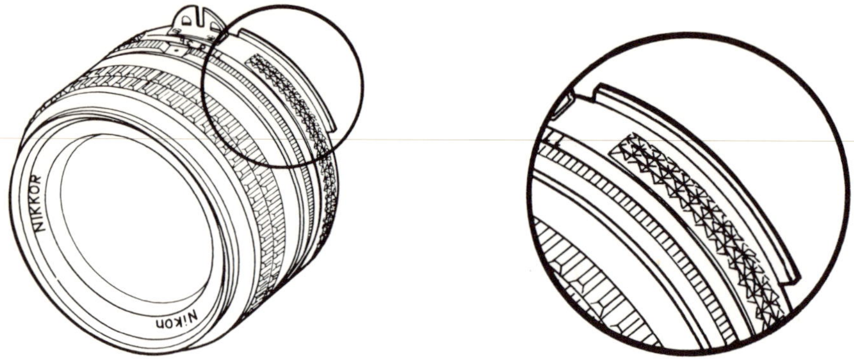

Newest AI-Nikkor lenses have meter-coupling ridge, slotted meter prong, and secondary aperture scale. In other respects they are similar to older Auto-Nikkors.

have an improved, rough, knurled-rubber focusing ring. In any case, with minor exceptions, the Auto-Nikkors and AI-Nikkors are optically alike, and on an older camera will work the same way. (But note: *Only* the AI-Nikkors will give automatic indexing with Nikon F2A and F2AS Photomic finders.)

All the normal lenses are very similar. They all stop down to *f*/16, with intermediate *f*-stops, and focus from approximately 1.5 feet to infinity (see the accompanying table). All have fully-automatic diaphragms that permit viewing, focusing, and metering at full aperture. When the shutter is released, the diaphragm stops down to the preselected aperture and reopens after the exposure. The lenses couple to any Photomic exposure meter. They take screw-in filters, lenshoods, and other accessories in the 52 mm size. The 55 mm *f*/1.2 and the 50 mm *f*/1.4 are constructed of seven optical elements; the 50 mm *f*/2 lens of six.

Nikon is one of a very few companies which not only makes its own lenses, but also its own optical glass in its Japanese factories. In fact, all parts of the lenses are made by Nikon. Because of the extreme control Nikon exercises, the Nikkors are among the most highly corrected lenses in the world, eliminating most aberrations over the full range of apertures and focusing distances. Nikon's exclusive "integrated coating" (IC), which is visible as the bluish or purplish cast of the front lens element and is actually a multiple coating of fluorides and other ingredients, is applied to various lens elements to improve light transmission and image contrast, and to reduce flare caused by internal reflections. Other remarkable improvements in lens design pioneered by Nikon include the "floating element" system and extra-low dispersion (ED) glass, which will be discussed in Chapter 3, "Lenses."

Suffice it to say that the normal Nikkors are superb lenses for most photographic applications, especially in low-level light. The principal choice among them depends upon your need for lens "speed": The *f*/1.4 is one stop "faster" than the *f*/2, and the *f*/1.2 is ½ stop faster than the *f*/1.4.

NORMAL NIKKOR and NIKON LENSES

Lens	Elements	Angle of View	Minimum f/stop	Minimum Focus	Filter Size	Weight
50 mm f/1.4	7	46°	f/16	17.7″	52 mm	9.2 oz
50 mm f/1.8	7	46°	f/16	19.7″	52 mm	14.5 oz
50 mm f/1.8 Series E	6	46°	f/22	24″	52 mm	4.8 oz
50 mm f/2	6	46°	f/16	17.7″	52 mm	7.8 oz

DEPTH-OF-FIELD TABLE FOR ALL 50 mm NIKKOR LENSES — FEET

Object Distance	f/1.4	f/2	f/2.8	f/4	f/5.6	f/8	f/11	f/16	Reduction Ratio 1 :
∞ (ft)	187′ —∞	131′ —∞	93′ 7″ —∞	65′ 6″ —∞	46′ 10″ —∞	32′ 9″ —∞	23′ 10″ —∞	16′ 5″ —∞	∞
30	25′ 11″ —35′ 8″	24′ 6″ —38′ 9″	22′ 10″ —43′ 11″	20′ 8″ —54′ 10″	18′ 5″ —81′ 11″	15′ 9″ —321′	13′ 5″ —∞	10′ 9″ —∞	175.5
15	13′ 11″ —16′ 3″	13′ 6″ —16′ 11″	13′ —17′ 9″	12′ 3″ —19′ 4″	11′ 5″ —21′ 10″	10′ 5″ —27′ 1″	9′ 3-7/8″ —39′	7′ 11-1/2″ —146′	86.88
10	9′ 6-1/8″ —10′ 6″	9′ 3-7/8″ —10′ 9″	9′ 7/8″ —11′ 2″	8′ 8-3/4″ —11′ 9″	8′ 3-5/8″ —12′ 7″	7′ 8-7/8″ —14′ 2″	7′ 1-3/4″ —16′ 9″	6′ 3-7/8″ —24′ 4″	57.33
7	6′ 9-1/8″ —7′ 3-1/8″	6′ 8″ —7′ 4-1/2″	6′ 6-1/2″ —7′ 6-3/8″	6′ 4-3/8″ —7′ 9-3/8″	6′ 1-5/8″ —8′ 1-3/4″	5′ 10″ —8′ 9-1/4″	5′ 5-7/8″ —9′ 8-3/8″	5′ —11′ 9″	39.61
5	4′ 10-5/8″ —5′ 1-1/2″	4′ 10″ —5′ 2-1/8″	4′ 9-1/4″ —5′ 3-1/8″	4′ 8-1/8″ —5′ 4-1/2″	4′ 6-5/8″ —5′ 6-1/2″	4′ 4-5/8″ —5′ 9-3/4″	4′ 2-3/8″ —6′ 2-3/8″	3′ 11″ —6′ 11-1/2″	27.78
4	3′ 11-1/8″ —4′ 7/8″	3′ 10-3/4″ —4′ 1-3/8″	3′ 10-1/4″ —4′ 1-7/8″	3′ 9-1/2″ —4′ 2-3/4″	3′ 8-5/8″ —4′ 4″	3′ 7-1/4″ —4′ 5-7/8″	3′ 5-3/4″ —4′ 8-1/2″	3′ 3-1/2″ —5′ 1-1/2″	21.86
3.5	3′ 5-3/8″ —3′ 6-3/4″	3′ 5″ —3′ 7″	3′ 4-5/8″ —3′ 7-3/8″	3′ 4-1/8″ —3′ 8-1/8″	3′ 3-3/8″ —3′ 9″	3′ 2-3/8″ —3′ 10-3/8″	3′ 1-1/4″ —4′ 1/4″	2′ 11-3/8″ —4′ 3-7/8″	18.90
3	2′ 11-1/2″ —3′ 1/2″	2′ 11-1/4″ —3′ 3/4″	2′ 11″ —3′ 1″	2′ 10-5/8″ —3′ 1-1/2″	2′ 10-1/8″ —3′ 2-1/8″	2′ 9-3/8″ —3′ 3-1/8″	2′ 8-1/2″ —3′ 4-3/8″	2′ 7-1/8″ —3′ 6-3/4″	15.94
2.5	2′ 5-5/8″ —2′ 6-3/8″	2′ 5-1/2″ —2′ 6-1/2″	2′ 5-3/8″ —2′ 6-5/8″	2′ 5-1/8″ —2′ 7″	2′ 4-3/4″ —2′ 7-3/8″	2′ 4-1/4″ —2′ 8″	2′ 3-5/8″ —2′ 8-7/8″	2′ 2-5/8″ —2′ 10-3/8″	12.97
2	1′ 11-3/4″ —2′ 1/4″	1′ 11-3/4″ —2′ 1/4″	1′ 11-5/8″ —2′ 3/8″	1′ 11-3/8″ —2′ 5/8″	1′ 11-1/4″ —2′ 7/8″	1′ 10-7/8″ —2′ 1-1/4″	1′ 10-1/2″ —2′ 1-3/4″	1′ 9-7/8″ —2′ 2-5/8″	9.996

OTHER BODY FEATURES

Film-advance lever. One stroke of 120° (135° on the Nikon F) cocks the shutter, advances the film, and operates the frame counter. On the Nikon F2, the lever also switches the Photomic meter on or off.

Frame counter. This feature indicates the number of pictures taken. It automatically resets to "S" (start) when the camera is reloaded.

Self-timer. This ten-second delaying mechanism permits vibration-free pictures without a cable release. It also lets the photographer get into the picture. On the Nikon F2, the self-timer is used with the shutter release to get extra-long shutter speeds of two to ten seconds.

Mirror-lock knob. This knob locks the reflex mirror in the "up" position. It is necessary for certain lenses, which extend into the camera body, and for vibration-free shooting.

Depth-of-field preview button. This button stops the lens down to the selected aperture in order to preview the depth of field at that aperture.

Shutter-release button. This button trips the shutter; it is also threaded for the Nikon cable release. On the Nikon F, it is surrounded by the A-R fingerguard: the A position is for advancing film; R is for rewinding. On the Nikon F2, it is surrounded by the T-L fingerguard: the T position activates the timer for long exposures; the L position locks the shutter; the central position is for standard operation.

Rewind crank. This handle folds out to rewind film quickly.

Accessory shoe. Found around the rewind crank, this shoe takes flash units and other accessories. A built-in electrical contact wires the camera for cordless flash units (the "hot" shoe).

Flash synchronization system. In addition to the hot shoe, both cameras have a single flash-synch terminal, which permits the attachment of flashbulb (M) or electronic-flash (X) units. The Nikon F2 has automatic-synch switchover; the Nikon F, a manual synch-selector ring. (See Chapter 6, "Flash and Electronic Flash," for details.)

Camera-back lock. This very secure means of opening and closing the camera is found on the baseplate, and must be unfolded and twisted to open the camera.

Tripod socket. Threaded to accept a standard tripod screw, this socket allows the camera to be mounted on a tripod for additional steadiness.

Battery chamber (Nikon F2 only). This chamber houses the batteries that power the meter. On the Nikon F, the batteries are in each finder/meter.

Rewind button (Nikon F2 only). This button releases the film-advance mechanism so the film can be rewound (Nikon F uses the A-R ring).

Lensmount system. This system consists of a rugged, universal Nikkor bayonet, a lens-release button, and an alignment index dot.

Finder-release button. This button permits easy interchange of finders.

Slotted take-up spool. This spool permits fast loading of film. Newer models have a multi-slotted spool, which is even more convenient.

Film pressure plate and film roller. Found inside the camera back, these devices insure maximum image sharpness by keeping the film absolutely flat.

Film-advance and shutter-release couplings (Nikon F2 only). Found on the baseplate of the F2, these features allow swift, sure linkage with the motor-drive unit (MD-2).

VIEWING AND METERING SYSTEMS

The unparalleled versatility of the Nikon cameras is principally due to the wide variety of viewfinders and exposure meters devised over the years for the F and F2 models. The interchangeable viewing devices provide normal viewing; enlarged viewing; viewing at unusual angles; a vast number of focusing aids, in the form of screens and eyepiece accessories; precise exposure measurement; and always a bright, clear image of 100 percent of the picture you are about to take. Most Nikon cameras are sold with one or another of the pentaprism viewfinders, usually of the Photomic metering type, so we will concentrate on those and will emphasize the latest models for the Nikon F2. It will be noted that earlier models, especially those for the Nikon F, are in many ways similar.

The Viewfinder

The Nikon F or F2 supplied with any of the Photomic finders, the eye-level pentaprisms, or the Action Finder (called the Sportsfinder on the Nikon F) give a large, clear image that is right side up and laterally correct (left is left and right is right). This image shows 100 percent of the scene to be photographed, and it clearly shows what is in and out of focus. The image magnification with the 50 mm lens set at infinity is 0.8×; with the 55 mm lens it is 1:1 (life size). These magnifications make it easier to follow a scene with the naked eye, and then look through the viewfinder, since there is no abrupt change of image size.

With the regular K screen mounted on the camera, the photographer sees a 3 mm diameter circle in the center of the image, bisected by a horizontal line. This is the split-image rangefinder spot: when the picture is out of focus, the two half-images do not align; when the scene is in focus, the split image reunites. Surrounding the split-image spot is a circular band (or "doughnut") of microprisms, 1 mm wide. This microprism band further assists focusing—it is actually a collection of small prisms—by breaking an out-of-focus image into a shimmering blur. When the lens is correctly focused, the image is sharp. The remainder of the screen consists of a matte Fresnel field, which, with a condenser lens, distributes light evenly over all parts of the viewfinder screen. (In older Nikon F2's and most Nikon F's, the standard focusing screen was the Type A, which is the same as the K screen without the microprism doughnut. Yet other screens are available, and will be covered shortly.) The screen also has an etched 12 mm circle, which indicates the area favored by the "center-weighted" meter of all recent Photomic finders.

The split-image rangefinder and microprism areas of the screen work best in average conditions, with subjects of definite detail, and at fairly large apertures. At smaller apertures with certain larger lenses, and in ultra-closeup photography, they will not work well or at all; at *f*/4.5 the split-image spot and, at *f*/8, the microprism generally darken. The matte field, however, can be used under any circumstances, and it has the advantage of focusing anywhere on the screen. An out-of-focus area looks blurry on it; an in-focus image looks sharp.

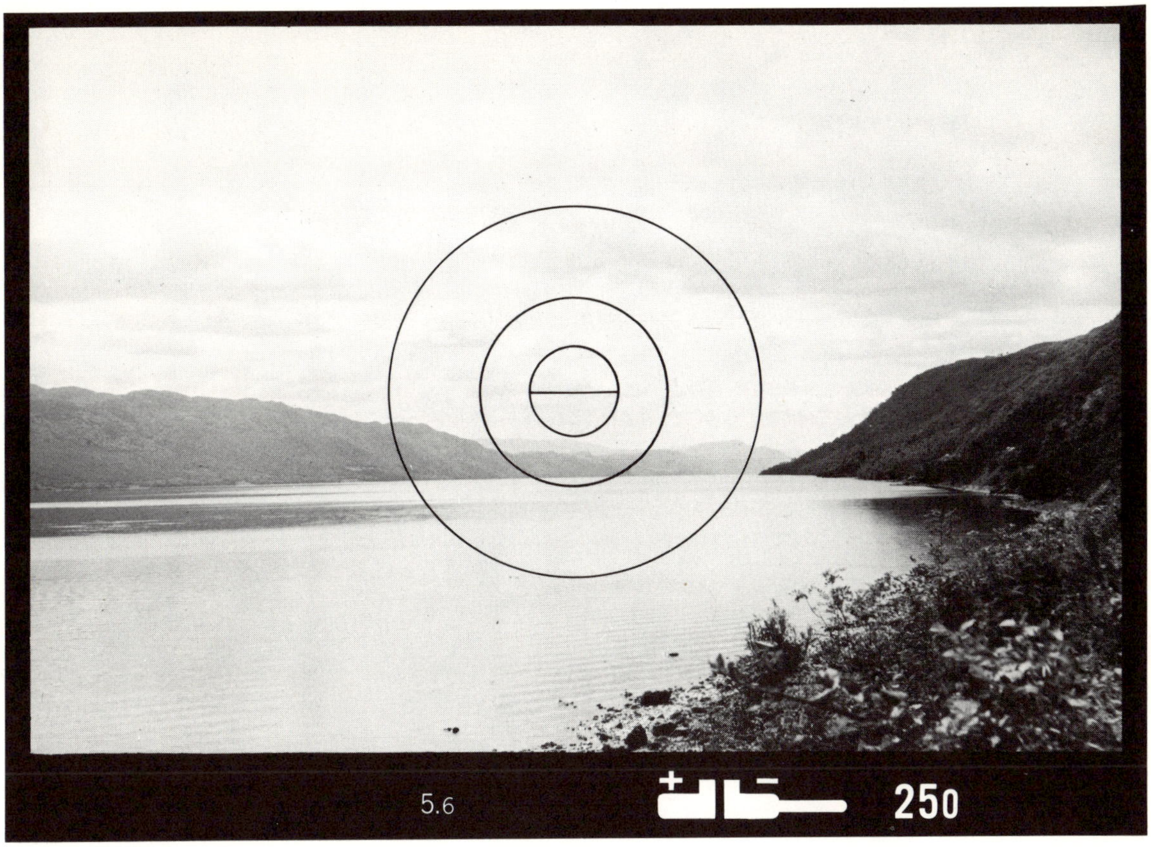

The viewfinder of the Nikon F2A Photomic is typical of the newer Nikon models: split-image rangefinder, microprism band, 12 mm metering circle, exposure information below picture area.

Interchangeable Focusing Screens

As noted above, there is a wide variety of focusing screens for the F and F2 to suit specific purposes. Although the K or A screen is suitable for general photography, certain circumstances and even individual preference suggest the use of one or another of the screens, as each has different optical properties and each type combines different focusing aids. Since some screens are better suited to focusing with certain lenses than others, and some require exposure compensation with yet other lenses, consult the accompanying charts to determine which screens to use with which lenses, depending upon the type of Photomic finder you have. There are presently 19 interchangeable Nikon screens, divided into 12 types.

Type A. Described above, this type is used for general photography.

Type L. This is the same as Type A, except the split-image rangefinder line is at a 45-degree angle. It is used for general photography.

Type B. A matte Fresnel field, with a 12 mm fine-ground central matte focusing circle, this type is used for long telephoto shots and close-ups at small apertures.

Type C. A fine-ground matte field with a 4 mm central clear spot and cross hair, its uses are photomicrography, photomacrography, and other applications requiring parallax focusing on aerial images.

Type D. This is a plain fine-ground overall matte field, for use with long lenses and close-ups.

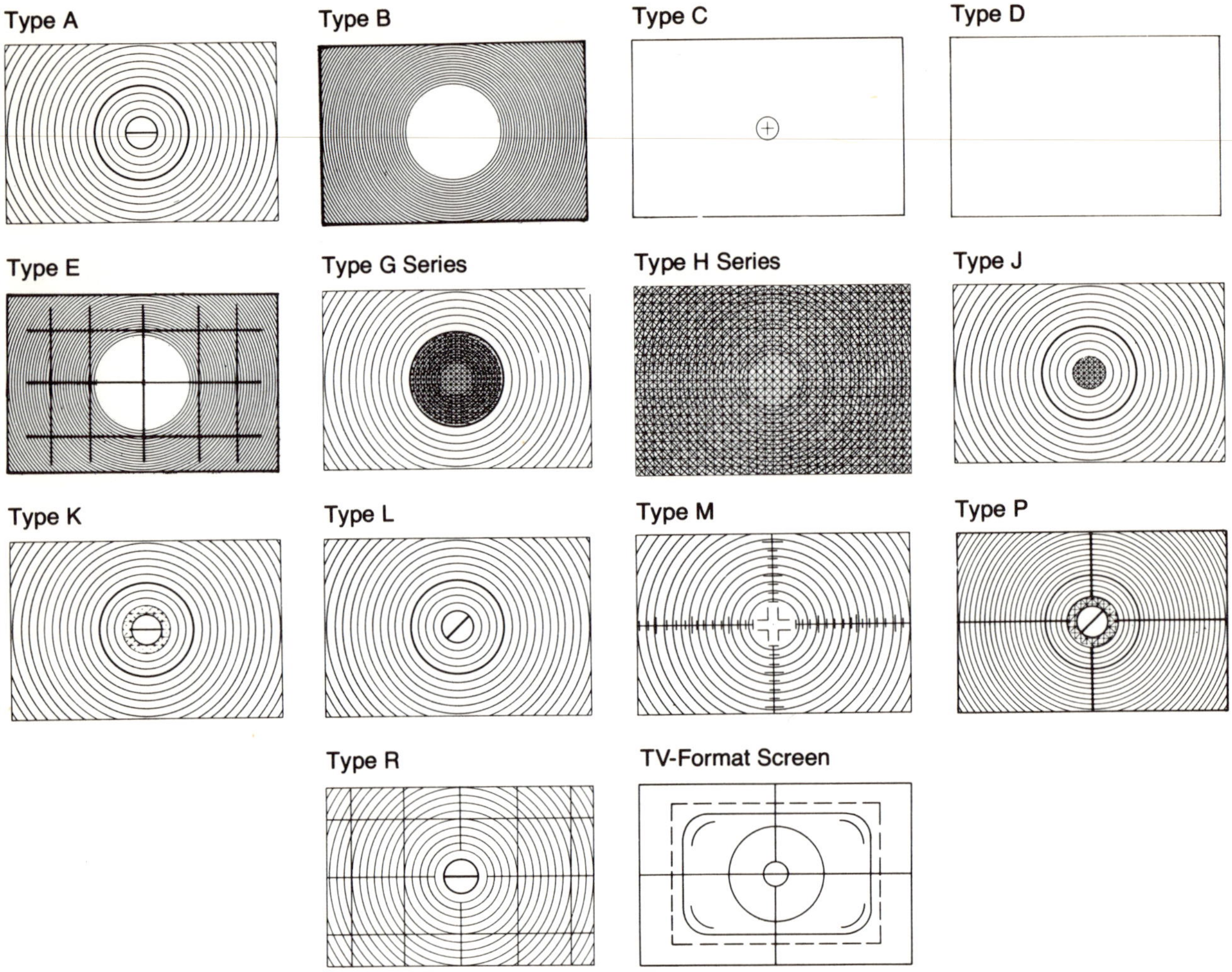

Interchangeable focusing screens for Nikon F3, F2, or F models. See text for details.

Type E. This is a matte Fresnel field with a 12 mm fine-ground matte central focusing circle and etched vertical and horizontal lines in a grid pattern. Useful for precision composition and architectural photography, it is ideal with PC-Nikkor lenses.

Types G1, G2, G3, and G4. Each of these four types has a clear Fresnel field with a 12 mm central microprism focusing spot. They are useful for focusing in very poor light. Four models are available for use according to the focal length of the lens. (See the accompanying chart.)

Types H1, H2, H3, and H4. Each of these types has a clear Fresnel field with an overall microprism pattern, which permits rapid focusing on any part of the screen in poor light. A Fresnel-free center spot is an additional feature. Four models are available for use with specific focal lengths. (See the accompanying chart.)

Type J. A matte Fresnel field with a 4 mm central microprism spot and a 12 mm (meter preference) etched circle, this type is used for general photography.

Type K. Described above, this type is used for general photography.

Type M. A fine-ground Fresnel field with a 5.5 mm clear spot and a double cross hair, as well as vertical and horizontal scales marked in 1 mm increments, this type is useful in dim light for focusing on aerial images, for close-ups, and for photomicrography.

Type P. The same as Type K, except that the

FOCUSING SCREEN SELECTOR CHART

= Excellent

= Acceptable

The image is brilliant from edge to edge, but the central rangefinder, microprism or cross-hair area is dim. Focus on the surrounding matte area.

= Acceptable

Slight vignetting or moire phenomenon (in the case of the microprism) affects the screen image. But the image on film shows no traces of this.

= Acceptable

Incompatible with any lens having a maximum aperture larger than f/2.8 since this decreases the efficiency and accuracy of the screen rangefinder. The in-focus image in the central spot may prove to be slightly out of focus on film. Focus on the surrounding matte area.

Caution: The rear surface of the screen is made of acryl resin. Special care should be taken to protect it from scratching or excessive pressure.

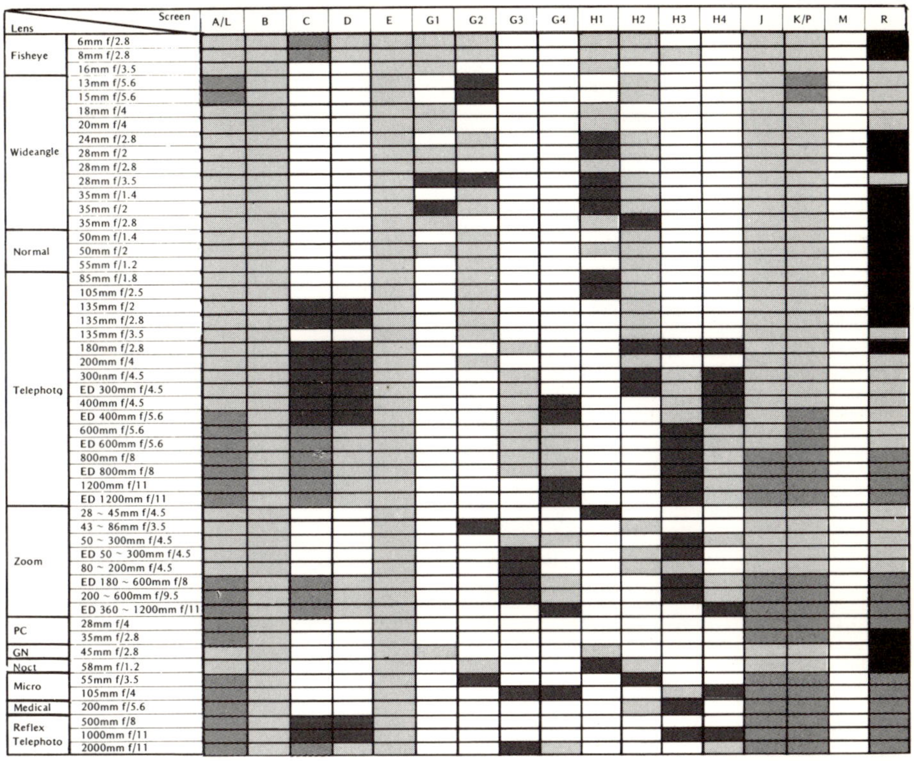

split-image rangefinder line is at a 45-degree angle, this type is used for general photography.

Type R. This is the same as Type A, but it has etched grid lines for precise composition and slightly different rangefinder prisms, making it suitable for lenses with smaller maximum apertures of *f*/3.5 to *f*/5.6.

Meter Indicators

Below the picture area of a Nikon F2 (or above that of a Nikon F), fitted with any of the Photomic finders, is a grouping of numbers with either a needle or symbols illuminated by light-emitting diodes (LED's). These indicators represent the principal function of the Photomic series of finders: through-the-lens exposure measurement. In all cases, the numbers refer to the shutter speed at which the camera is set as well as the lens aperture (on F2 Photomics). The function of the needle or LED's will be described in detail shortly, but let us say here that when the needle is centered or the LED's correctly illuminated, the camera is set for an unerringly accurate exposure, regardless of lens, film, or scene.

THE PHOTOMIC METERS

All Photomic viewfinders built for Nikon F and F2 cameras since 1964 are through-the-lens reading, maximum-aperture meters. You can take your readings with the diaphragm open with any AI-Nikkor or Auto-Nikkor, and the lens will automatically "stop down" to the shooting aperture as you release the shutter. Only the original Photomic finder of 1962 did not read light coming through the lens; thereafter, every Photomic finder took its readings directly from the focusing screen.

Direct reading automatically compensates for any filter, attachment, or extension device placed in front of or behind the lens, thereby ending forever such headaches as "exposure factors" and calculations. Moreover, every Photomic since the Photomic TN of 1967 has been "center-weighted"; that is, it takes 60 percent of its measurement from the central 12 mm of the viewing screen. (This is why most screens have an etched 12 mm circle.) Since a photographer usually places the most important part of the subject at or near the center of the screen, this is where the principal measurement counts. Even if the main subject is to the side, it is still easy to center the subject while metering, then switch back to the desired position before shooting.

The center-weighted meter is not a "spot" meter, which would measure only a tiny, prescribed area of the scene; nor is it an "averaging" meter, which would give equal weight to all parts of the area in view. The averaging meter often gives undue emphasis to background illumination or extraneous objects in the field of view. The spot meter, on the other hand, takes in so small an area that several readings must be made of a broader scene, averaged mentally, then set on the camera. To do so is tricky and time-consuming. Center-weighting gives 40 percent of its consideration to the rest of the scene—so extreme variations in brightness or contrast are included in its calculations—but the principal concentration is on the central 1/8 portion of the screen. Thus, the meter is less likely to be "fooled" by excessive backlighting, or extreme brightness falloff toward the edges of the screen.

Nikon F Photomic, Photomic T, and TN

These three finder/meters, introduced in 1962, 1964, and 1967, respectively, gradually incorporated the basic components of the modern Photomic meters. The first combined the viewfinder and the cross-coupled Cds meter; the second introduced through-the-lens measurement; and the third incorporated the center-weighted principle. All three have very similar needles, which are to be centered in a notch for correct exposure and are visible through the eyepiece or in a window on top of the finder.

The *Photomic* was a direct-reading meter with an external Cds cell, which was pointed at the subject or could be used as an incident light meter. It could be set for film speeds from ASA 10 to ASA 1600, and had provisions for dialing in filter factors. An acceptance-angle converter was used to change the light-collecting angle of the meter to correspond with lenses of 35 mm to 135 mm focal length.

The *Photomic T* was an "averaging," through-the-lens meter, with a measuring range of EV 1 to EV 18 with the 50 mm *f*/1.4 lens at ASA 100, and a film-speed range from ASA 10 to ASA 1600. This model introduced full-aperture metering, though it could be used as a stop-down meter with non-auto lenses and non-coupled accessories. The finder required a rather complicated method of attaching lenses, necessitating manual cross-coupling of lens and meter indexes. An aperture window on the back of the finder assured proper indexing, but the meter had to be re-indexed with every change of lens or film speed.

The *Photomic TN* was the first Photomic meter to center-weight the exposure measurement, taking 60 percent of the reading from a 12 mm central circle of the screen. The measuring range of the TN was EV 2 to EV 17 with the 50 mm *f*/1.4 lens at ASA 100, and the range of film speeds was greatly expanded from ASA 20 to ASA 6400. This finder can be distinguished from the earlier Photomic T by an engraved white "N" behind the meter "off" switch, and a smaller, battery-check button in front of it. The mechanical operation of the TN was like that of the T, including the awkward lens–film-speed indexing, but exposure procedures anticipated the more sophisticated Photomic FTN.

Nikon Photomic FTN

The most advanced finder for the original Nikon F, the Photomic FTN combined the center-weighted exposure measurement of the FT with several dramatic improvements. The measuring range of the FTN is EV 2 to EV 17 with the 50 mm *f*/1.4 lens at ASA 100, with a film-speed range of ASA 6 to ASA 6400. When lenses are changed, the FTN automatically indexes the film speed to the maximum aperture (from *f*/1.2 to *f*/5.6). The

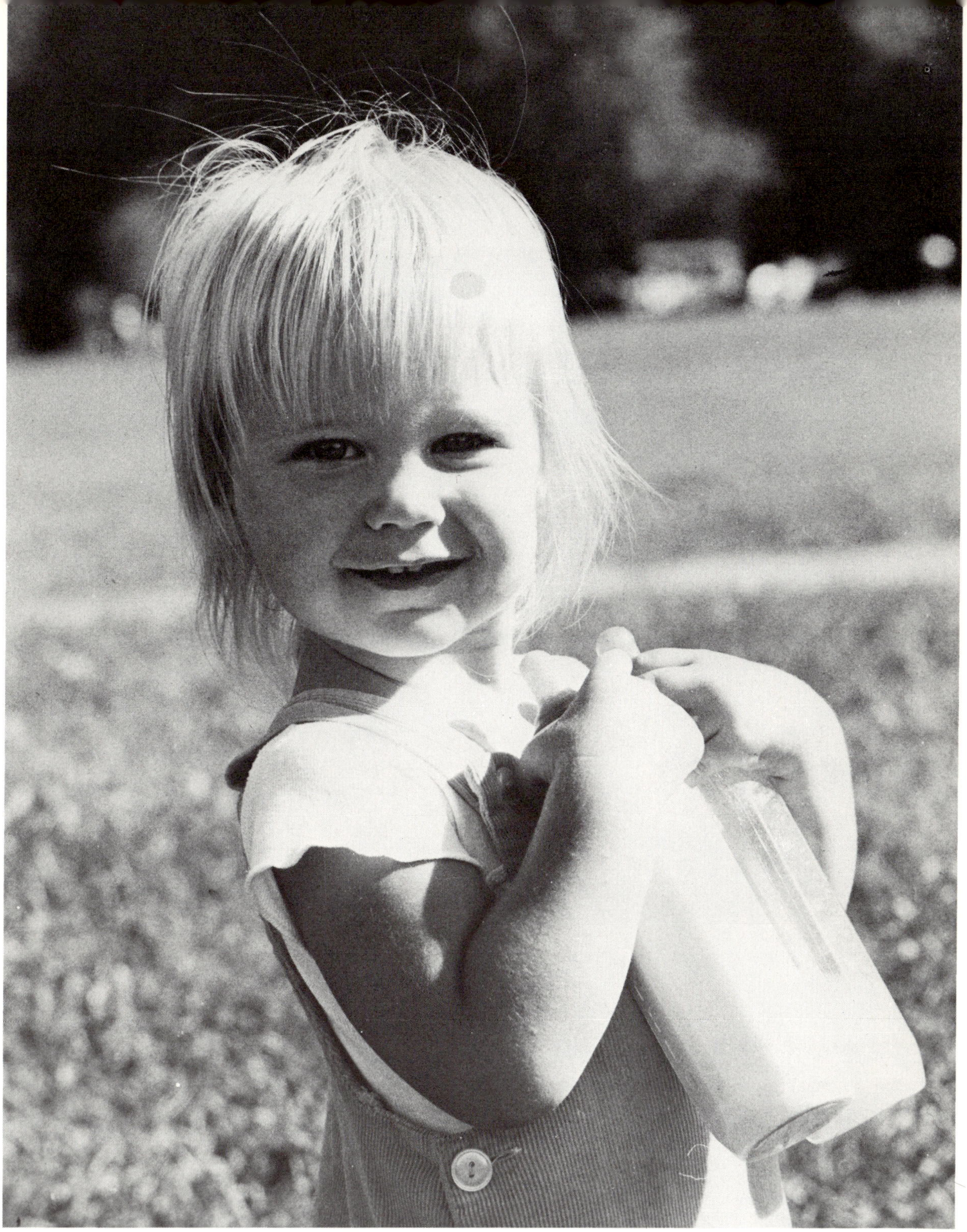

A hard-to-meter shot: The bright summertime glare would swamp an averaging meter, causing underexposure of the little girl's face, but Nikon's center-weighted meters take the shadow areas into account, with a slight loss of highlight rendition, even compensating for a filter factor. Taken on Ilford FP-4 (ASA 125), through a medium yellow filter, at 1/125 sec. and *f*/5.6, with the 105 mm Nikkor.

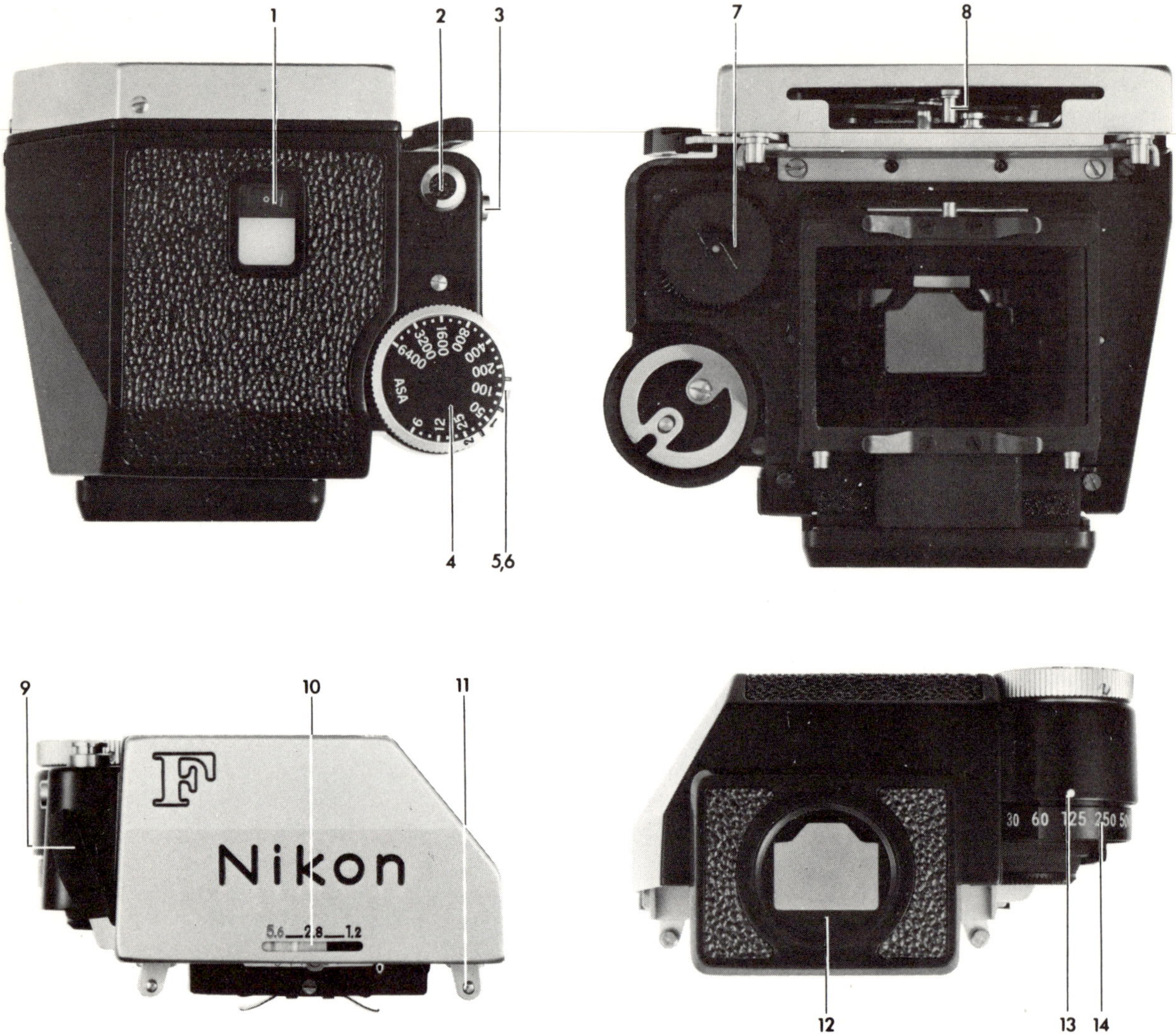

Parts Nomenclature for Photomic FTN Finder

1. Meter window: houses the meter needle for exposure determination and battery checking
2. Meter switch-off button
3. Meter switch-on button
4. ASA film-speed dial: for setting the film speed from ASA 6–6400
5. ASA scale index ring: marked with a red triangular index and exposure-correction scale for exposure compensation with certain lens-focusing screen combinations
6. Shutter-speed selector: turns in either direction for setting the desired shutter speed
7. Battery-chamber cover
8. Coupling pin: connects the meter mechanism to the lens diaphragm for full-aperture exposure measurement
9. Finder-lock lever: press to remove or attach the finder
10. Maximum-aperture scale: check to verify if the meter is set for the maximum aperture of the lens used
11. Clamps: for positioning the finder on the camera
12. Viewfinder eyepiece: accepts screw-in finder eyecup and eyesight correction lenses
13. Shutter-speed index
14. Shutter-speed scale

finder itself must still be indexed to the lens. The shutter-speed range, which is visible through the eyepiece, is from four seconds (at "T"), and two seconds (at "B"), through the regular range of one to 1/1000 sec. The meter switch has been combined with the battery-check button, and a pincer clamp with a large, locking lever has been added to fasten the finder on the camera more securely. This finder is easily distinguished from the older ones by its maximum-aperture scale (*f*/1.2 to *f*/5.6) on the front of the finder. Like all Photomic finders except the latest, the FTN links to the coupling prong of Auto-Nikkor lenses by means of a coupling pin on the bottom front of the finder.

The Photomic FTN is powered by two 1.3V mercury batteries (Mallory PX-13, PX-625, or equivalent) inserted into the bottom of the finder. Next to the ASA scale is an index that permits compensation for transmission differences of certain lens/screen combinations, from −½ stop to +2 stops. As with previous models, the finder/meter gives full-aperture readings by centering a needle in the eyepiece—or another on top of the prism—in a notch, either by adjusting the shutter speed or the aperture. The FTN can also give stop-down readings with lenses or accessories that cannot be coupled with the meter.

Nikon F2 Photomic (DP-1)

The first of the Photomic finders for the Nikon F2, this finder brings to the newer camera all the advantages the Photomic FTN gave the Nikon F, plus a few of its own. The meter, of center-weighted, through-the-lens Cds design, has a measuring range of EV 1 to EV 17 with the 50 mm *f*/1.4 lens at ASA 100. Its film-speed range is ASA 6 to ASA 6400. The finder automatically indexes a new lens (with maximum apertures from *f*/1.2 to *f*/5.6) to a preset film speed. The finder itself must be indexed to the lens, but this procedure has been much simplified. The meter couples to Auto-Nikkor lenses via the standard Nikon coupling pin (which can be used even with the latest AI-Nikkors). A maximum-aperture indicator window, on the front of the meter, assures proper coupling and indexing. The full aperture range of the meter is *f*/1.2 to *f*/32, and the range of shutter speeds is one second to 1/2000 sec., plus "B" (two seconds). It is capable of being adjusted to compensate for various lens-screen transmission factors.

The F2 Photomic finder takes full-aperture readings with any Auto-Nikkor or AI-Nikkor and is capable of stop-down measurement with non-coupled lenses or other attachments. It is powered by the two 1.5V silver-oxide batteries (Mallory MS-76, Eveready S-76, or equivalent) in the Nikon F2's baseplate. The camera's film-advance lever acts as the on-off switch, but the finder has its own battery-check button. (Incidentally, the F2 model Photomics *cannot* be used on a Nikon F body.)

Correct exposures are obtained by centering a needle in a notch, visible below the picture area in the finder eyepiece—which also has over (+) and under (−) exposure indicators—by varying either the shutter speed or the aperture. Also visible in the finder are the actual shutter speed and *f*-stop at which the camera is set. A second meter window, on top of the prism, shows the needle when the camera is viewed from above.

A very useful innovation in the DP-1 finder is the built-in flash ready light, which connects with Nikon electronic-flash units, via a special ready light contact. This light illuminates when the flash unit is fully charged and ready to fire. The finder also takes the Photomic Illuminator (DL-1), which provides extra light to read the interior scales in poor illumination. The round eyepiece of the finder can also accept a number of other accessories. (See Chapter 4, "Nikon Accessories.") A new Nikon F2 Photomic comes supplied with a Type A focusing screen. It has the same secure type of clamp and finder-release lever as the earlier FTN, and can be distinguished from other Photomic finders by its battery-check button. All F2 Photomic finders are black with a white "Nikon" on them.

Nikon F2S Photomic (DP-2)

An entirely new concept in Nikon finder/meters, the F2S Photomic presents two startling innovations: First, it eliminates the meter needle entirely, replacing it with solid-state light-emitting diodes (LED's), which glow to indicate correct exposure; second, the F2S is made to be linked with the EE Aperture Control Attachment (DS-1), which

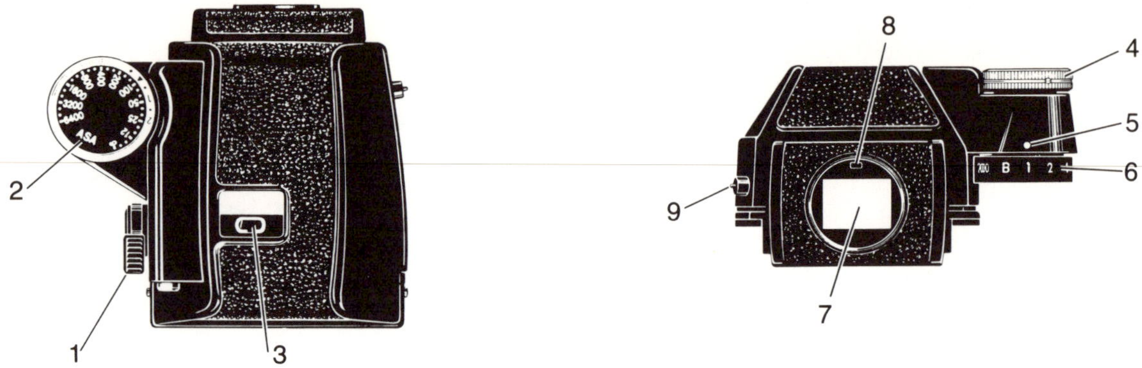

Top and Rear Views of the Photomic Finder DP-1

1. Finder-release lever: press to remove the finder
2. ASA film-speed dial: for setting the film speed, from ASA 6–6400
3. Meter window: for exposure control when settings are made away from the eyes
4. Shutter-speed selector
5. Shutter-speed index
6. Shutter-speed scale
7. Finder eyepiece: accepts the screw-in finder eyecup, eyesight correction lenses, and the eyepiece magnifier
8. Ready light: shows when the Nikon speedlight is fully charged without having to move the eye from the viewfinder
9. Ready-light contact

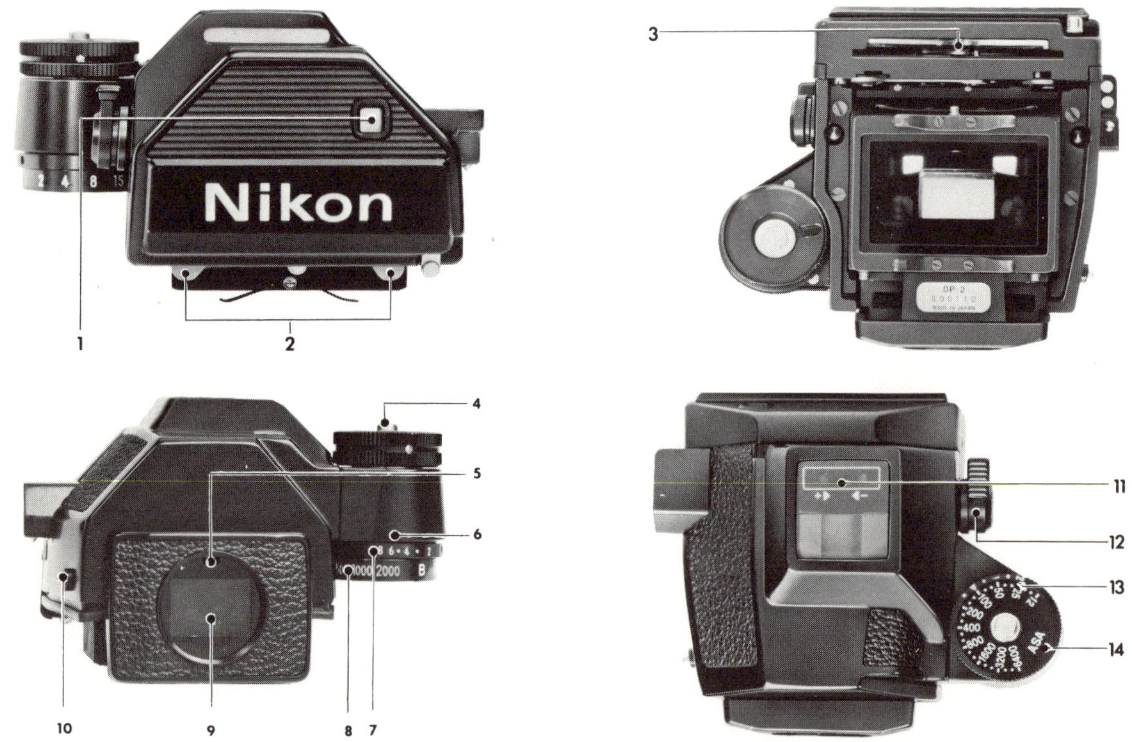

Parts Nomenclature of the Nikon F2S Photomic Finder DP-2

1. Maximum-aperture indicator
2. Clamps
3. Meter-coupling pin
4. Shutter-speed selector
5. Ready light
6. Shutter-speed index
7. Shutter-speed scale (for extra-long exposure)
8. Shutter-speed scale
9. Viewfinder eyepiece
10. Ready-light contact
11. Meter window
12. Finder-release lever
13. ASA film-speed index ring
14. Film-speed scale

converts the Nikon into an automatic-exposure camera.

Because the LED's can be read in light in which meter needles cannot, and because they require less power to operate than the needle, the actual sensitivity of this center-weighted, through-the-lens Cds meter has been greatly expanded. Its measuring range is EV −2 to EV 17 with the 50 mm *f*/1.4 lens at ASA 100, and the film-speed range is ASA 12 to ASA 6400. Although this finder also must be indexed to each lens, it then indexes lenses to any film speed automatically. The meter couples to Auto or AI-Nikkors, with maximum apertures of *f*/1.2 to *f*/5.6, by means of a standard Nikon meter-coupling pin. Proper indexing and coupling are assured by checking a maximum-aperture indicator window on the front of the meter housing. The full aperture range of the meter is *f*/1.2 to *f*/32, and the shutter-speed range has been expanded incredibly. It now includes one second to 1/2000 sec., plus "B," in normal operation, but a special provision for extreme low-light metering gives readings from two to ten full seconds at the maximum aperture of the lens in use, to correspond with the fullest capacity of the F2 shutter and self-timer. A separate extra-long shutter-speed scale appears on the finder for that purpose.

Like the simpler F2 Photomic, the F2S is capable of full-aperture or stop-down measurement, and is powered by the silver-oxide batteries in the Nikon body. The camera body also houses the on-off switch, and in this case, an automatic battery checker. The F2S also has the same flash ready light, which can be augmented with the Photomic Illuminator (DL-1) as well as all the other Nikon eyepiece accessories. It can also be adjusted to compensate for lens-screen transmission factors.

The principal operational difference, in fact, lies in the two LED's in the finder. They are arrow-shaped red pointers below the picture area; the left-hand one (marked "+") represents overexposure; the right-hand one (marked "−") represents underexposure. Shutter speed and aperture—both also visible in the finder—are adjusted until *both* LED's glow, indicating correct exposure. In a separate meter window atop the finder, a second set of LED's (in this case dots, not arrows) repeats the basic exposure information.

As noted above, the F2S makes direct contact with the EE Aperture Control Attachment (DS-1), which activates the lens diaphragm ring automatically, by means of a servomotor, in accordance with the shutter speed selected and the light information gathered by the meter. This actually turns the Nikon F2S Photomic into a fully automatic, shutter-priority camera: The mechanism itself selects the proper exposure, which can, of course, be overridden at the photographer's discretion. (More on the EE attachment will be found in Chapter 4, "Nikon Accessories.") Early models of the Nikon F2S Photomic were supplied with a Type A focusing screen; later ones came with a Type K screen. The now-standard clamp and finder-release lever are integral parts of the F2S Photomic, which can be distinguished by its high profile and lack of battery-check button.

Nikon F2Sb Photomic (DP-3)

A thorough redesign of the earlier F2S, the F2Sb improves the basic performance of that meter, while adding many new features. This finder/meter paves the way for all current metering systems. The principal changes are electronic: The F2Sb abandons Cds for the much-improved silicon photodiodes (SPD's), which give greater stability, quicker response, and more accurate measurement in very poor light. A monolithic integrated circuit and functional resistance element have contributed to an easier-to-use and more accurate LED system, and greater overall compactness.

The various ranges of the F2Sb Photomic are the same as those for the F2S; see the preceding section for details. Note that the lowest EV measurable, EV −2, represents an exposure of *eight full seconds* at *f*/1.4 with an ASA 100 film! Like its predecessor, the center-weighted, through-the-lens F2Sb also shares the following features: auto-indexing of lens to film speed (but manual indexing of meter to lens); coupling to Auto or AI-Nikkor via a meter-coupling pin; a maximum-aperture indicator window; an extra-long shutter-speed scale; full-aperture or stop-down metering; adjustment for lens-screen transmission characteristics; power from batteries in the camera body, regulated by a switch in the film-advance lever (which is also the battery-checking device); a built-in flash ready light; and, most important of the similarities, F2Sb accepts the same EE Aperture Control Attachment (DS-1), by means of a set of EE contacts.

Where the F2Sb differs principally, as a result of extensive internal changes, is in the actual metering operation. Within the finder eyepiece are *three* LED's, marked "+," for overexposure; "0," for correct exposure; and "−," for underexposure. These LED displays yield *five* exposure gradations, from more than one *f*-stop over or underexposure, through 1/5 to one stop, to correct exposure. In brief, shutter speed and/or aperture, which are both visible in the finder, are adjusted until the desired exposure is indicated by the LED's. (See the next chapter, "Operating the Camera," for details.) A separate "correct exposure" indicator on top of the finder glows to indicate proper settings only. This indicator is activated (and the internal LED's are *de*activated) when the F2Sb's new eyepiece shutter is closed. This handy device allows you to close off the eyepiece when the camera is on a tripod or in any unmonitored situation, in order to prevent stray light that would throw off the exposure from entering the highly-sensitive metering system from behind.

Another convenient refinement in the F2Sb is the built-in scale illuminator. A switch on top of the finder causes the shutter-speed indicator in the finder to glow red; this allows it to be read in the worst light, without the accessory Photomic Illuminator. The eyepiece of the F2Sb, however, can be fitted with any of the other standard eyepiece accessories. A new Nikon F2Sb Photomic is supplied with a Type K focusing screen as standard equipment, and can be distinguished from the earlier finder by its flatter profile and its illuminator and eyepiece-shutter switches.

Nikon F2AS Photomic (DP-12)

The "new generation" of Nikon cameras, introduced in 1977, all feature, as noted, automatic aperture indexing of lens with camera (AI) and aperture direct readout (ADR); that is the principal difference between the F2AS Photomic finder (DP-12) and the earlier F2Sb (DP-3). As meter systems, however, they are nearly identical. This finder, and the match-needle F2A Photomic, are natural descendants of their predecessors. They combine the metering qualities of the former models with the simplified operation of the latest Nikon mechanical advances.

Thus, the principal distinction of the F2AS Photomic is in mounting the lenses and checking the aperture. When attaching a new AI-Nikkor to the F2AS Photomic, it is not necessary to index the meter to the maximum aperture of the lens; merely putting the lens on the camera (see the next chapter) automatically sets the meter for the proper readings. (*Auto-Nikkors will not index*, nor can they be used for full-aperture metering, though they can be adapted to the AI system for a slight fee. Otherwise, they must be used in the stop-down mode, locking up the meter's coupling lever. This also applies to fixed-aperture lenses, manual-aperture lenses, and certain accessories such as bellows units.) The easiest way to recognize the F2AS Photomic finder is by the black flange in front (marked "AS" in white letters), on which is found the coupling-lever lock/release, as well as the coupling lever itself, which replaces the old Nikon lens-coupling pin. The F2AS also has no maximum-aperture indicator window.

When the lens is on the camera, you can look down through the eyepiece of the finder directly onto the second aperture scale of an AI-Nikkor to see the *f*-stop setting. The F2AS is also different from the F2Sb in that it requires a different model EE Aperture Control Attachment (in this case DS-12) to effect the same conversion of the Nikon F2 into a shutter-priority auto-exposure camera.

In all other respects, the F2AS is the same as the F2Sb; consult the two preceding sections of this chapter for detailed specifications. In brief, the F2AS has the same measuring ranges, obtained by the same sophisticated through-the-lens, center-weighted, silicon-diode metering system. A further similarity is that the display is of the three-LED, five-position type, with a secondary "correct exposure" indicator on top of the finder, actuated by closing the eyepiece shutter. The eyepiece of the F2AS has a built-in flash ready light and a separate scale illuminator, for lighting up the shutter-speed index in the finder. Like other Photomic models, the F2AS may be fitted with a variety of eyepiece accessories. The Nikon F2AS Photomic is supplied with a Type K focusing screen as standard equipment.

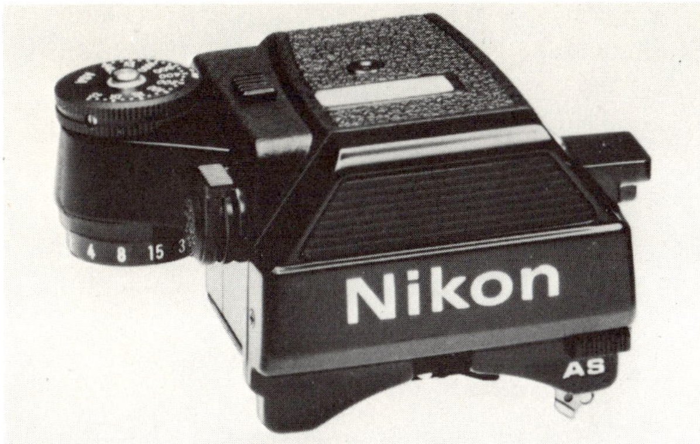

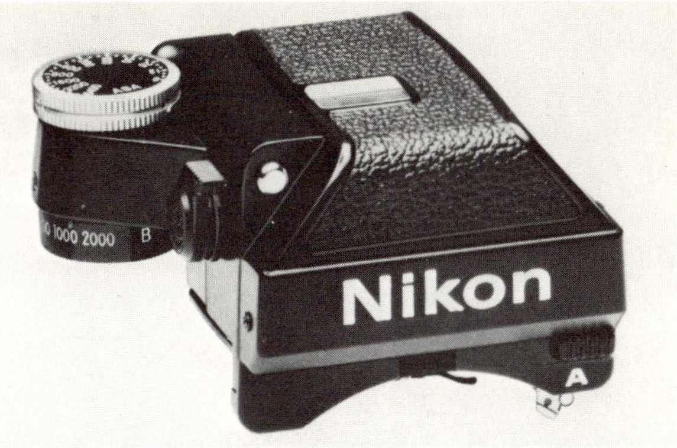

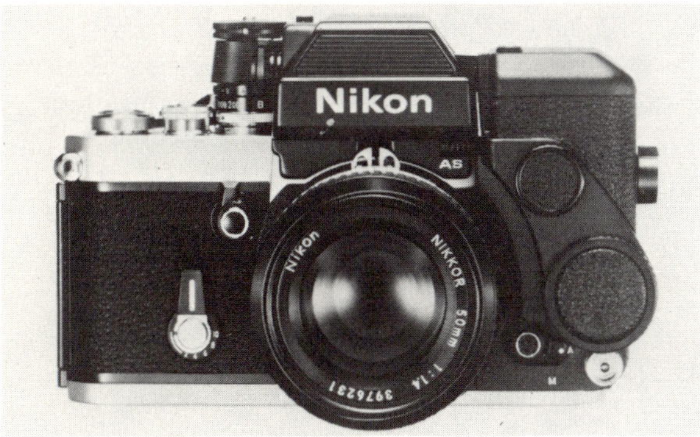

Latest Photomic finders, F2AS (DP-12) and F2A (DP-11), above. At left, fully equipped Nikon F2AS Photomic with the EE Aperture Control Attachment (DS-12).

Nikon F2A Photomic (DP-11)

The match-needle F2A Photomic finder of 1977 brings together the Cds, needle-centering mode of the earlier F2 Photomic with the automatic aperture indexing (AI) and aperture direct readout (ADR) of the LED-display F2AS Photomic. It is a more economical alternative to the F2AS, for those photographers who do not need the extreme light sensitivity of the latter, or who do not wish to use their Nikon F2 as an auto-exposure camera.

The principal innovation in the F2A is in mounting lenses and checking apertures. As with all AI-system cameras (or finders), merely attaching an AI-Nikkor automatically indexes the meter to the maximum aperture of the lens (see Chapter 2 for details), so the meter is set to give full-aperture readings according to the film speed and the light entering the lens. Again be warned: *Auto-Nikkors will not index with the meter*, nor will they permit full-aperture metering; but they can be used in the stop-down mode, as can fixed-aperture Nikkors, manual-aperture lenses, and other bayonet-mounted accessories, such as extension tubes or bellows. Auto-Nikkors *may* be adapted for AI and ADR by Nikon, for a modest sum. The easiest way to identify the F2A is by the black flange in front (marked "A" in white), on which is the coupling-lever lock release, and the new Nikon coupling lever itself, which replaces the previous lens-coupling pin. The F2A has no maximum-aperture indicator window, since none is needed.

With an AI-Nikkor on the camera, you can see the actual aperture at which the lens is set through the finder eyepiece; that is ADR. In every other respect, the F2A is identical to the F2 Photomic. (Consult the relevant section, above, for details.) Briefly, the F2A has the same meter-range specifications and the same needle-centering method of exposure determination, both through the eyepiece and on top of the finder. It is also powered by batteries in the camera body (and it has a similar battery-check button), which are turned on or off by means of the film-advance lever. The finder is attached to the camera with the same sure clamps (though they are covered), and released with an identical finder-release lever.

Like the other Photomic finders, the F2A will accept a number of eyepiece accessories (see Chapter 4), particularly the Photomic Illuminator (DL-1), which gives the scales in the finder extra illumination in poor light. A built-in flash ready light connects to Nikon Speedlight units, by means of a special contact on the side of the meter; it signals when the flash unit is fully charged. A new Nikon F2A Photomic camera is supplied with a Type K focusing screen as standard equipment.

OTHER VIEWFINDER TYPES

There are a variety of non-metering finders for both Nikon F2 and Nikon F cameras that serve special purposes, as indicated by type. Similar (but *not* identical) versions are available for each camera.

Eye-Level Finder (DE-1)

This is a "straight" eye-level pentaprism for the Nikon F2 body. Like the Photomics, the eye-level shows 100 percent of the image at 0.8× with the 50 mm Nikkor. It also has the same built-in flash ready light as the Photomic finders. The eyepiece takes all standard eyepiece accessories.

Waist-Level Finder (DW-1)

This finder is intended for use when the F2 camera must be handled from above, as in macro work, or on a tripod, or even upside-down, as in shooting over a crowd. It folds into a very flat, compact shape and opens at the touch of a button. A built-in flip-up magnifier aids critical focusing by magnifying the central part of the image 5×.

6× Focusing Finder (DW-2)

Intended principally for macro work with the Nikon F2 and Type C and M (cross hair) focusing screens, the 6× Finder is a waist-level type viewer that magnifies the entire image 6×. It can be used for any highly-critical focusing, and with any screen, and it provides −5 to +3 diopter adjustment, to suit the eyesight of the individual photographer.

Action Finder (DA-1)

The Action Finder, as its name suggests, is designed for sports and other fast-moving events, with the Nikon F2 held as much as 2½" away from the eye. The truly huge picture it presents in its rectangular eyepiece is ideal for photographers with thick glasses (or goggles) who have difficulty seeing the entire screen.

Nikon F Finders

Finders of the same type as the four above are available for the Nikon F. The F version of the Action Finder is called the Sportsfinder. *Only* the 6× finder for the F2 can be adapted for the F.

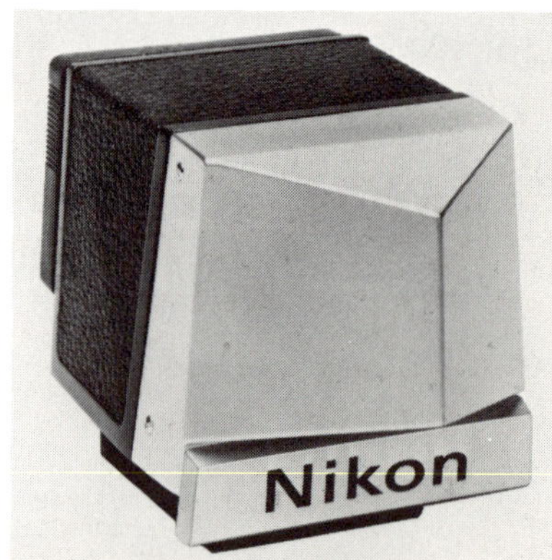

Non-metering finders for Nikon F2. Below, left to right: Eye-level; Waist-level; and 6x Focusing Finder. At right: the Action Finder. Finders for Nikon F are similar.

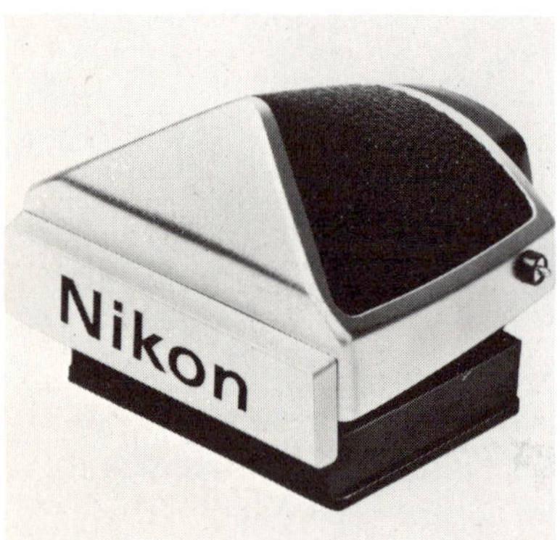

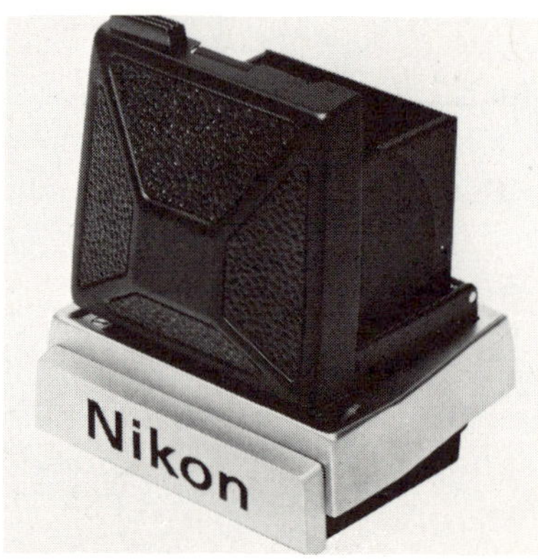

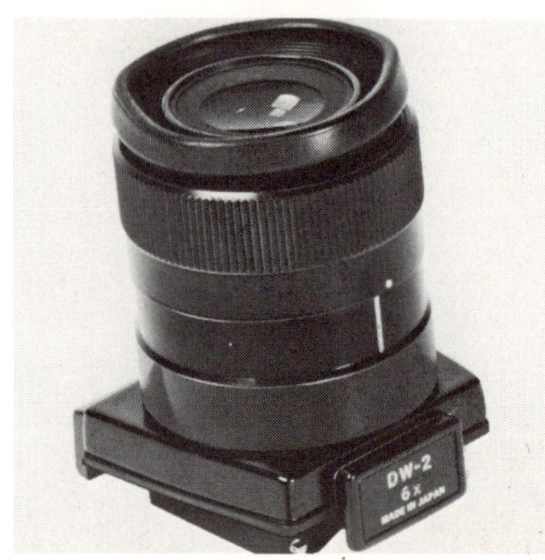

If the Nikon F2 of 1972 was considered evolutionary, the Nikon F3, introduced in 1980, is revolutionary in concept for Nikon, and for 35 mm photography. It is the first professional-level Nikon to incorporate the latest electronic and mechanical components, automation, and miniaturization, resulting in a camera as easy to operate as the simplest amateur machine but capable of more sophisticated photography than ever before. The Nikon F3 has interchangeable viewfinders, but exposure-metering and auto-exposure capabilities are built into the camera body itself. In other words, regardless of the finder—and there are several—the camera retains auto-exposure and manual metering abilities. There are a greater number of accessories for the F3 than ever before, and the camera itself has capacities found on no other Nikon.

The F3 retains many familiar features from earlier models, and many accessories are compatible. Most particularly, Nikon owners will be relieved to know that the lensmount remains the same, and that all AI-Nikkors and earlier Auto-Nikkors will fit the F3 without adjustment. The (aperture-preferred) automatic-exposure system of the camera is, in fact, geared to give full-aperture automatic exposure, aperture-direct readout (ADR), and automatic aperture indexing (AI) with AI-Nikkors, and stop-down automatic exposure with Auto-Nikkors and older lenses.

But the emphasis of this camera is on its differences from earlier Nikons. The Nikon F3 has an incredibly sensitive silicon metering system that reads light *through* the reflex mirror (and eliminates exposure compensation for different finders or screens). The F3 also features an electronic shutter-speed range (8 seconds to 1/2000 sec), with mechanical speeds ("X"—1/80 sec, and "T") that do not rely on battery power; an energy-saving liquid crystal display (LCD) that indicates shutter speeds and over- or underexposure; quartz timing on manually selected speeds; automatic flash synchronization and flash metering with "dedicated" Nikon units; a multiple exposure lever; the ability to draw all its power from a new motor-drive unit; and many other new features. All this is accomplished in a package far smaller than any other professional system camera; the F3 measures only 148.5 × 96.5 × 65.5 mm (5¾" × 2¾" × 1⅜") with the standard eye-level prism, and weighs only 24 oz (680 g).

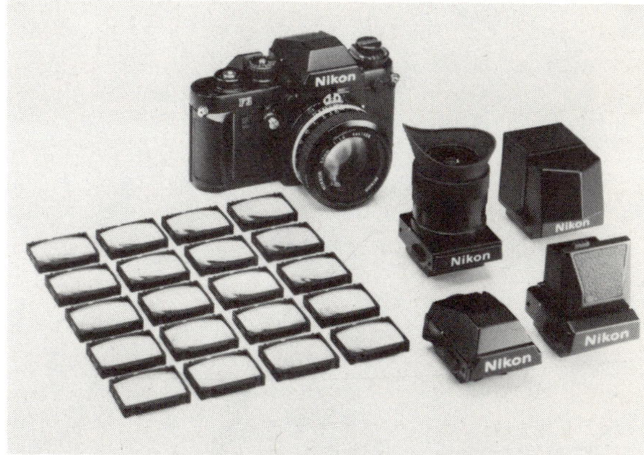

The Nikon F3 with its array of interchangeable viewfinders and focusing screens.

To complement the new camera, Nikon has brought out two new lenses in the normal focal length, the 50 mm *f*/1.8 and *f*/1.2 AI-Nikkors. While similar to the lenses they replace, they are smaller, lighter, and have several improved features. The 50 mm *f*/1.8, for example, is only 37 mm (1.5 in) long and weighs 220 g (7.8 oz). It also has a smaller minimum stop, *f*/22. The faster 50 mm *f*/1.2, which replaces the 55 mm *f*/1.2, is 47.5 mm (1.8 in) long and weighs only 390 g (13.8 oz). It focuses down to .5 m (19.6 in).

Shutter

The Nikon F3 has a horizontal focal-plane shutter with curtains made of quilted titanium foil. The meter takes its flash reading from the surface of the curtain. It has two independent electronic timing systems: In the automatic-exposure mode, a microprocessor sets stepless, *continuously variable* speeds from eight seconds to 1/2000 sec. In other words, depending on exposure conditions, a precisely correct shutter speed for that exposure is set, even between the standard settings—for example,

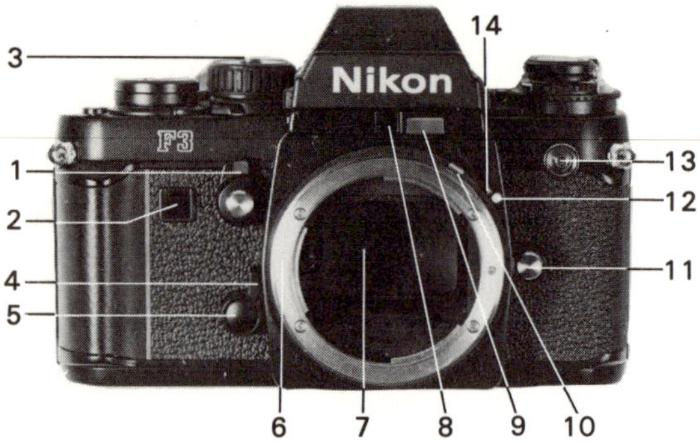

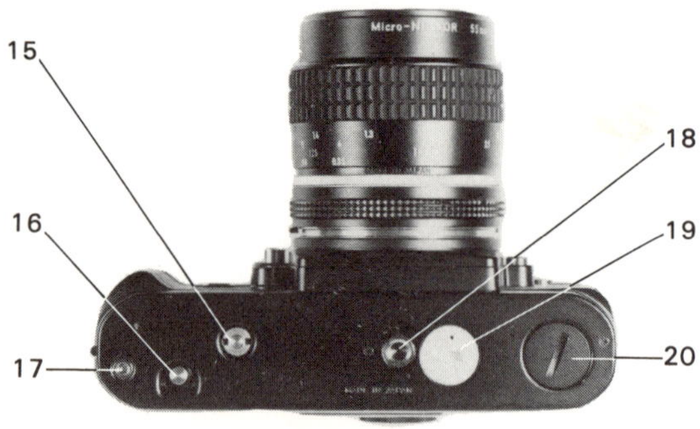

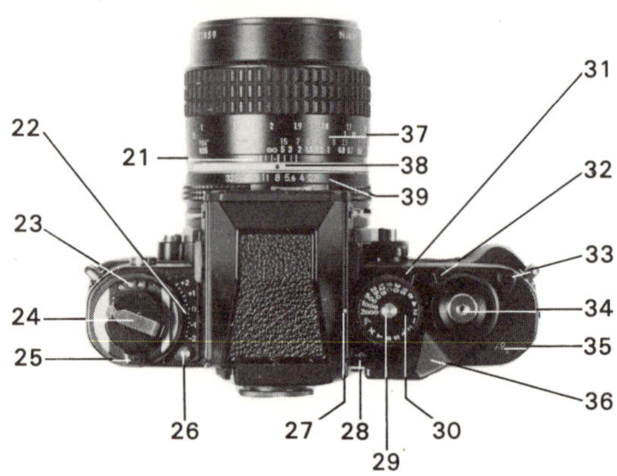

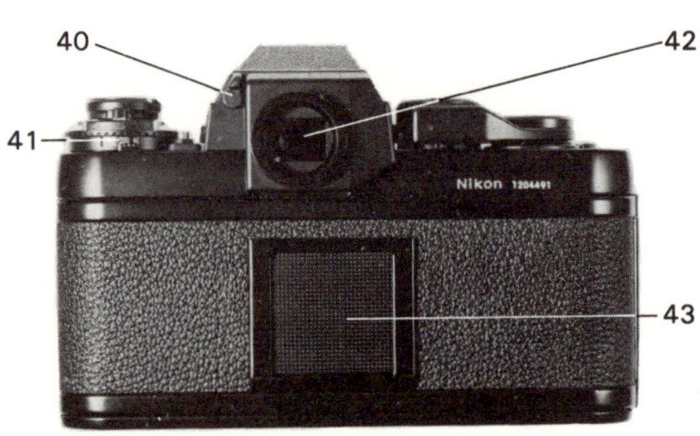

NIKON F3—PARTS NOMENCLATURE

1. **Mirror lockup lever**
2. **Self-timer LED**
3. **Shutter-speed dial locking button**
4. **Backup mechanical release lever**
5. **Exposure memory lock button**
6. **Lens mounting flange**
7. **Reflex mirror**
8. **ADR window**
9. **Viewfinder illuminator**
10. **Meter coupling lever**
11. **Lens release button**
12. **Lens mounting index**
13. **Flash sync. terminal**
14. **Meter coupling lever release button**
15. **Motor drive coupling**
16. **Film rewind button**
17. **Motor drive positioning hole**
18. **Tripod/motor drive coupling socket**
19. **Battery chamber lid**
20. **Motor drive coupling cover**
21. **Depth-of-field indicators**
22. **Exposure compensation scale**
23. **Hot-shoe contacts**
24. **Film rewind crank**
25. **Camera back lock lever**
26. **Exposure compensation locking button**
27. **Shutter speed index**
28. **Film plane indicator**
29. **Shutter speed dial**
30. **Shutter-speed scale**
31. **Self-timer lever**
32. **Power switch**
33. **Multiple exposure lever**
34. **Shutter release button**
35. **Frame counter**
36. **Film advance lever**
37. **Distance scale**
38. **Aperture/focusing index**
39. **Aperture ring**
40. **Eyepiece shutter lever**
41. **ASA film speed scale**
42. **Viewfinder eyepiece**
43. **Memo holder**

1/48 sec, or 1/327 sec. When manual shutter speeds are set, a quartz-controlled timing device sets exact stepped speeds of eight seconds, four seconds, two seconds, one second, 1/2, 1/4, 1/8, 1/15, 1/30, 1/60, 1/125, 1/250, 1/500, 1/1000, and 1/2000 sec. There are also manual settings for B ("bulb": the shutter stays open as long as the shutter-release button is pressed), T ("time": the shutter stays open until the dial is reset), and X, the proper synchronization speed for electronic flash, which is 1/80 sec. A separate, unique, backup mechanical shutter release allows you to set 1/60 sec. and T, independent of battery power.

On the shutter-speed dial, next to the film-advance lever, all the functions of the shutter are indicated: A *green* "A" sets the shutter for automatic exposure. Full seconds are in *orange*—8, 4, 2, and 1—as is the "B"; fractional seconds are indicated by the lower half of the fraction in *white*—2, 4, 8, 15, 30, 125, 250, 500, 1000, and 2000—except for "60," which is *red*, to indicate the fastest speed for synchronizing electronic flash, other than "X" (1/80 sec.). The "X" and "T" are in white.

The shutter is ordinarily fired by pressing the electromagnetic shutter release, a button at the hub of the film-advance lever. (This also turns on the meter/auto-exposure system.) The release button is threaded to accept a standard cable release. The backup mechanical shutter-release lever is to the left of the lensmount (camera facing you). You can use it to fire the shutter at "T," or to obtain 1/60 sec. at any other setting. It may be used with the camera switched off, or if the batteries have run down. A fourth way to fire the shutter is to use the self-timer, which will be discussed shortly.

Other Body Features

Because the F3 *is* a Nikon, it draws on the fine tradition of earlier top-of-the-line Nikons, the F and F2, for many of its more ordinary components. To avoid needless repetition, those parts which are identical to, or nearly the same as, those on the previous models, are merely referred to here. For a fuller description, the reader should see pages 19 and 20. Look at the present illustrations for the location on the F3 of: *the film-advance lever* (the F3's has a stroke of 140° and can be wound in several short strokes); *the frame counter*; *the mirror-lock lever*; *the depth-of-field preview button*; *the rewind crank and knob* (which on the F3 doubles as *the camera-back lock*); *the accessory shoe*; *the tripod socket*, *battery chamber*, and *rewind button*, all on the baseplate; *the lensmount system*; *the finder-release system* (works differently from previous models); and inside the camera, *the take-up spool*, *film pressure plate*, and *film roller*. A set of *couplings* for motor-drive units is on the baseplate, as on previous models, but in different positions; motor-drive units are *not* interchangeable with earlier cameras.

Some other body features, apart from those connected with viewing and exposure, unique to the F3 follow:

Flash-synchronization system. The hot shoe on the Nikon F3 has *three* electrical contacts: one makes the flash contact, the second is for a viewfinder ready-light indicator, and the third triggers a through-the-lens flash-duration control. The last two features are designed to make the F3 fully automatic with certain "dedicated" Nikon SB speedlight units. Like earlier models, the F3 also has a standard, threaded PC flash-synch terminal, and will take adapters for standard (ISO) or Nikon F2 hot-shoe units. The camera switches over automatically from electronic-flash (X) to flashbulb (M) synchronization.

Self-timer. The Nikon F3 self-timer is electronic and controlled by a lever at the base of the shutter-speed dial. When it is set, the shutter-release button activates the timer, which in turn starts a bright red LED blinking on the front of the camera. The delay is about ten seconds; after about eight, the blinking speeds up to warn you that the exposure is about to be made.

Multiple-exposure lever. The F3 permits the easiest multiple exposures of any Nikon. Simply pushing the lever (next to the film-advance hub) forward after your first shot lets you re-cock the shutter without advancing the film. (The frame counter doesn't move, either.)

Electrical system. The very complex electronics of the F3's meter, auto-exposure system, and shutter are all driven by two 1.5 V silver-oxide batteries (Eveready EPX-76, D76, or equivalent). Although the camera is extremely modest in its energy demands, "button" sized batteries do run down. But when the camera is fitted with the new *MD-4 Motor Drive*, it derives *all* its power from that unit's own eight AA (penlight) batteries.

The viewing system of the Nikon F3 is the most advanced and the most efficient of any Nikon. The several types of viewfinders, focusing screens, and other optical aids combine to provide the brightest, clearest, easiest-to-focus image ever found in a Nikon. Each of these components—especially designed for the F3 alone—is smaller, lighter, and *much* easier to remove and replace than ever before. Regardless of the combination employed, they all produce an image that is 100 percent of the scene to be recorded on the film: no "cutoff" whatsoever. As indicated above, each has full auto-exposure and data readouts, above the image area.

The Viewfinders

The Nikon F3 is ordinarily supplied with the standard *Eye-Level Pentaprism Viewfinder* (DE-2), which yields a right-side-up and laterally correct image, 0.8× life-size with the normal 50 mm lenses set at infinity. This image size makes it easy to follow a scene with the naked eye, then switch to the viewfinder, since there is no abrupt change of magnification. With the standard K screen on the camera, you will see a 3 mm diameter circle in the center of the frame, bisected by a horizontal line—the split-image rangefinder spot. When the picture is in focus, the half-images in the circle align; when it is not, the image is broken into two parts. Around the split-image spot is a one-millimeter-wide band of microprisms. These fracture an out-of-focus picture into a shimmering blur. When the lens is correctly focused on the subject, the shimmer stops and the image looks sharp. The rest of the screen consists of a matte Fresnel field, which can also be used for focusing, since it shows in-focus images sharp and out-of-focus images blurry, though this distinction is not as clear as with the split-image or the microprisms. With its condenser lens, the Fresnel distributes light evenly over the whole screen; there is no vignetting in the corners. An etched circle 12 mm in diameter indicates the area emphasized by the camera's "center-weighted" metering system.

The split-image and microprism work best under average conditions; under certain other circumstances, they will not work well or at all, such as with lenses of fairly small maximum aperture, at the smaller apertures of any long lens, and in close-up photography. This microprism or split-image "blackout" can be overcome by focusing with the matte field, which works under all conditions. Another method is to switch to one of the 19 more specialized focusing screens made for the F3. These will be discussed shortly.

The DE-2 finder has other useful features. A built-in eyepiece shutter lets you close off the eyepiece to exclude extraneous light from the metering system when the eyepiece is not blocked by your eye, as when mounting the camera on a tripod or copy setup and exposing with a cable release, remote release, or the self-timer. A tiny lamp inside the finder lets you read the shutter/aperture settings in even the dimmest light. The full range of exposure information provided in the F3 viewfinders will be detailed in the section on "Metering and Auto-Exposure System."

There are at present four other viewfinders for the Nikon F3: the (DA-2) *Action Finder*, the (DW-3) *Waist-Level Finder*, the (DW-4) 6× *High-Magnification Finder*, and the (DE-3) *High-Point Finder*. The first three finders are nearly identical with those for the Nikon F2; they are not, however, interchangeable with the earlier models. Unlike them, the special finders for the F3 retain exposure information in the eyepiece, and they are attached and detached with greater ease. The new *High-Eyepoint Finder* (DE-3) allows you to hold the camera an inch from your eye, yet see the entire picture and the exposure readouts clearly. It gives the same 100 percent coverage as the other finders, at about 0.7× magnification with the normal lens.

Interchangeable Focusing Screens

Again, the interchangeability of Nikon focusing screens follows a traditional pattern: the same *types* of focusing screen (that is, A—R) are available for the F3 as for the F2. See pages 21 and 22 for the specifications of those screens, which use various focusing aids to suit different lenses (or different viewing conditions). Screens for the F3, though of the same specifications, are *not* interchangeable with the F2 models. Like the viewfinders, they have been redesigned to make insertion and removal much easier. Moreover, since the F3 measures light irrespective of the viewing apparatus, there is no longer any "screen-compensation factor" to consider in matching screen to lens.

METERING AND AUTO-EXPOSURE SYSTEM

The heart of the Nikon F3 is its sensitive, accurate, and reliable light-measurement and exposure-control system. Nikon designers took the best parts of the systems developed for the F2, EL2, and FE and added new features found on no other camera. The result is an automatic electronic mechanism of greater versatility and ease of operation than any previous professional camera.

The Meter

The meter itself is based on a silicon photodiode (SPD) that takes 80 percent of its through-the-lens reading from the central 12 mm circle (in the viewfinder). But that reading is not taken *at* the viewfinder; rather, light from the lens passes *through* 50,000 microscopic "holes" in the reflex mirror, where 8 percent of it is reflected downward by a secondary mirror and focused on the SPD cell at the bottom of the mirror box. The purpose of this strange route is to bypass light-transmission variables in the viewing system; thus the meter works the same with any number of lens/viewfinder/screen combinations and eliminates "exposure compensations." The 80 percent concentration on the central 1/8 of the screen is an improved version of Nikon's long-successful center-weighted meter bias (see pages 23 and 24 for details).

From the cell, the exposure information goes via a special flexible printed circuit to the shutter and the viewfinder display. This circuit and a new temperature-compensating circuit—both unique to the F3—make its meter the most reliable around, especially because there are no moving parts.

The exposure range of the meter is EV 1 to EV 18 with a 50 mm *f*/1.4 lens and ASA/ISO 100 film. Its full aperture range is *f*/1.2 to *f*/32, and its shutter-speed range is 8 seconds to 1/2000 sec. The meter will couple with film speeds of ASA/ISO 12 to 6400, and a built-in exposure-compensation dial programs the system to give exposures from +2EV to −2EV (or *f*/stops) above or below the indicated ones, in 1/3-step increments.

The F3's meter gives full-aperture readings (and indexes automatically) with all AI-Nikkor lenses; it works in the stopped-down mode with all other Nikkors and accessories. Moreover, the same SPD cell that measures natural light *automatically* provides electronic-flash metering and exposure control (see Chapter 6 for details).

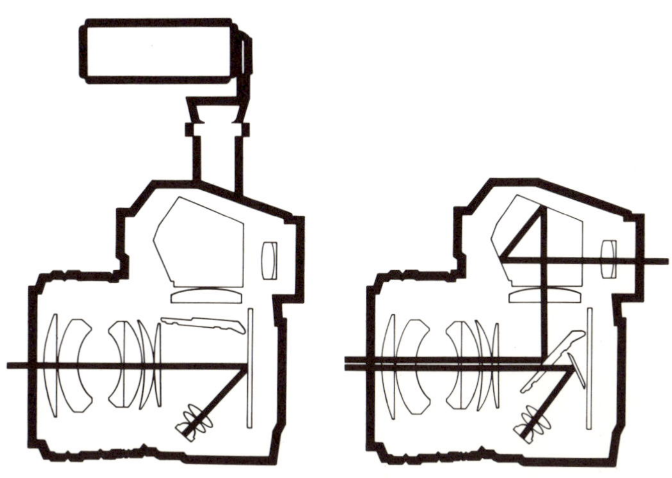

Unique metering system of the Nikon F3 reads light through the reflex mirror, also operates with "dedicated" flash units.

Viewfinder Display

By far the most "different" aspect of the F3's meter is the way it communicates its information to you. A liquid-crystal display (LCD)—the first in *any* camera—replaces both meter needles and LED's. This energy-saving and easy-to-see display simplifies exposure information dramatically. (The one minor flaw in an LCD is its sensitivity to extremes in temperature. Below freezing, it slows down considerably; above 60 C (140 F) it blackens. After six or seven years, it must be replaced.) When you push the shutter-release button, the display lights up (and stays lit for 16 seconds). Depending on the exposure mode, it shows the following:

In automatic-exposure mode: The LCD gives the nearest whole shutter speed selected by the meter ("125," for example) for the correct exposure. If the exposure-compensation dial has been used, the display shows the *compensated* setting. If light conditions are beyond the meter's range, the display is "+2000" for overexposure and "—8—" for underexposure.

In manual-metering mode: The display shows the *actual* shutter speed set on the camera, with the letter "M." A "+" or "−" also indicates whether that setting is above or below the setting for a correct exposure. A display of "−+" indicates the right setting. Thus, 1/125 sec., if it were the correct setting, would read "−+125." Fractional seconds are distinguished from full seconds as follows: 1/8 sec = "8"; 8 seconds = "8−." The X setting shows as "+80"; the B and T settings display as "M−." The "M80" setting automatically shows at the beginning of every roll of film until the frame-counter reaches "O," and the shutter will open only for 1/80 sec. for the first (usually blank) exposures. This speeds up loading the camera considerably.

The viewfinder also displays the aperture at which the lens is set in a small window (ADR), when an AI-Nikkor is mounted on the camera. A flash ready-light LED will glow when specific "dedicated" Nikon units are attached to the camera, fully charged, and turned on. There is also a built-in illuminator lamp, to be used in extremely dim light to see both the LCD and the ADR window.

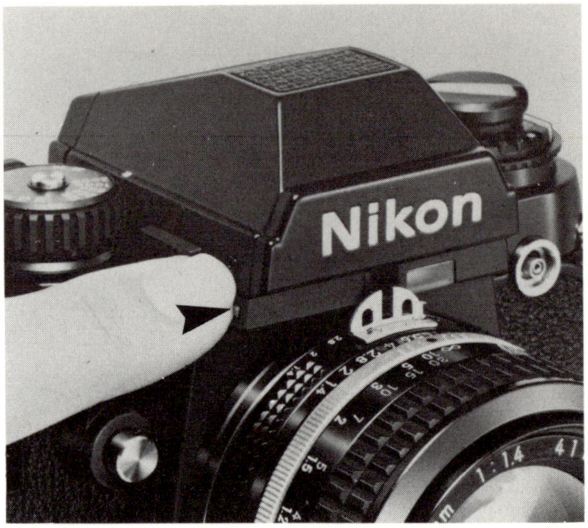

Viewfinder illuminator lets you see exposure information display in the dimmest light. Just push red button in.

Automatic Exposure

Using the F3's metering system to obtain perfectly exposed pictures automatically is far easier than describing it. Details will be given in the next chapter; here, it is sufficient to say that with the camera's aperture-preferred system, you turn the camera on, select an aperture, focus, and shoot. In the vast majority of cases, that's all. The meter selects the appropriate shutter speed, based on the aperture, the lighting on the subject, and the film speed; the shutter reacts instantaneously; and the picture is taken. The specific cases where more effort on your part is required are: when you are not using an AI-Nikkor (you must use the stop-down method); when the light is *extremely* contrasty (you may wish to employ the exposure-compensation control); when your main subject is lit in a peculiar way or is off to the side, out of the 12 mm central circle (you can "lock-in" an exposure via the memory-lock lever); or when, for various reasons, you must expose the picture at some very different setting (the F3 has fully manual controls).

The Nikon FM combines all the latest advances of 35 mm camera design into one extremely small package. One of the most "modern" Nikons of all, the FM combines the AI and ADR lens system, with the standard Nikon bayonet, a blazing fast shutter, the latest gallium metering cells and an LED-meter display, and adaptability to motorized photography. The only features it does not have are interchangeable viewfinders and automatic exposure control, but it packs the features it does have into a body about 5½" × 2⅜" × 3½", weighing only 20.8 oz. (A full-size Nikon F2AS, for example, measures about 6" × 2½" × 4", and weighs 29.6 oz.)

Many of the features of the Nikon FM are the same as those of the Nikon F2, so the reader is referred to previous sections of this chapter for detailed descriptions. These features include the film-advance and rewind mechanism, as well as film-flatness provisions; a frame counter; a self-timer; a depth-of-field preview lever; a shutter release; an accessory shoe (ISO-type, on top of the prism, with built-in "hot shoe" flash contact); a tripod socket; a battery chamber, with the same two 1.5V silver-oxide batteries (Mallory MS-76, Eveready S-76, or equivalent); a film-advance and shutter-release coupling, for motorized operation; and, of course, the classic Nikkor bayonet lensmount, which takes all Nikon SLR lenses from the earliest, made in 1959, to the current AI-Nikkors. The camera comes supplied with the same choice of normal AI-Nikkors as the F2: the 50 mm *f*/2 or *f*/1.4, or the 55 mm *f*/1.2. The FM also shares with other Nikons an oversized instant-return mirror, a similar viewfinder and metering system, to be described below, and a huge array of accessories, which will be discussed in Chapter 4. Certain other FM features apart from the camera's size are, however, quite distinctive.

Shutter

The shutter is of the vertical focal-plane type, made of metal, with speeds of one second, 1/2, 1/4, 1/8, 1/15, 1/30, 1/60, 1/125, 1/250, 1/500, and 1/1000 sec., plus B (on bulb: the shutter stays open as long as the button is depressed). On the shutter-speed dial, the top of the fraction is omitted, so the dial reads B, 1, 2, 4, 8, 15, 30, 60, 125, 250, 500, and 1000. The "125" is red, indicating the maximum electronic-flash synchronization speed of 1/125 sec. This high "X"-synch speed is made possible by the traverse—the time it takes the shutter to expose the entire film gate—of seven milliseconds, the fastest of all focal-plane 35 mm reflexes. The shutter-release button is next to the film-advance lever. It is surrounded by a finger-guard, which is also a shutter-mode selector (manual, motorized, or locked).

Flash-Synchronization System

The Nikon FM is synchronized for electronic flash *only*, at speeds up to 1/125 sec., as indicated above. In addition to the "hot shoe" mentioned earlier, there is a standard Nikon threaded flash-synch terminal, which will take any unit with a PC cord.

Multiple-Exposure Control

One feature unique to the Nikon FM is the ease with which double or multiple exposures are made. A multiple-exposure button, next to the shutter-speed dial, permits recocking the shutter without advancing the film. All controls on the camera can be reset between exposures, and this procedure can be repeated indefinitely.

Motor-Drive Linkage

To facilitate use of the FM's own compact Motor-Drive Unit (MD-12), the camera has a shutter coupling, a drive coupling, and a set of electrical contacts on the baseplate. As a consequence, the Nikon FM may be fitted for motorized operation with absolutely no modifications or special adjustments.

Viewing and Metering Systems

The viewfinder of the Nikon FM is a gold mine of information for the photographer. It combines a

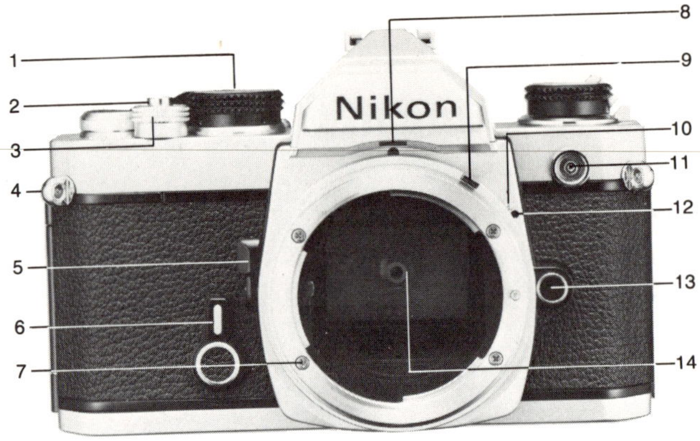

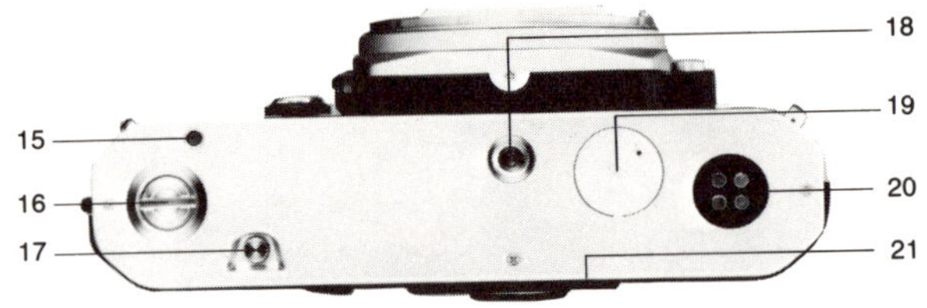

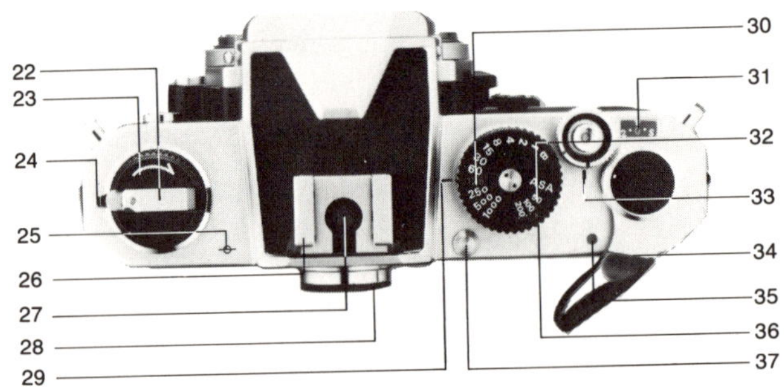

Parts Nomenclature for the Nikon FM

1. Shutter-speed/ASA selector ring
2. Shutter-release button
3. Shutter-release finger-guard/mode selector
4. Neckstrap eyelet
5. Depth-of-field preview lever
6. Self-timer lever
7. Lens-mounting flange
8. Lens aperture-direct-readout window
9. Meter coupling lever
10. Meter coupling lever release
11. Sync terminal (cover provided)
12. Lens-mounting index
13. Lens-release button
14. Reflex mirror
15. Motor drive shutter coupling
16. Motor drive coupling
17. Film-rewind button
18. Tripod socket
19. Battery chamber lid
20. Motor drive electrical contacts
21. Memo holder
22. Film-rewind crank
23. Film-rewind knob
24. Safety lock
25. Film-plane indicator
26. Hot sync shoe
27. Hot-shoe contact
28. Viewfinder eyepiece
29. Shutter-speed index
30. Shutter-speed selector
31. Frame counter
32. ASA film-speed window
33. Shutter operation-mode index
34. Film-advance lever
35. Meter ON index
36. ASA film-speed index
37. Multi-exposure button

bright, clear, easy-to-focus image with full exposure information, via an LED display and scale indexes of shutter speed and aperture.

The fixed, eye-level pentaprism finder gives a bright image that is right side up and laterally correct. The screen is 93 percent of the actual image, the remainder being the area usually covered by a slide mount. Focusing aids in the viewfinder are a central split-image rangefinder; a surrounding microprism band; and an overall matte Fresnel field. (This is the same arrangement as on the standard K screen supplied with the Nikon F2. Consult the section "The Viewfinder," earlier in this chapter for details.)

The meter indicators in the finder eyepiece consist of a shutter-speed scale to the left of the picture area; an aperture window above it, which shows the actual *f*/stop when an AI-Nikkor is on the camera (ADR); and a five-position, three-LED signal system indicating correct, over, and underexposure. The next chapter, "Operating the Camera," discusses the uses of these exposure indicators. They are the same as the ones found on the Nikon F2AS Photomic.

The meter itself is of the center-weighted through-the-lens type, again similar to those of the Photomic finders. Where it differs is in its gallium photodiodes (GPD's), which have a uniform and nearly instantaneous response to light of widely varying intensity. Its measuring range is EV 1 to EV 18 with the 50 mm *f*/1.4 Nikkor at ASA 100, and the film-speed range is ASA 12 to ASA 3200. It couples with any AI or Auto-Nikkor, over a full aperture range of *f*/1.2 to *f*/32, by means of the new meter-coupling lever built onto the lensmount. The FM meter is capable of full-aperture or stop-down measurement. A switch built into the film-advance lever turns it on and off.

THE NIKON EL2

The Nikon EL2 was a fully electronic automatic-exposure camera of the "aperture-priority" type with automatic aperture indexing (AI). Not only does it take the full range of Nikkor lenses, it has an advanced, silicon photodiode (SPD) meter with exposure compensation; an amazingly accurate, continuously variable shutter; and it is convertible, by means of the Auto Winder AW-1, into a semi-motorized camera as well.

The Nikon EL2 has the standard Nikon bayonet lensmount, which takes not only AI-Nikkors but Auto-Nikkors and all older Nikkor SLR lenses (though it offers full-aperture metering only with the latest lenses). The camera is supplied with either of the three normal lenses. Like the Nikon F2, the EL2 has a similar film-advance and rewind mechanism and film-flatness provisions; a frame counter; a ten-second self-timer (which is combined with a memory lock); a depth-of-field preview button; a mirror-lockup lever; a shutter-release button; an accessory shoe, with a built-in ISO "hot shoe" flash contact; a flash-synchronization system, with automatic switch over from "M" to "X" synch; and a tripod socket. For a more detailed description of these features, consult the appropriate sections of this chapter on the Nikon F2.

Shutter

The shutter of the EL2 is of the downward-vertical focal-plane type, made of metal, and controlled electromagnetically. In auto-exposure mode, its speeds are stepless and continuously variable from eight full seconds to 1/1000 sec. This means that the meter selects the precise shutter speed to insure correct exposure, no matter how "odd" the duration—for example, 1/17 sec. 1/251 sec., or 1/989 sec. In manual mode, the shutter has equally precise, stepped speeds of eight seconds, four seconds, two seconds, one second, 1/2, 1/4, 1/8, 1/15, 1/30, 1/60, 1/125, 1/250, 1/500, and 1/1000 sec., plus B (bulb: the shutter stays open as long as the shutter release is pressed). On the shutter-speed dial, full seconds are orange: 8, 4, 2, and 1; fractional seconds omit the upper half of the fraction—2, 4, 8, 16, 30, 125, 250, 500, and 1000—and are white, except "125," which is red to indicate the maximum electronic-flash synchronization speed of 1/125 sec. The "B" setting is

NIKON FE—PARTS NOMENCLATURE

1. Shutter-speed dial lock
2. Shutter release button
3. Shutter-release fingerguard
4. Neckstrap eyelet
5. Depth-of-field preview lever
6. Self-timer/memory lock
7. Reflex mirror
8. Lens mounting flange
9. Lens aperture direct readout window
10. Meter-coupling lever
11. Meter-coupling lever release
12. Synch terminal (cover provided)
13. Lens-mounting index
14. Lens-release button
15. Focusing screen holder release
16. Motor-drive shutter coupling
17. Motor-drive coupling
18. Film-rewind button
19. Tripod socket
20. Battery-chamber lid
21. Motor-drive electrical contacts
22. Memo holder
23. Distance scale
24. Focusing ring
25. Aperture ring
26. Meter-coupling ridge
27. Aperture/distance scale index
28. Meter coupling shoe
29. Depth-of-field indicators
30. Aperture-direct-readout scale
31. Exposure-compensation index
32. Exposure-compensation scale
33. Film-rewind crank
34. Film-rewind knob
35. Safety lock
36. Film-speed scale index
37. ASA film-speed scale/dial
38. Exposure-compensation ring
39. Power-check lever/lamp
40. ASA film-speed dial lock
41. Accessory shoe
42. Hot-shoe contact
43. Shutter-speed index
44. Shutter-speed scale
45. Frame counter
46. Multi-exposure lever
47. Film-advance lever
48. Meter ON index
49. Film-plane indicator
50. Viewfinder eyepiece (with ready-light)
51. Ready-light contact

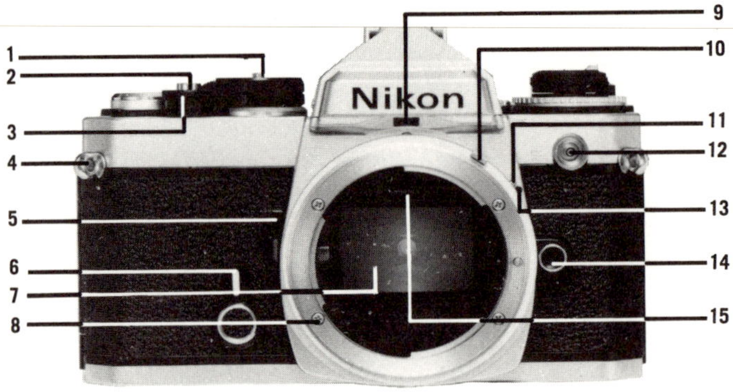

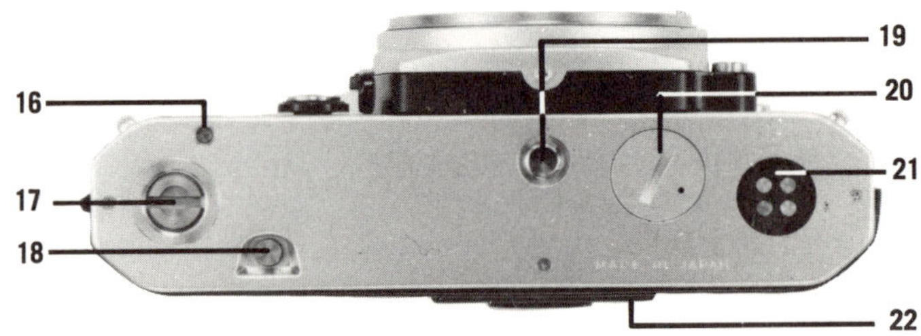

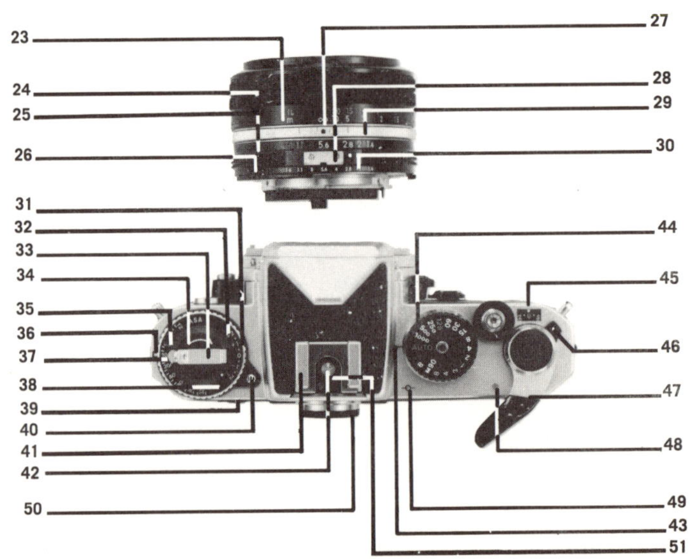

white, and a green "A" sets the shutter for automatic operation. A mechanical speed of 1/90 sec. is automatically set if the battery runs down. The shutter-release button is surrounded by a finger-guard, which doubles as the auto-winding mode switch/shutter-release lock.

Electrical System

The electronics of the EL2 operate the entire camera, not just the meter. A 6V silver-oxide type 544 battery is inserted in the bottom of the mirror chamber, through the lensmount. A battery-check button on the rear of the camera lights a small lamp when there is sufficient power in the battery. The electrical system is turned on or off by a switch in the film-advance lever, or another in the shutter-release lock.

Automatic Film-Advance Linkage

The Auto Winder AW-1 requires several electrical and mechanical couplings built into the baseplate of the camera. No modifications are needed to run the EL2 as an auto-exposure camera at up to 2 fps.

Viewing System

The viewfinder of the Nikon EL2 is a fixed, eye-level pentaprism with a large, clear, easy-to-focus image, as well as exposure information. The image is right side up and laterally correct, with a screen area approximately 92 percent of the actual scene, the remainder being the amount usually covered by a slide mount. The focusing aids are the same as those of a Nikon "K" screen: a central split-image rangefinder, surrounded by a microprism collar, on a matte Fresnel field. (See "The Viewfinder" section on the Nikon F2.)

Metering and Auto-Exposure System

The meter indicators in the viewfinder are a little different from those of other Nikons, owing to the automatic-exposure provisions of the EL2. A shutter-speed scale appears to the left of the image area, with two needles: one green, one black. A red area marked "A" is at the top of the scale; another, marked "B", is on the bottom. In auto mode, the green needle remains in the "A" zone, and the black needle points to the shutter speed being selected by the meter. In manual mode, the green needle points to the actual shutter speed set on the camera, while the black needle indicates the "proper" setting for correct exposure. Causing the needles to overlap produces a balanced exposure.

The meter itself is of the center-weighted through-the-lens type, using extremely sensitive silicon photodiodes. It is much like the meter of the Nikon F2AS Photomic. The metering range is EV 1 to EV 18 with the 50 mm *f*/1.4 Nikkor at ASA 100, and its film-speed range is ASA 12 to ASA 3200. The meter indexes automatically, and controls exposure automatically, with any AI-Nikkor over an aperture range of *f*/1.2 to *f*/32. With AI-Nikkors, the meter takes full-aperture readings; with other Nikkors the stop-down method of metering (and exposure control) is used.

The auto-exposure provision of the camera may be overridden by the exposure "memory lock," built into the self-timer lever, which allows you to freeze the shutter-speed setting. Also, an exposure-compensation ring will program the meter to yield exposures from +2 EV to −1 EV (or *f*-stops) above or below the indicated exposure.

THE NIKON FE

The Nikon FE is a compact, fully electronic automatic-exposure camera, which packs all the features of the EL2, and then some, into the body of the tiny FM. In fact, the FE is almost indistinguishable from the non-automatic FM, except for its film-speed and exposure-compensation controls, which are around the rewind crank, rather than on the shutter-speed dial. Like all the new Nikons, the FE uses the AI lenses, and it also has aperture direct readout (ADR), so the *f*-stop chosen is visible in the finder. The camera may be used with the compact Motor-Drive Unit (MD-12), like the FM, to give up to 3.5 fps continuous sequences.

Most of the mechanical features of the camera are identical to those of the FM, which are in turn based on the Nikon F2: film advance, rewind, and flatness provisions; frame counter; self-timer; depth-of-field lever; shutter release; battery chamber (for the standard two 1.5V silver-oxide Mallory MS-76 or equivalent batteries); couplings for motor drive; and standard Nikkor bayonet lensmount, among others.

In operation, however, the FE is like the EL2, providing fully automatic exposure control or match-needle metered manual photography. In practice, nearly all the operations of the Nikon FE are the same as those for the EL2, so in this and the next chapter it will be assumed that whatever is stated for one will apply to the other, unless specifically noted. The FE has, of course, several advanced features of its own

Shutter

The shutter is the identical one to that of the EL2. The only difference is in the control, which adds a mechanical "M90," that is, 1/90 sec. to the electronic speeds (and to the scale in the viewfinder). The green "A" has been replaced by the word "AUTO."

Electrical System

The electrical system is also like that of the EL2, but uses standard 1.5V batteries. An improved battery-check lever on the back of the camera lights an LED when the batteries are at full charge. Flipping out the film-advance lever turns on the power. The circuitry is of the solid-state type, using a monolithic integrated circuit (IC) and a functional resistance element (FRE) for great reliability.

Viewing System

The viewfinder of the FE is, again, like that of the Nikon EL2, with one major improvement: There are three user-interchangeable focusing screens. These are the standard Nikon "K" screen, as well as the "B" and "E" (see page 22 for illustration). The screens are interchanged very simply through the lensmount opening. This gives greater versatility to a fixed-prism camera.

Metering and Auto-Exposure System

The meter indicators in the viewfinder are the same scale-and-needle arrangement found in the EL2, and work in the same manner (see next chapter). The FE adds a window above the screen in which the *f*-number set on the lens appears. The silicon photodiode meter is also the same and operates within the same ranges. The FE also has the "memory lock" and exposure-compensation control, but the compensation range has been expanded to +2 EV to −2 EV.

Other Features

The *flash-synchronization system* is essentially that of the Nikon FM. With the *Nikon SB-10 Flash Unit*, however, when the FE is in "AUTO" mode it automatically switches to a synched 1/90 sec. speed, and a flash ready-light glows in the viewfinder. You need not reset the shutter-speed dial. (With other flash units, you must set manual speeds of 1/125 sec. or slower.)

A new *multiple-exposure lever* is mounted with the film advance. Activating it permits you to take repeated shots on the same frame.

The Nikon EM, introduced in late 1979, is the simplest Nikon ever made. This is not to suggest that the camera was simply conceived or that it is an inferior device, but for the first time a Nikon is as easy to operate as a box camera; it is also modestly priced. But the EM *is* a Nikon, taking Nikon's lenses and accessories and contains some of the subtlest and most ingenious components found in photography. The body is a marvel of the designer's art, stressing ease of use, great elegance, and diminutive size.

The EM is the smallest Nikon ever, measuring merely 134.5 × 85.9 × 54 mm (5⁵⁄₁₆″ × 3³⁄₈″ × 2⅛″) without lens, and weighing but 460 g (16½ oz). The specially made Series E 50 mm *f*/1.8 lens adds 25 mm (1″) and less than 135 g (5 oz) to the whole. The camera is the lightest fully-automatic SLR made. An aperture-preferred automatic, the EM has manual speeds of 1/90 sec. and "B," a special 1.5 EV "backlight" control, and a unique SONIC (Sound and Optical Nikon Indicator Circuit) system—in other words, an under- and over-exposure warning system that not only *shows* you the faulty setting—it also beeps!

Many of the mechanical features of the EM are essentially the same as on other models: film advance, rewind, and flatness provisions; frame-counter; self-timer; shutter release (electromagnetic); battery chamber, for two 1.5 V silver-oxide MS-76 batteries; motor-drive couplings; and standard Nikon bayonet lensmount. There are, of course, some differences: There is no depth-of-field preview button, no mirror lockup, and no standard PC flash contact; but these are compensated for by many of the camera's unique qualities.

Series E Equipment

A new line of compact, inexpensive lenses and accessories has been created just for the EM, though the camera can be used with the full battery of AI-Nikkors and many other pieces of standard Nikon apparatus. The current Series E *Nikon* lenses (as distinguished from *Nikkors*), in addition to the normal 50 mm *f*/1.8, are: a 28 mm *f*/2.8, a 35 mm *f*/2.5, a 100 mm *f*/2.8, and a remarkable 75-150 mm *f*/3.5 zoom. (The Nikon EM will *not* take Auto-Nikkors or older meter-coupled lenses; its meter-coupling lever does *not* flip out of the way and would be damaged. By the same token, Series E lenses will work on any AI/ADR Nikon/finder combination, but *not* with older meters, as the lenses do not have a meter-coupling *prong*.) Among the Series E accessories are: the *Nikon SB-E* electronic flash, a pocket-size auto unit that actually sets the camera shutter *and* is regulated itself by the lens aperture selected—another unique feature; and the Nikon *Motor Drive MD-E*, which can drive the film-wind mechanism continuously at about two frames per second, using just six AAA batteries. The MD-E weighs just 8.2 oz (185 g), but it can power 50 rolls of 36-exposure film through the camera on one set of batteries.

Shutter

The EM's shutter is of the vertical focal-plane type, with metal blades and electronically controlled continuous speeds ranging from 1 second to 1/1000 sec. (Seiko MFC). Since the camera is intended to be used principally in the auto mode, no separate shutter-speed dial is provided, but manual settings of 1/90 sec ("M90") and B, the bulb setting which makes the shutter stay open as long as the button is pressed, can be set. "M90" is used principally for flash-synch, but also as an emergency backup since it, like B, works independently of battery power. The film-wind lever, which also cocks the shutter, can be wound in many short strokes as well as one long one—the first multiple-stroke lever with such a shutter.

Viewing System

The viewfinder is a fixed silver-coated pentaprism that shows an image brighter and clearer than those of most cameras, with standard Nikon viewing aids and exposure information. The image is right side up and laterally correct, and covers about 93 percent of the scene to be recorded on film. The rest is the outermost edge usually cov-

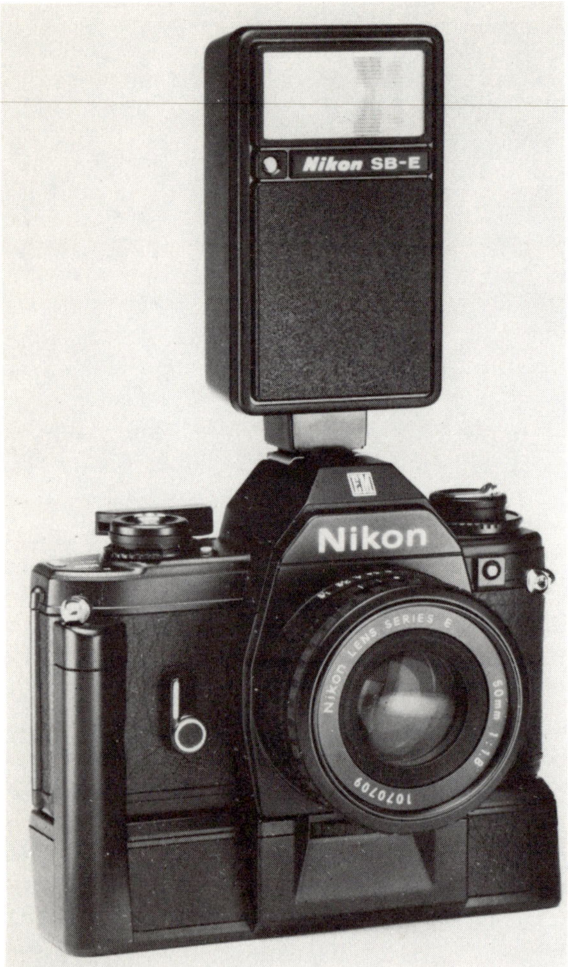

Ultra-compact, ultra-simple automatic Nikon EM, shown here with the Series E lens, winder, and flash.

ered by a slide mount. The focusing aids are those of the Nikon "K" screen: a split-image rangefinder spot, surrounded by a microprism band, on a matte Fresnel field.

Metering and Auto-Exposure System

The meter indicator in the viewfinder consists of a shutter-speed scale to the left of the image area with a single black needle. The needle points to the speed set by the meter for a correct exposure. Shutter speeds between 1/60 sec. and 1/1000 sec. are in black; the speeds below 1/30 sec. and an area above 1/1000 sec. are in red, to indicate over-exposure or a very slow shutter speed/under-exposure. When speeds are in these "alert" zones, the SONIC system noted above emits an audible pulsating beep. When the exposure is corrected, the beep stops. There is also a flash-ready LED in the finder, which lights up when a "dedicated" electronic flash unit (like the SB-E) is ready to fire, and blinks if the *f*/stop on the lens is beyond that unit's range. This is a feature found on no other camera.

The meter itself is a center-weighted silicon photodiode (SPD) type, with a metering range of EV 2 to EV 18 with the standard lens and an ASA/ISO 100 film; its film-speed range is ASA/ISO 25 to 1600. It indexes automatically with any AI-Nikkor, Series E Nikon, or non-meter-coupled lens, at full aperture *only*, as there is no stop-down provision. An override of +1.5 EV is possible with the camera's "backlight" button. The meter is activated by a slight push on the shutter-release button and remains on for 20 seconds after the button is released. For the first one or two (blank) exposures on a roll of film, the meter/auto-exposure provision is cut out; the camera fires at 1/90 sec. until the frame counter reaches "1."

Other Features

The *flash-synchronization system* consists of a "hot" shoe that works at the manual "M90" (1/90 sec.) setting with most units, but with the SB-E unit made for the camera, it passes information back and forth, as described above, and programs both flash and camera to yield perfect exposures.

A *battery-check button* and corresponding LED, and a built-in *memo-holder* round out the EM's provisions.

CHAPTER 2

Operating the Cameras

In this chapter the physical manipulations needed to operate the various Nikon cameras will be described. In the interests of clarity and brevity, the "why's" and "wherefore's" will be discussed in later chapters devoted to various aspects of photography.

The Nikon system was put together by people very much aware of "human engineering." They intended to make cameras that were fine instruments but easy to handle, for even the finest instruments are essentially worthless if they can be operated only with great difficulty. Nikon engineers have succeeded admirably in making all the Nikon models a joy to use. Once a Nikon owner has mastered a few simple procedures, he or she may forget about the means and get on with the object: making good pictures. The functions of each camera are remarkably self-evident, and once you decide what you are going to do, the camera itself helps you do it. The simple procedures that must be learned are: loading (and unloading) the camera with film; setting and using the exposure meter; viewing (composing) the scene and focusing the camera; setting the camera controls; shooting the picture; changing lenses; and, where applicable, changing finders, automatic exposure, and motorized operation.

In this chapter, as elsewhere, the various Nikon models, which operate in a very similar fashion, will be discussed simultaneously, with distinctions being made where necessary. Newer models will be stressed, and operations peculiar to one or two models will be discussed at the end of the chapter.

LOADING AND UNLOADING

Always load and unload the camera in subdued light. This does not mean in impenetrable gloom, but stay out of direct sunlight or the glare of light bulbs.

Open the back. On Nikon F and F2 cameras, twist the "O/C" key on the bottom plate; the Nikon F back and bottom plate comes off completely; the Nikon F2 back swings open. For other models: Unlock and pull up on the rewind knob; the back will swing open. In any case, pull up the rewind knob. The frame counter will automatically reset to "S" (start).

Insert the film cartridge. With the rewind knob up, drop the cartridge, projecting end *down,* into the film chamber on the left. Push the rewind knob back down, making sure the claw engages the film spool.

Insert the film into the take-up spool. Draw the film from the cartridge across the back of the camera to the take-up spool on the right. Insert the end of the film into any of the slots on the spool (older cameras have a single slot). Make sure the film is engaged.

Advance the film. Slowly wind the advance

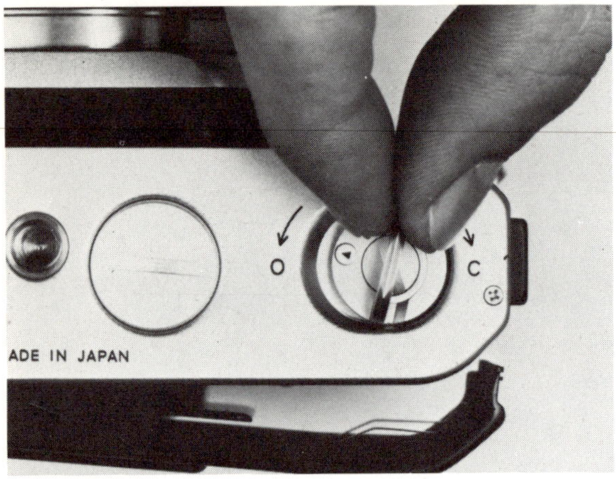

A. Open back (F, F2).

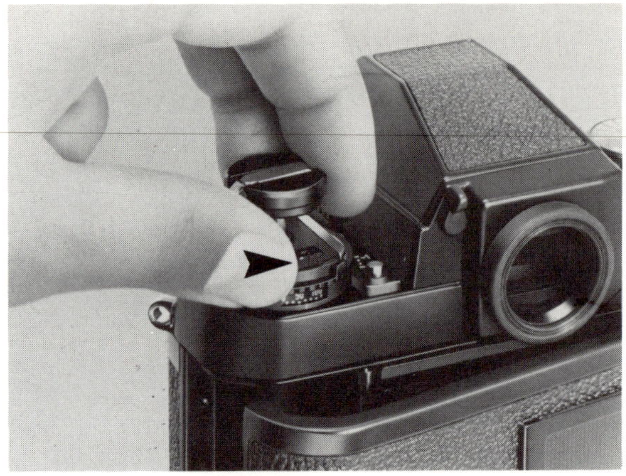

B. Open back (F3, FE, FM, EM, EL2).

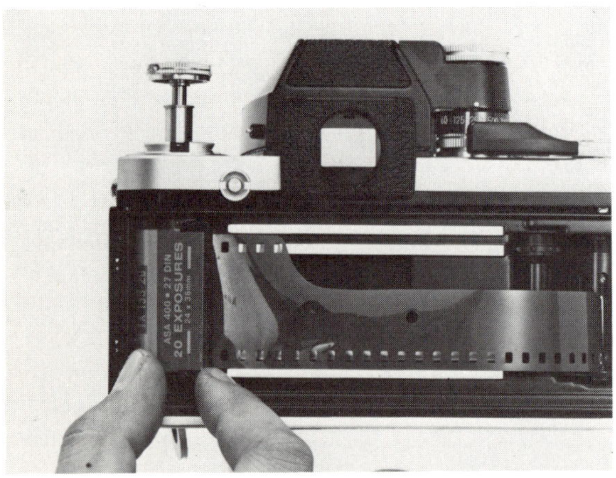

C. Insert film.

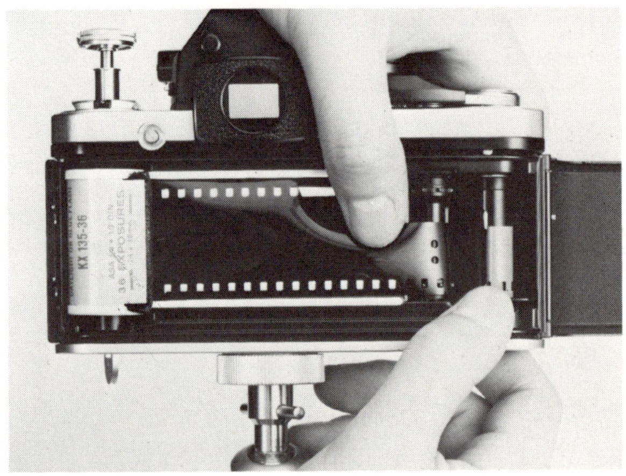

D. Attach to take-up spool.

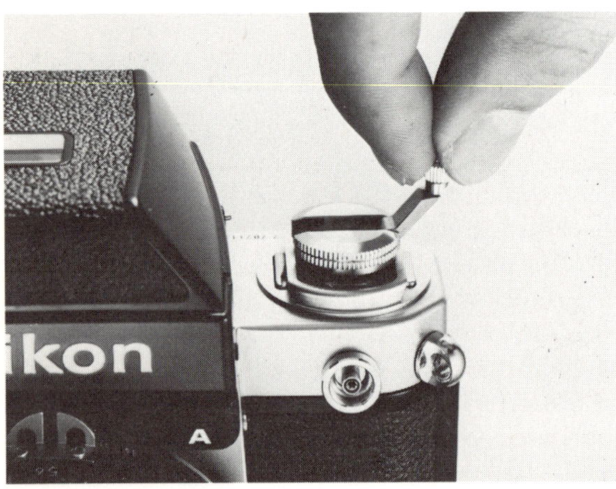

E. Take up slack.

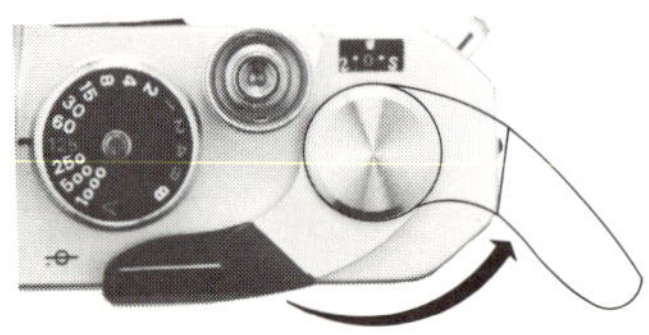

F. Advance film.

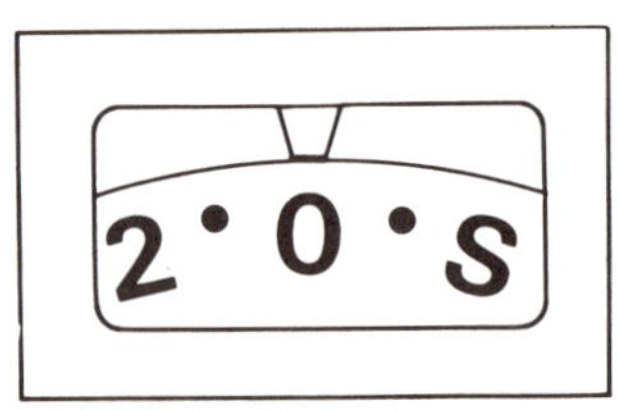

G. Counter at "0."

Loading any Nikon camera. See text for details. Note that Nikon F, F2 open by turning key on bottom. With all other models, pull up on rewind knob. F3 and EM bypass meter in loading sequence, so shutter does not stay open and delay loading.

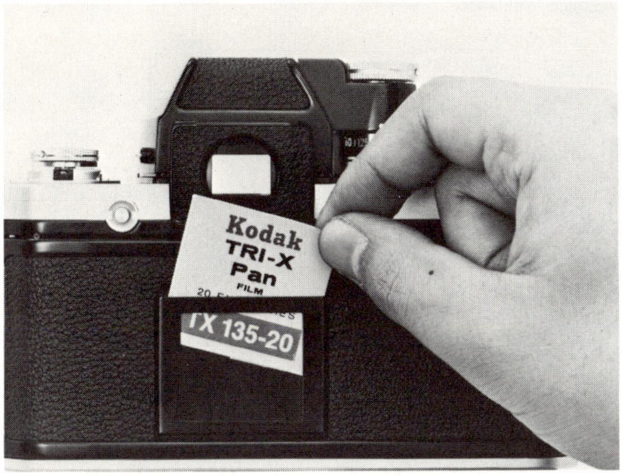

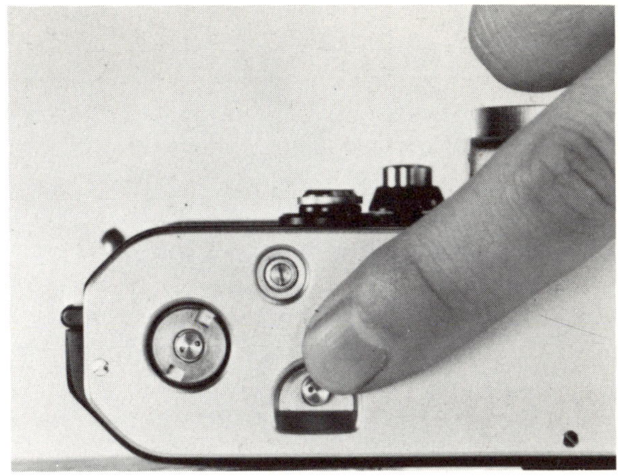

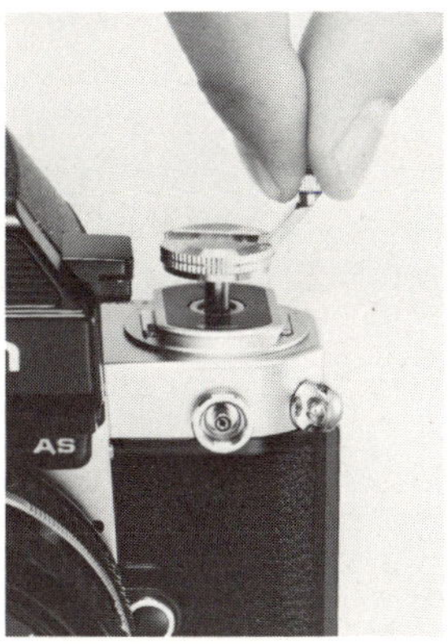

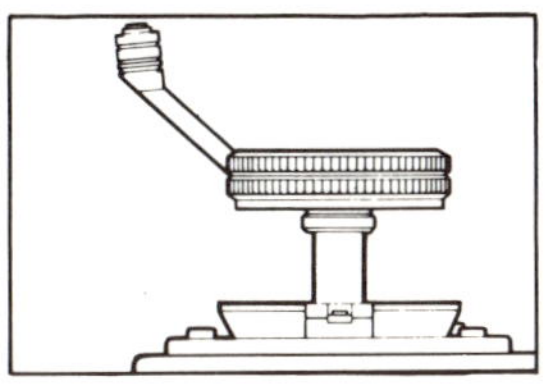

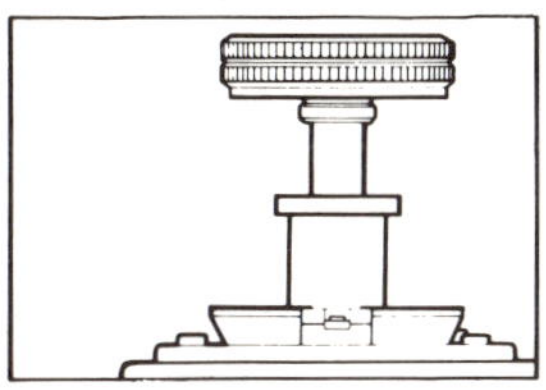

Insert film-box top in memo holder. To unload, press rewind button (on Nikon F, turn A-R ring to "R") and turn crank. On Nikon F2, raise crank to first notch to rewind, second notch to remove film.

lever; the film will go *over* the sprocket wheels and *under* the take-up spool (emulsion side out). See that the top and bottom sprocket teeth both engage parallel perforations. Release the shutter when the advance lever stops; then wind it again.

Take up the slack. Press down gently on the sprocket teeth protruding through the film perforations. Unfold the rewind crank and gently turn it in the direction of the arrow to take up the film slack. When it will turn no farther, stop.

Close the back. When both perforations are engaged, and if the film is advancing smoothly, swing the back shut and turn the key or push down the snap, thus locking the camera.

Blank exposures. Wind the film-advance lever twice, releasing the shutter each time. The frame counter should now indicate "0," and the camera is ready to go.

Rewinding. When the last frame (20 or 36) has been exposed, the advance lever will "bind" in mid-swing. *Do not force it further.* Push in the rewind button on the base of the camera; it will click and stay put. The film is now free of the advance mechanism. (On the Nikon F only, there is no rewind button; turn the A-R ring, instead, to "R.") Flip up the crank on the rewind knob and turn it slowly in the direction of the arrow.

Unloading. When the tension of the crank suddenly ceases, turn the crank once or twice more; then pull up the rewind knob or twist the O/C key to open the camera back. The film cartridge will drop out easily.

SETTING THE EXPOSURE METER

Before setting the meter on any Nikon camera with one built in (or in a Photomic finder), you must first know the sensitivity of the film you are using. Film sensitivity, or "speed," is usually expressed in this country as an "ASA number"; the higher the number the "faster," or more sensitive, the film. ASA stands for the American Standards Association, now actually named the American National Standards Institute. Some European films are rated in "DIN numbers" (Deutsche Industrie Norm). The new ISO combines both numbers. This information is usually printed on the film package, and sometimes on the cartridge, too. The meter must be coordinated with the speed of the film in use to indicate the correct exposure. (A further discussion of film speed will be found in Chapter 5.)

On the various Nikon cameras and finders, the ASA film-speed dial is in different places, and extends through different ranges, but the principle is the same: A circular scale with the various ASA numbers (or dots, representing intermediate values) must be made to align with an index mark. For example, on the Photomic finders and the Nikon FM, the dial is on the same knob as the shutter-speed dial. The scale on the Nikon F3 has numbers and dots representing the ASA ratings of all films in common use, including "pushed" speeds: 12 · · 25 · · 50 · · 100 · · 200 · · 400 · · 800 · · 1600 · · 3200 · · 6400. The dots represent the ASA speeds 16, 20, 32, 40, 64, 80, 125, 160, 250, 320, 500, 640, 1000, 1250, 2000, 2500, 4000, and 5000.

Set the dial. On all but the earliest Photomic finders for the Nikon F, merely lift and rotate the film-speed dial so that the proper ASA number is adjacent to the index mark (usually a red triangle). The Nikon F3, FE, EM, and EL2 have the film-speed dial around the rewind crank. On the early Nikon Photomic, Photomic T, and Photomic TN, the speed must be aligned with a number engraved on the dial representing the maximum aperture of the lens in use *each time* the lens is changed.

Test the meter battery. Again, depending upon the model you own, press the battery-check button or move the film-advance lever to the offset position. The meter needle (in finders that use them) should swing to the right edge of the notch or beyond (the center of the Nikon Photomic FTN), or the LED should glow. If this fails to happen, replace the battery or batteries.

Turn on the meter. On the F3, and older Photomic finders, use the "ON" switch. On the newer Photomics, the Nikon FM, FE, or EL2, merely moving the film-advance lever to the standoff position, uncovering the red dot on the body, turns the meter on. It should then respond to changes in light.

COMPOSING AND FOCUSING

Look through the viewfinder eyepiece. You will see exactly what the camera "sees." The viewfinder magnifies the image 0.8×, or nearly life-size, with the normal lens, and shows you 92 to 100 percent coverage, depending on the camera model. The life-size image facilitates your looking at the scene before you with your naked eye, then switching to the camera without being jarred by a sudden change of image size. Thus, you can "follow-focus," or watch a scene entering your viewfinder area and catch it at the critical moment.

Focus the image. When you have the picture you want in the viewfinder, bring it into focus by rotating the focusing ring right or left, until the shimmering microprism image clears and looks like a single picture, or until the split image in the rangefinder spot is brought into alignment, depending upon which screen you have on the camera. (See the table on the opposite page.) You may focus using the rest of the screen, but the rangefinder or microprism is most critical.

Exposure measurement via full-aperture method
Exposure measurement via stop-down method
Exposure measurement not possible; lens/screen combination permits only focusing operation
Blank space indicates lens/screen combination cannot be used

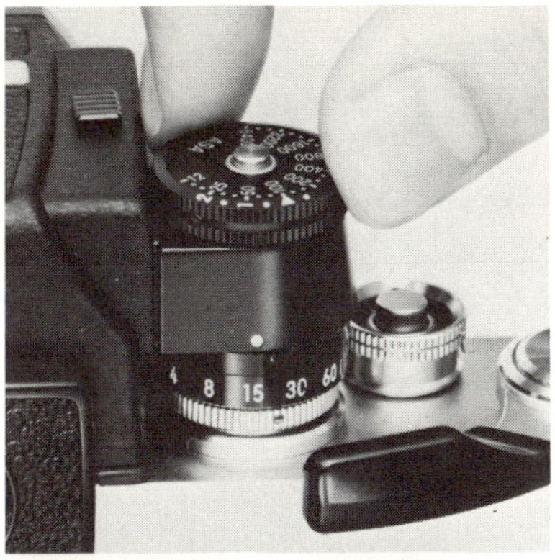

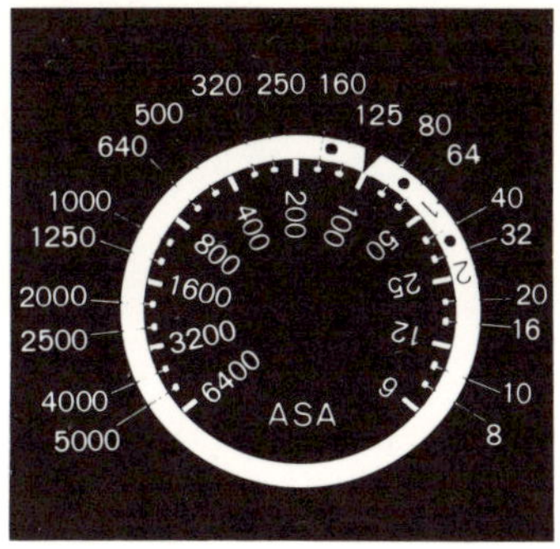

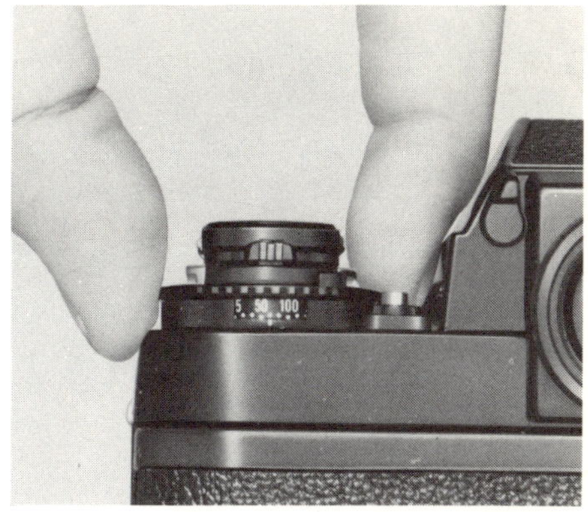

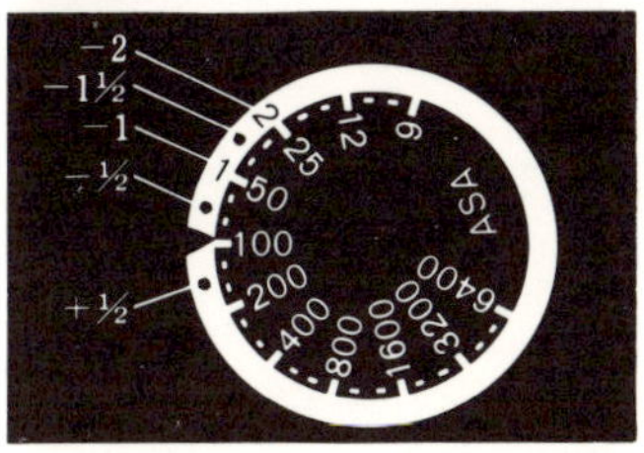

Top: to set exposure meter on any Nikon, align ASA/ISO speed with index. Dots represent intermediary speeds. Dial on automatic models is around rewind crank. Left: exposure on Photomic (F and F2) finders can be compensated +½ to −2 stops for various lens/screen combinations. This *kind* of compensation (in the table below) is *not* required for the F3.

EXPOSURE COMPENSATION FOR VARIOUS LENS/SCREEN COMBINATIONS (F & F2 ONLY)

Lens	Screen	A/L	B	C	D	E	G1	G2	G3	G4	H1	H2	H3	H4	J	K/P	M.	R
Fisheye	6mm F2.8	0	0	−½	−½	0	0	0			0	0			0	0		0
	8mm F2.8	0	0	−½	−½	0	0	0			0	0	0		0	0		0
	16mm F3.5	0	0			0	−½				0				0	0		0
Wideangle	13mm F5.6	0	0			0		−1				−½			0	0		0
	15mm F5.6	0	0			0		−1½				−½			0	0		0
	18mm F4	0	0			0	−1				−1				0	0		0
	20mm F4	0	0			0	−1				−½				0	0		0
	24mm F2	0	0			0		0			+½	0			0	0		0
	24mm F2.8	0	0			0		0			+½	0			0	0		0
	28mm F2	0	0			0	+½	+½			+½	+½			0	0		0
	28mm F2.8	0	0			0	−½				0				0	0		0
	28mm F3.5	0	0			0	−½	−½			0	0			0	0		0
	35mm F1.4	0	0			0		+½			+½	+½			0	0		0
	35mm F2	0	0			0	+½	0			+½	0			0	0		0
	35mm F2.8	0	0			0	0				0	0			0	0		0
Normal	50mm F1.4	0	0			0		+½				+½			0	0		0
	50mm F2	0	0			0	+½	+½			+½	+½			0	0		0
	55mm F1.2	0	0			0		0				0			0	0		0
Telephoto	85mm F1.8	0	0			0		+½			+½	+½			0	0		0
	85mm F2	0	0			0		+½			+½	+½			0	0		0
	105mm F2.5	0	0			0		0			+½	+½			0	0		0
	135mm F2	0	0	0	0	0		+½				+½			0	0		0
	135mm F2.8	0	0	0	0	0		0				+½			0	0		0
	135mm F3.5	0	0			0		−½				+½			0	0		0
	180mm F2.8	0	0	0	0	0			0			0	0	0	0	0		0
	200mm F4	0	0	0	0	0		−1½				−1			0	0		0
	300mm F4.5	0	0	0	0	0			−1½			−1½	−1	−1½	0	0		0
	ED 300mm F4.5	0	0	0	0	0			−1½			−1½	−1	−1½	0	0		0
	400mm F4.5	0	0	0	0	0									0	0		0
	※ED 400mm F3.5	0	0	0	0	0			−1	−½			0	−½	0	0		0
	ED 400mm F5.6	0	0	0	0	0									0	0		0
	600mm F5.6	0	0	0	0	0									0	0		0
	※ED 600mm F5.6	0	0	0	0	0									0	0		0
	ED 600mm F5.6	0	0	0	0	0									0	0		0
	800mm F8	0	0	0	0	0									0	0		0
	ED 800mm F8	0	0	0	0	0									0	0		0
	1200mm F11	0	0	0	0	0									0	0		0
	ED1200mm F11	0	0	0	0	0									0	0		0
Zoom	28~45mm F4.5	0	0			0					0				0	0		0
	43~86mm F3.5	0	0			0		−½				−½			0	0		0
	50~300mm F4.5	0	0			0			−2				−1½		0	0		0
	ED50~300mm F4.5	0	0			0			−1			−1½	−½		0	0		0
	80~200mm F4.5	0	0			0			−1			−1½	−½		0	0		0
	ED180~600mm F8	0	0	0	0	0									0	0		0
	200~600mm F9.5	0	0	0	0	0									0	0		0
	ED360~1200mm F11	0	0	0	0	0									0	0		0
PC	28mm F4	0	0			0									0	0		0
	35mm F2.8	0	0			0									0	0		0
GN	45mm F2.8	0	0			0	0				0				0	0		0
Noct	58mm F1.2	0	0			0		0			0	0			0	0		0
Micro	55mm F3.5	0	0			0									0	0		0
	105mm F4	0	0			0									0	0		0
Medical	200mm F5.6	0	0			0									0	0		0
Reflex Telephoto	500mm F8	0	0	0	0	0									0	0		0
	1000mm F11	0	0	0	0	0									0	0		0
	2000mm F11	0	0	0	0	0									0	0		0

※Internal focusing type

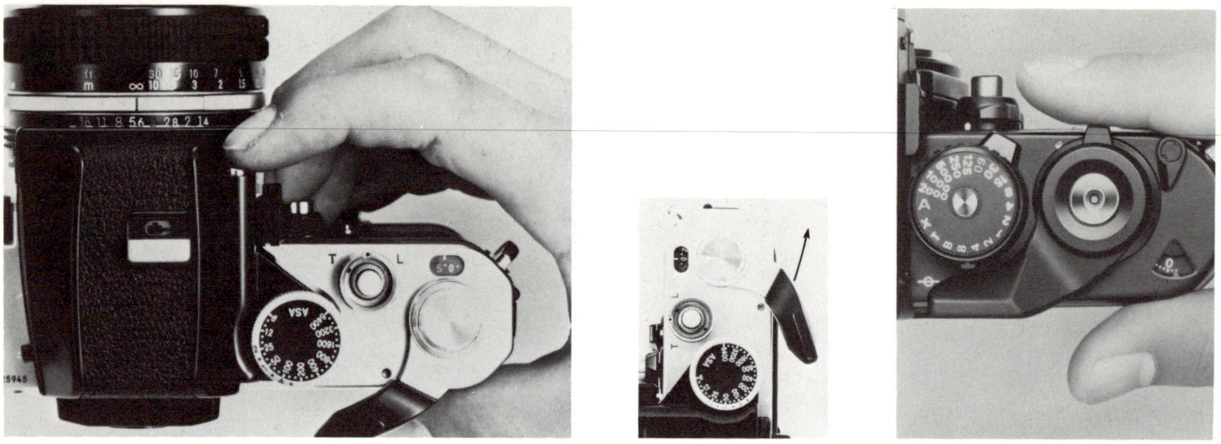

Testing meter batteries. On F2 and F2A, push button and pull out wind lever. On F2S, F2Sb, F2AS, and FM, pull out lever only. On FE and EL2, push button in back. On F3 and EM, turn camera on, touch shutter button.

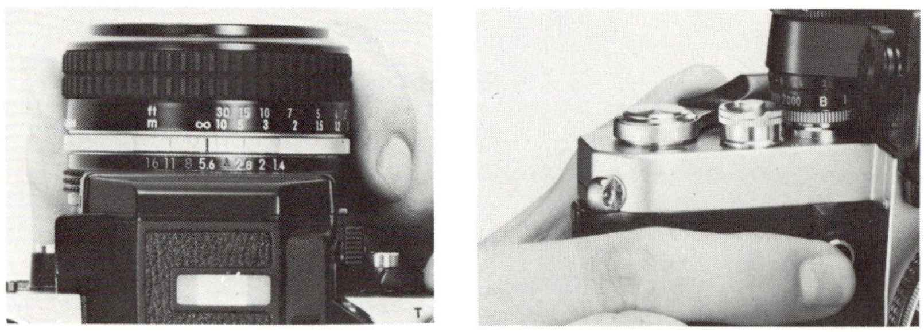

To focus, turn focusing ring on lens until image is sharp. To preview depth of field, push in preview button or lever.

It is best to turn the focusing ring past the point of sharpest focus, then back. This allows you to zero in on the subject with added accuracy. The Nikon is then focused for that subject at that distance, which may be read in feet or meters on the distance scale on the lensbarrel. (In using infrared film, that distance setting must then be moved to the red dot or line on the depth-of-field scale.) Nevertheless, other areas of the scene may not be in focus.

Check the depth of field. To determine how much of any given composition is in focus, you may observe the extent of focus (called the "depth of field") visually by depressing the depth-of-field preview button or lever, on the left side of the camera front or lensmount, as the camera faces you. This causes the automatic diaphragm of an AI-Nikkor or Auto-Nikkor to close down to the aperture that has been set, which in turn reveals the depth of field. Manual Nikkors can be stopped down merely by turning their aperture rings. Releasing the preview button returns the diaphragm to full aperture. (A depth-of-field scale, in color-coded lines, is also engraved on every Nikkor lens. Its use, and the relationship of aperture to depth of field, will be examined in the chapters "Lenses" and "Basic Photography.")

METERING THE SCENE

Your photograph is now composed and focused. The next step is obtaining the correct exposure. Depending on the model of the camera or finder, and the type of lens you are using, Nikon offers a number of metering possibilities, but the object is generally the same: to bring some indi-

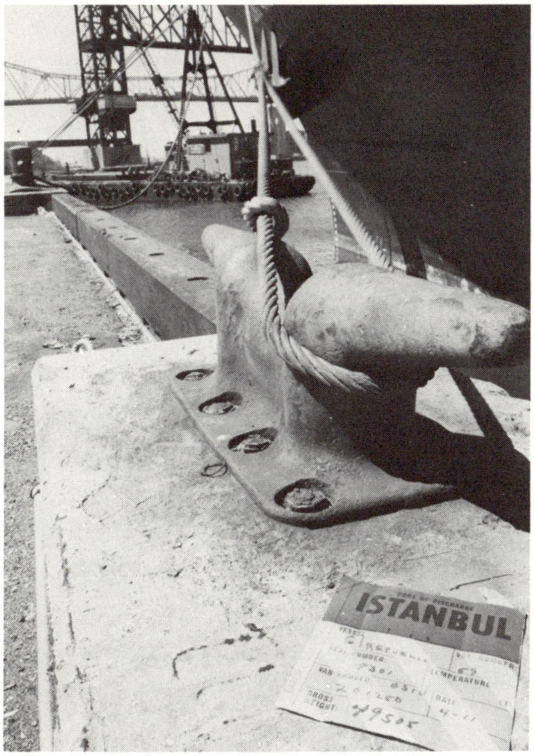

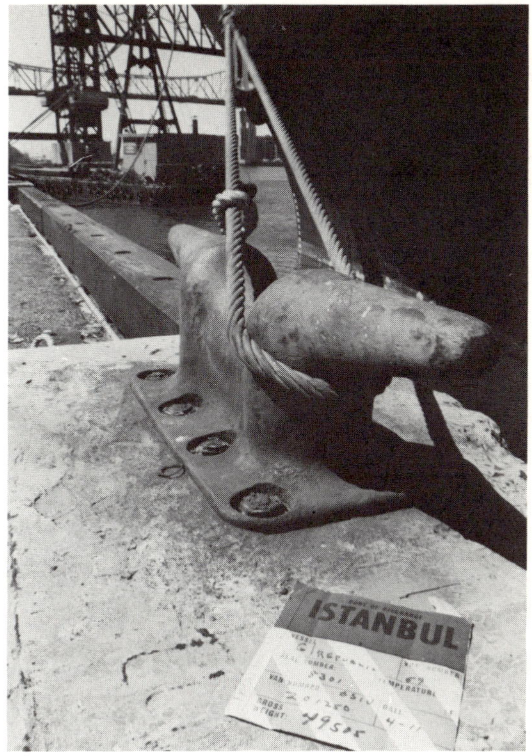

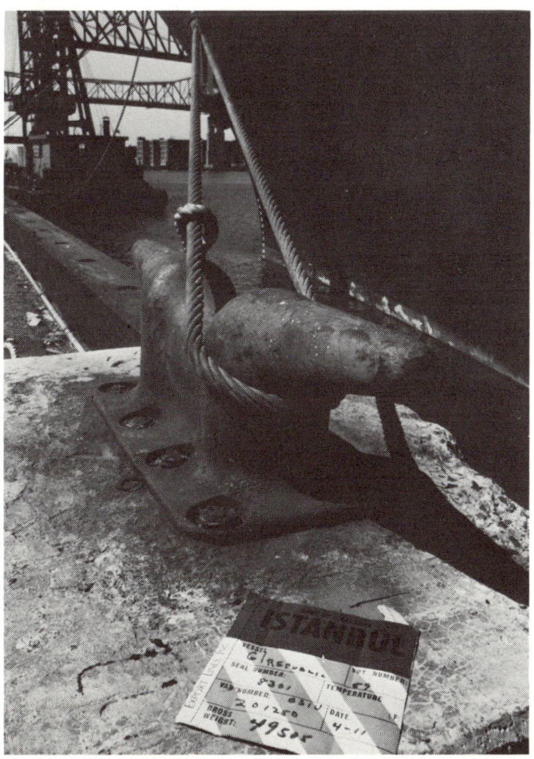

Metering the scene. Any Nikon meter will give you the "correct" exposure, but there are times when slight over- or underexposure will show certain aspects of the picture to better advantage. Here, exposure at top right is balanced for *all* elements in the photo, but one stop overexposure (top left) gives more detail in the ship's hull, while one stop underexposure (left) emphasizes the striped, exotic bill of lading. All taken at *f*/11, for front-to-back depth of field, at shutter speeds of 1/60, 1/125, and 1/250 sec. on Plus-X, with a medium yellow filter; 28 mm Nikkor.

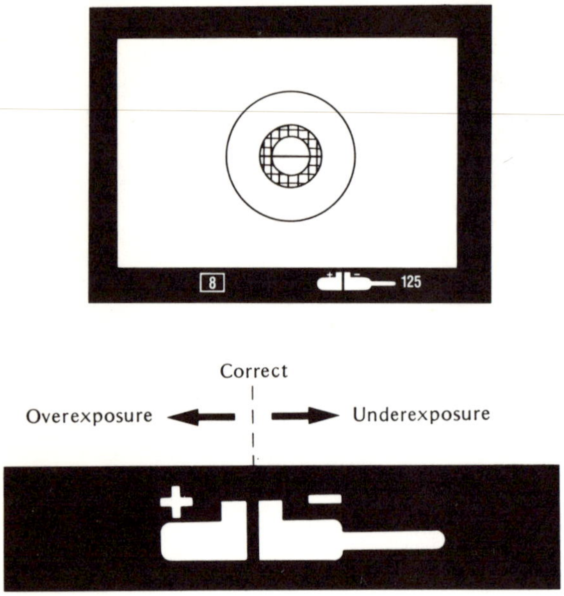

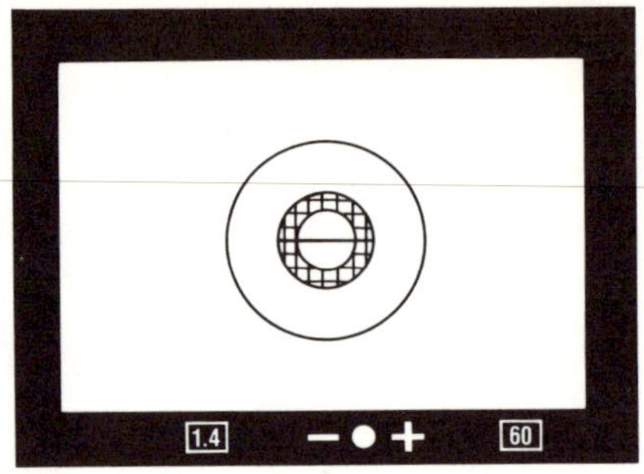

− ● +	Overexposure by more than 1 f-stop
− ● +	Overexposure by 1/5 to 1 f-stop
− ● +	Correct Exposure
− ● +	Underexposure by 1/5 to 1 f-stop
− ● +	Underexposure by more than 1 f-stop

Meter display of Nikon F2A Photomic. Over/under indicator is also on top of prism. Similar meter needle is found on older F2 Photomic, must be centered for correct exposure.

Meter display of Nikon F2AS and F2Sb Photomics. LED's, which replace the meter needle, indicate correct exposure when middle diode is lit.

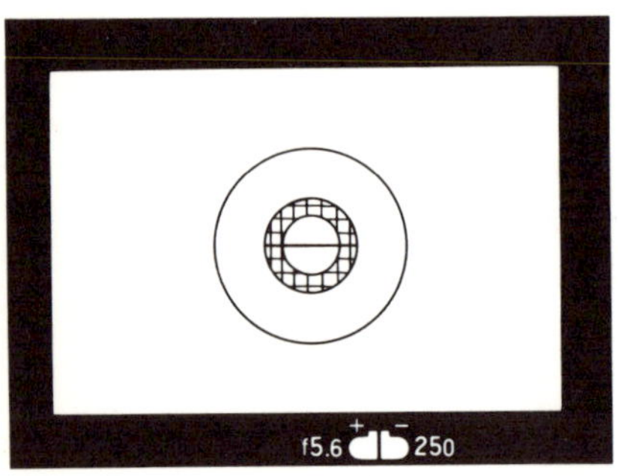

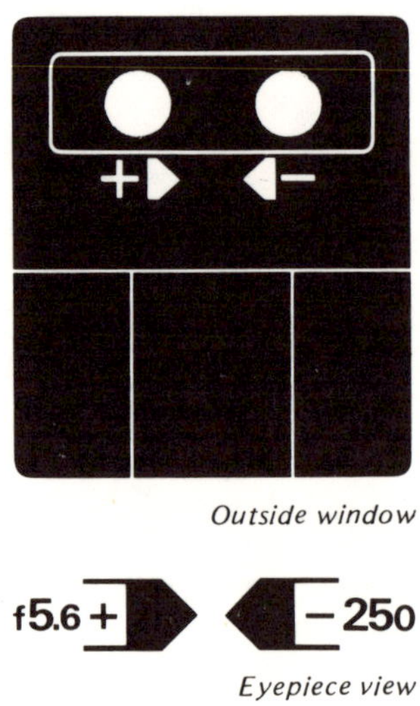

Above: meter display of Nikon F2 Photomic. Center needle for correct exposure. Right: Nikon F2S Photomic required both diodes to light for proper exposure; arrow-shaped in viewfinder; dots atop prism.

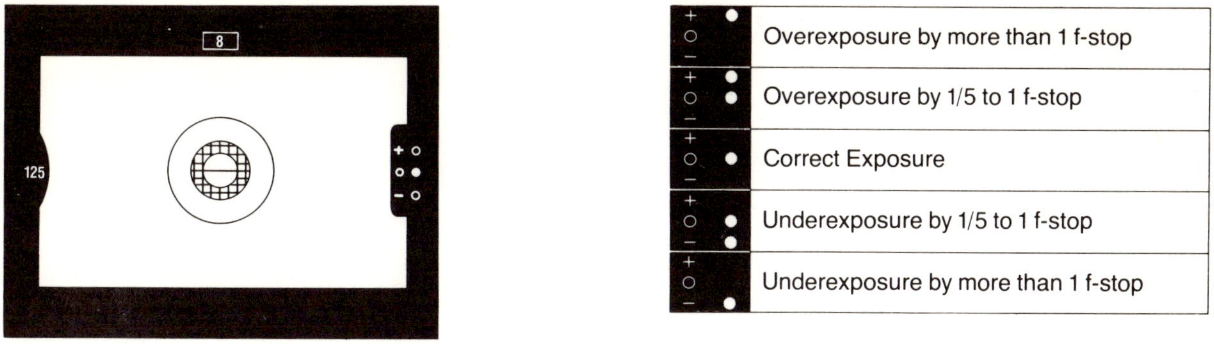

Meter display of Nikon FM is similar to that of F2AS, requires lighting of central diode for correct exposure.

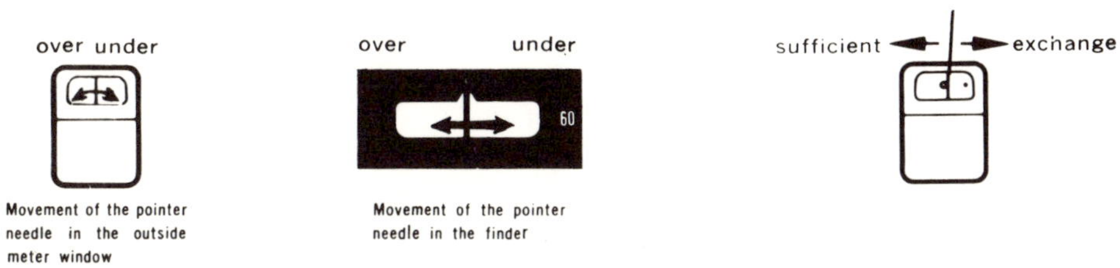

Nikon FTN Photomic used needle-centering method of determining proper exposure; also incorporated battery-check.

cator in the viewfinder to a "correct" position, by varying the shutter speed and in most cases the aperture of the lens. When that is done, the "right" amount of light will strike the film. (There are exceptions to correct exposure, but they will be discussed later.)

Meter Display

In every Nikon exposure meter, various indicators for correct, over, or underexposure are displayed. Nikon has used a number of systems in their SLR's over the years, but two basic types dominate: *needle centering* and *LED display*. The exceptions are the F3, FE, EM, and EL2, which require different metering because of their auto-exposure provisions and will be discussed separately. The following cameras (or finders) indicate correct exposure by centering a needle in a notch in the viewfinder (and often, a second one on top of the camera): Nikon F Photomic; Photomic T, TN, and FTN; Nikon F2 Photomic and F2A Photomic. In all these cameras, when the needle points upright, the exposure is correct; when it points to the left, overexposure is indicated; when to the right, underexposure.

The Nikon F2S, F2Sb, and F2AS Photomic, and the Nikon FM, all use a form of LED display. The F2S uses two diodes, the left for overexposure, the right for underexposure. To get proper exposure, you must vary the controls until *both* light simultaneously. The F2Sb, F2AS, and FM use a more advanced three-diode system, marked "+" (overexposure), "0" (correct exposure), and "−" (underexposure). Correct exposure is indicated by the central "0" being illuminated. When the "0" and either the "+" or "−" are lit simultaneously, the meter indicates over or underexposure by 1/5 to one full *f*-stop. When the "+" or "−" are lit alone, it means over or underexposure by more than one *f*-stop. All three cannot light together, nor can the "+" and "−" light at the same time.

Full-Aperture Metering

The most convenient way to measure light is with the lens at maximum aperture, for this method leaves the picture at its brightest and requires no complicated operations. But it does necessitate an automatic-diaphragm lens coupled to the meter. For this reason, an *AI-Nikkor* lens *must* be used with the Nikon Photomics F2A and F2AS, the Nikon F3, FE, FM, EM, and EL2. The same type of coupling is made when an *Auto-Nikkor* is used on any of the other Nikon Photomic SLR's.

Preselected shutter speed. If you have determined the shutter speed, simply change the aperture setting (*f*-stop) until the needle lines up or the proper LED glows red. If no change in aperture will cause this to happen, select another shutter speed and try again.

Preselected aperture. If, on the other hand, you know what aperture you want, set it. Then try the various shutter speeds until the needle or LED indicates correct exposure. Again, if you can't get proper exposure at any shutter speed (or if the speed is inconveniently slow), start with another *f*-stop.

An exception to these operations takes place when the light is too dim for the meter to give a proper reading (when it is below the range for the lens and film being used). With most Nikons, the "B" setting indicates time exposures longer than two seconds. Trial and error is the solution. With the extra-long shutter-speed scale on the Nikon F2S, F2Sb, and F2AS Photomics, however, it is possible to *measure* longer exposures (to ten seconds), and then use the self-timer to get them with the shutter set at "B." Depress the shutter-speed lock and continue to turn the dial. When the proper LED lights, read the speed indicated on the long-speed scale, then set that speed.

Stop-Down Metering

When a lens has no automatic diaphragm or does not couple to the Nikon meter, light measurement is still possible by the stop-down method, in which the aperture is closed down physically. Since the meter is designed to measure light with the lens open, however, this is a little tricky. The

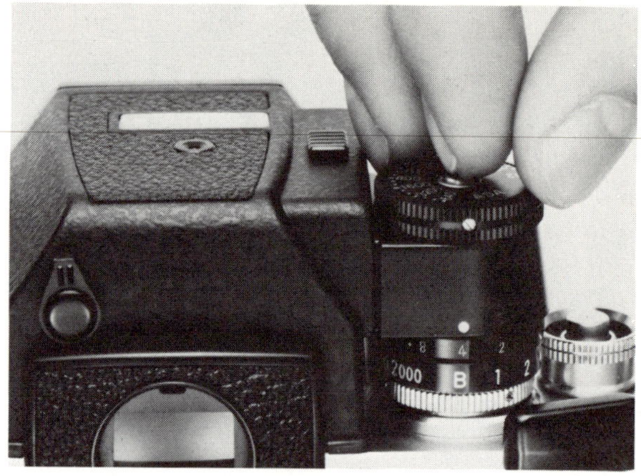

Measuring long exposures on F2 models.

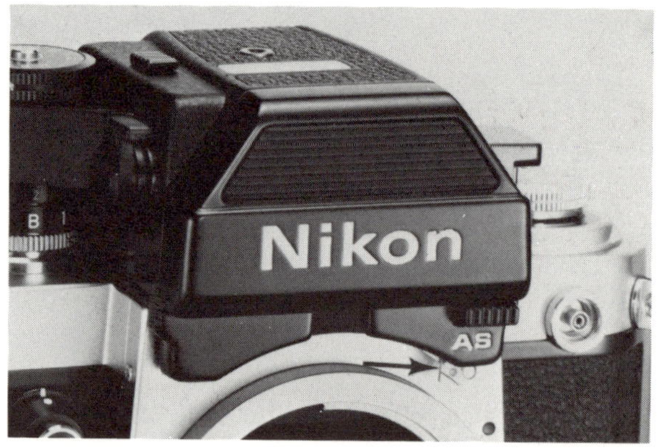

Stop-down metering with F3, FE, EM, F2A, F2AS, and FM. See text for details.

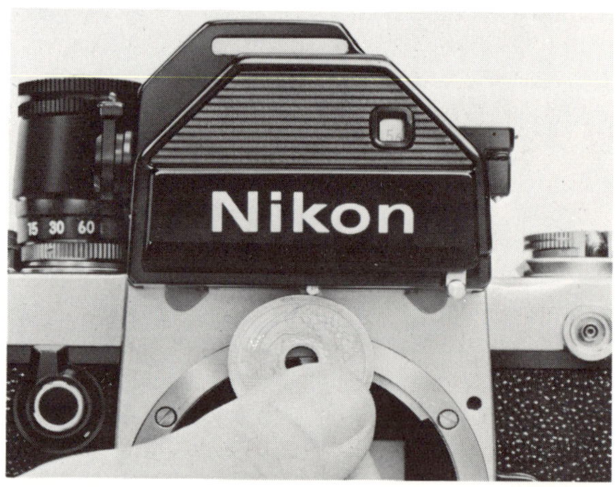

Stop-down metering on older model Photomics. See text for details.

method varies from model to model, so we will present a brief outline here of how it is done.

Stop-down metering must be used on the Nikon F2A and F2AS Photomics, the FM, FE, and EL2 when *any* other lens but an Al-Nikkor is mounted on the camera *directly*. If a bellows or other extension device is used—even with an Al lens—stop-down metering is required. On other Nikon models, anything but an Al-Nikkor *or* Auto-Nikkor requires stop-down measurement.

Nikon F2A, F2AS Photomics, and FM. For non-coupled auto lenses: (1) Push the meter-coupling lever up and to the *right* until it locks in position. (2) Set the shutter at the desired speed. (3) Depress the depth-of-field preview button and hold it down while setting the aperture. (4) When the indicator shows the proper exposure, release the depth button and shoot. For lenses with no diaphragm, vary the shutter speed alone. For bellows units, manual lenses, and the like, merely set the desired shutter speed and close down the diaphragm until the indicator shows the proper exposure.

Nikon F2, F2S, and F2Sb Photomics. (1) Push *up* the meter-coupling pin, until "5.6" appears in the maximum-aperture indicator window. (2) Then adjust the *f*-stop and/or shutter speed as in full-aperture metering.

Nikon F Photomic FTN. (1) Push up the meter-coupling pin to bring the red index on the front of the meter to the engraved "5.6" position. (2) Then adjust as in full-aperture metering.

Nikon F Photomic T, TN. (1) Set the ASA number of the film in use to the red dot position.

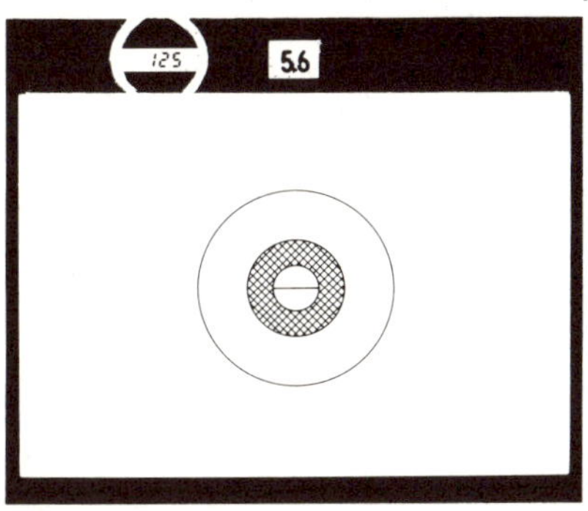

Viewfinder/meter display of Nikon F3. LCD window (top left) gives shutter, exposure information; ADR window (top center) shows *f*/stop set on lens. Other auto models use needles and scales.

(2) Move the meter-coupling pin to the *right* until it clicks into place; the aperture window on the back should show "1." (3) Use the preview button to stop down the lens, and adjust the aperture and the shutter as in full-aperture metering.

Nikon F Photomic. Push the slider to simulate diaphragm action. When the needle is centered, read the *f*-stop in the window and set the lens accordingly.

Metering/Auto-Exposure with Automatic Models

The Nikons capable of automatic exposure display and use exposure information quite differently from other models, although their meters are similar to other Nikons's, and the nature of the information is the same. Currently, the auto-exposure models are the Nikon F3, EM, FE, and EL2. All models but the EM can be used in the metered-manual mode as well.

Detailed descriptions of the meter displays are given for each model in Chapter 1. Here we will restrict our discussion to their use. There are four basic ways to use the meter/exposure systems of all these Nikons (except the EM): *auto mode, full-aperture*; *manual mode, full-aperture*; *auto mode, stop-down*; and *manual mode, stop-down*. The EM is designed to provide *only* full-aperture automatic exposure; it has limited manual capability and *no* stop-down provision.

Automatic mode, full-aperture (Al-Nikkor only). This is the most convenient way to use the camera, for the meter selects and sets the proper

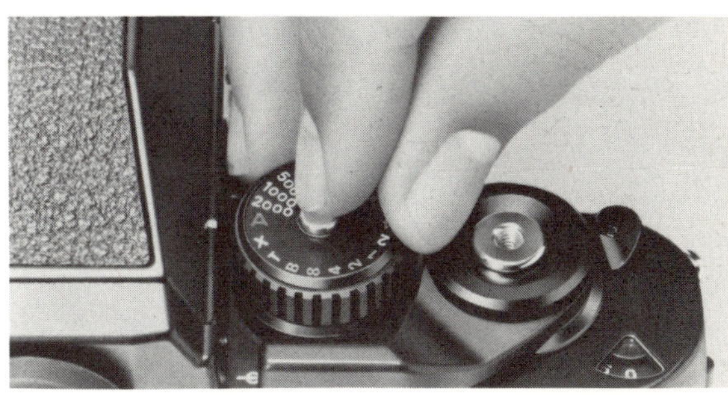

To get any auto model's shutter-speed dial off "AUTO," push in dial lock, then rotate dial to desired speed.

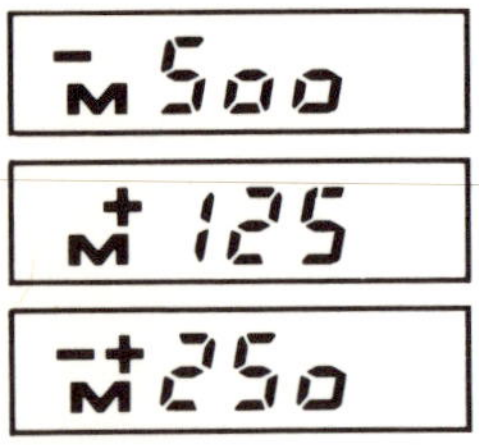

Meter display. On FE or EL2 (left), green needle stays on "A" in auto mode, black needle indicates shutter speed. In manual mode, green needle indicates speed set, black needle indicates "correct" speed. Vary *f*/stops until needles overlap. On F3 (above), LCD shows shutter-speed and (in manual mode) "+" or "−" to indicate over- or underexposure. Vary shutter or aperture until "− +" appears.

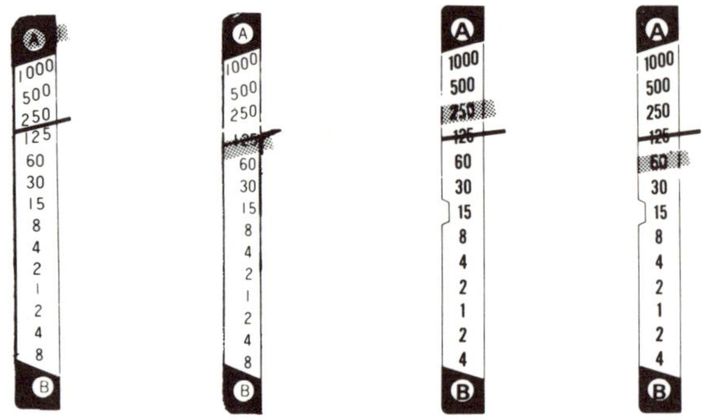

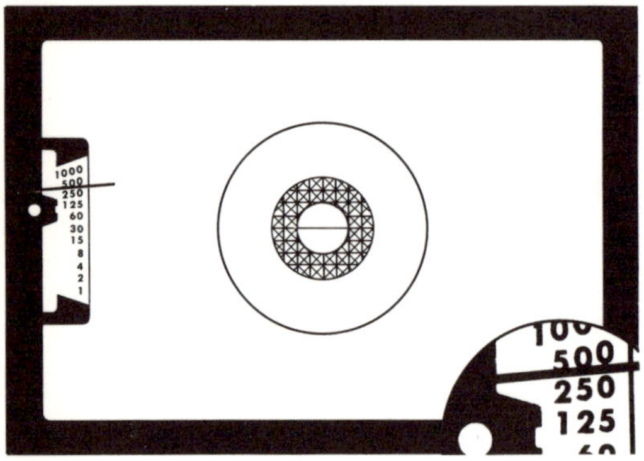

Meter display of Nikon EM. Needle points to shutter speed selected; "SONIC" system warns of over- or under-range lighting. Red LED in center is flash-ready and warning signal.

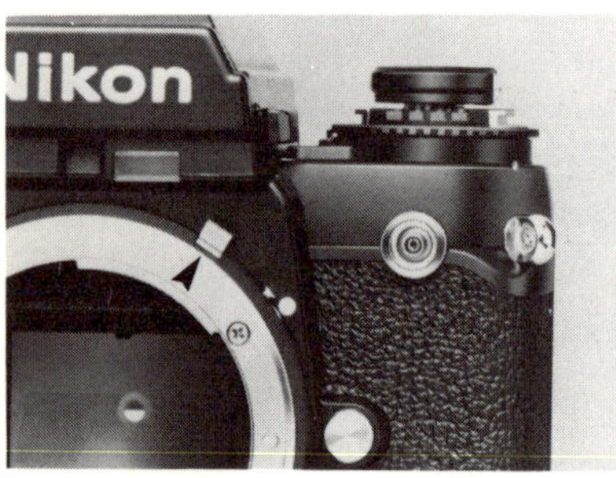

Meter-coupling lever up.

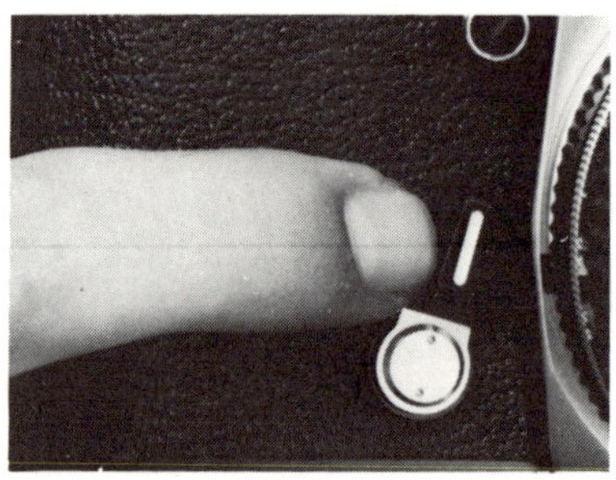

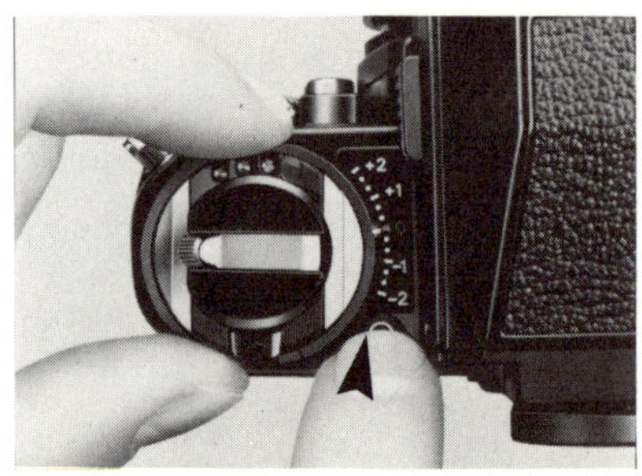

FE Memory lock (left) and F3 exposure compensation ring (right) are shown here. EM uses a "backlight button."

exposure. (1) Set the shutter-speed dial to "A" or "Auto." In the FE or EL2 the green needle will move to "A" in the finder. In the F3, the LCD will turn on, and in the EM the needle will be activated, by gentle pressure on the shutter-release button. (2) Select any aperture; the meter will select the shutter speed, which is indicated by the meter needle or LCD. To change the shutter speed, vary the aperture. Each camera has its own method of warning of over- or underexposure.

Manual mode, full-aperture. To choose your own settings, as per the instructions for the other Nikons, (1) select a shutter speed and set it. The meter indicator will tell you which speed you have set. (2) Vary the aperture until the meter indicates correct exposure: in the F3, the "− +" will show; in the FE and EL2, the black and green needles will overlap. (3) You may reverse this procedure, starting with an *f*/stop. As the EM has only the "M90" and "B" manual settings, this option is very limited.

Automatic mode, stop-down metering (non-AI lenses). (1) Lock up the meter-coupling lever, as with the Nikon F2A. (2) Set the shutter to "A." (3) Hold the depth-of-field preview button down while selecting the aperture. In the F3 the LCD and in the FE and EL2 the black needle will indicate the meter-chosen shutter speed. (4) Either keep the preview button down or switch to the memory-lock button, but keep one depressed when you make the exposure. (5) With fixed-aperture lenses, steps (3) and (4) are not needed. Stop-down metering *cannot* be done with the Nikon EM.

Manual mode, stop-down metering (non-AI lenses). (1) Lock up the lever. (2) Select and set a shutter speed. (3) For the F3, hold the preview button in and adjust the aperture until the "−+" shows or for the FE and EL2, the black needle overlaps the green one. (4) Release the preview button and make the exposure. Again, this *cannot* be done with the EM.

Exposure compensation. Various lighting and shooting situations call for exposures different from those set by the meter. To retain automatic operation yet vary the exposure, you may use the memory lock or the exposure-compensation dial. The former will hold a particular reading as long as it is pressed in; just push the lever or button, recompose, and take the picture. The latter lets you consistently shoot at up to 2 EV's (or *f*/stops) above or below the meter reading. (The range of the EL2 is −1 to +2 EV.) Just turn the dial, which is around the rewind knob, until the desired degree of compensation is opposite the index mark. On the F3, the lock button must be pushed before the pointer will turn, and settings are in 1/3 stop increments; on the FE and EL2, just lift the milled ring and turn—the settings are 1/2 stop apart. *Be sure to reset the exposure-compensation dial to the neutral "O" position, when you have finished taking compensated pictures.*

The EM has a simplified exposure-compensation system. Pushing the *backlight button* automatically produces 1.5 EV (or *f*/stop) more exposure, for subjects in shadow with glaring backgrounds. such as skylight.

High-Contrast Metering

In all the instances above, we have assumed an average scene for the center-weighted meter readings. Where the main subject is much darker or lighter than the rest of the scene and is *not* in the center, take the initial reading from the subject and set the camera controls accordingly. Then recompose the scene, using the settings obtained in the original measurement. Disregard the meter if it now shows under or overexposure. With the auto models, use the memory lock to freeze the readings before recomposing. Reasons for selecting particular shutter speeds of *f*/stops will be discussed in Chapter 6.

If the main subject of the photograph is *much* darker than the surroundings, it may be underexposed, unless you take your readings directly from the subject. In any case, center such subjects while metering; they may be re-composed to the sides for shooting.

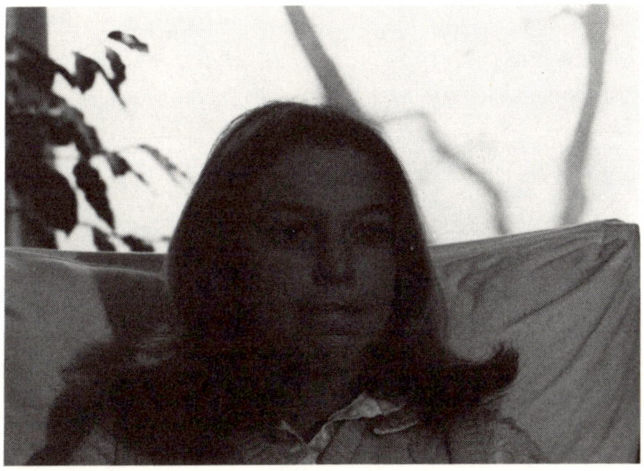

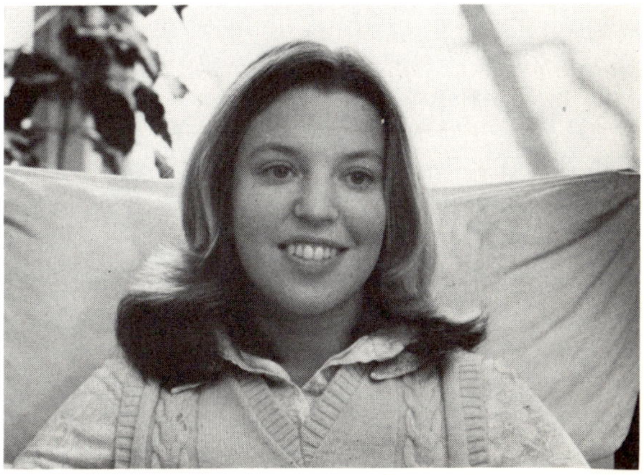

SET THE APERTURE

The aperture ("lens opening," or "*f*-stop") is set by rotating the diaphragm ring so that the desired *f*-number is aligned with the index on the barrel, in front of the aperture scale. When centering the needle or watching the LED's in the viewfinder, just rotate the ring, without regard to the numbers. There are definite click-stops at each *f*-stop and each half-stop (except between the widest and next-widest aperture). The range of apertures differs on different lenses, but each successive full *f*-stop represents twice (or half) the light-admittance of the previous number. In most Nikon finders, the *f*-number selected may be seen above the picture area.

SET THE SHUTTER SPEED

The shutter speed is set by turning the whole shutter-speed dial until the desired time is opposite the index mark (or until the needle or LED is correct in the viewfinder). In most Nikon finders, the shutter speed may be seen on the scale above or below the picture area. This dial has definite click-stops at each number. Be sure the dial snaps into each setting; an intermediate setting will throw the shutter off, except for the Nikon F2, which has intermediate settings between 1/80 sec. and 1/2000 sec. The times on the dial represent twice (or one-half) the previous time. On cameras with Photomic finders, the shutter-speed dial of the body is covered up, but the finder's shutter-speed dial acts the same way. The scale is visible on the cylindrical shaft of the dial, from the rear (shooting) position.

To set *extra-long shutter speeds* on any Nikon F2 camera, set the shutter-speed dial at "B," turn the T-L fingerguard to "T," then set the self-timer to the desired time, from two to ten seconds. Press the shutter release; the shutter will stay open for the indicated number of seconds, then close.

SHOOTING THE PICTURE

Hold the camera steady. This sounds elementary, but camera-shake is the largest cause of fuzzy pictures. Whether the camera is vertical or horizontal, rest it against your face and grip it firmly with both hands. Dig your elbows into your ribs (but not too tightly) or prop them upon an immovable surface.

Take a deep breath. Then let half of it go. If you try to hold the whole breath, you'll start trembling.

Squeeze, don't jab. The shutter-release button should lie beneath your right index-finger. Don't stab at it, but squeeze it gently. The actual release of the shutter should surprise you.

At slow shutter speeds, use a tripod. Don't trust your ability to hold the camera steady. When you use a tripod, release the shutter by means of a *cable release* or the *self-timer*, for particularly vibrationless exposures.

Self-Timer

To set the self-timer on any Nikon but the F3, turn the self-timer lever to the left. On the Nikon F and F2, dots or numbers will reveal the amount of delay (two to ten seconds on the F2). Then press the self-timer release, and after the appropriate delay, the shutter will go off. The Nikon FE, FM, and EL2 have no separate self-timer release; after the lever has been cocked, just push the shutter-release button. The Nikon F3 has an electronic timer activated by a switch at the base of the shutter-speed dial. Turn the switch and push the shutter release; an LED on the front of the camera blinks to indicate the timer is working. Remember to turn the timer switch *off* after the exposure, or before, if you wish to bypass it.

Multiple Exposures

All Nikons are capable of making more than one exposure on the same frame. On the Nikon F2, make the first exposure, then press the rewind button and advance the film-wind lever. The shutter will cock; the film will not move. Make the next exposure. On the Nikon F, turn the A-R ring to "R," then turn the rewind crank one full rotation, which will move the film backwards one frame.

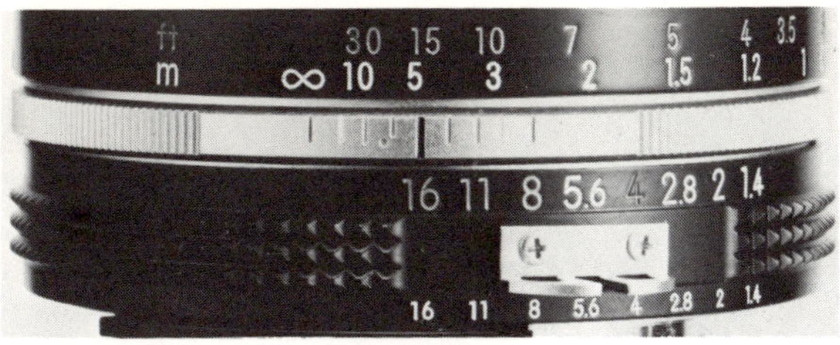

Setting the aperture on any Nikkor lens. Rotate diaphragm ring until *f*-number aligns with index; here, *f*/16.

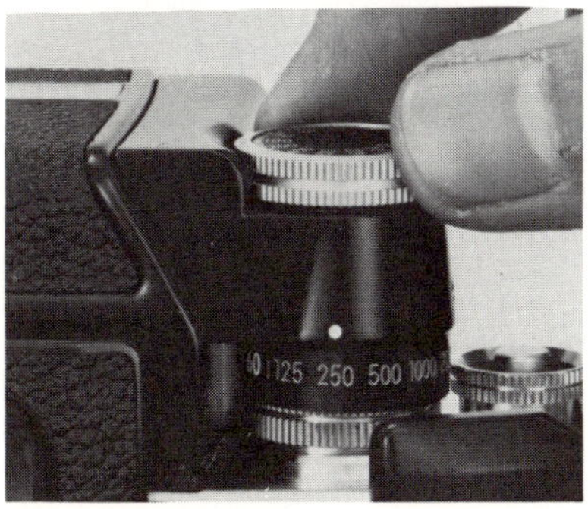

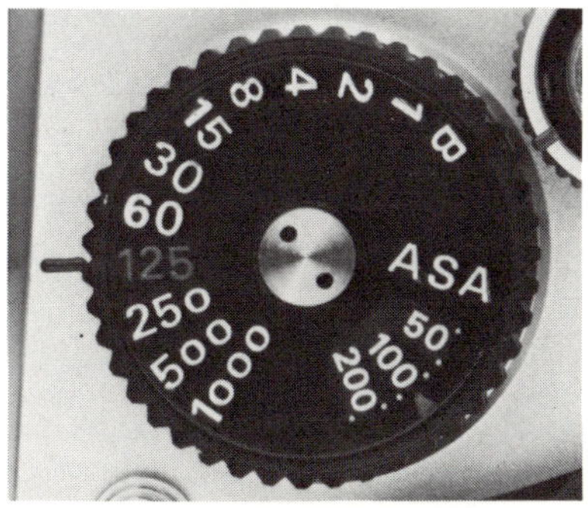

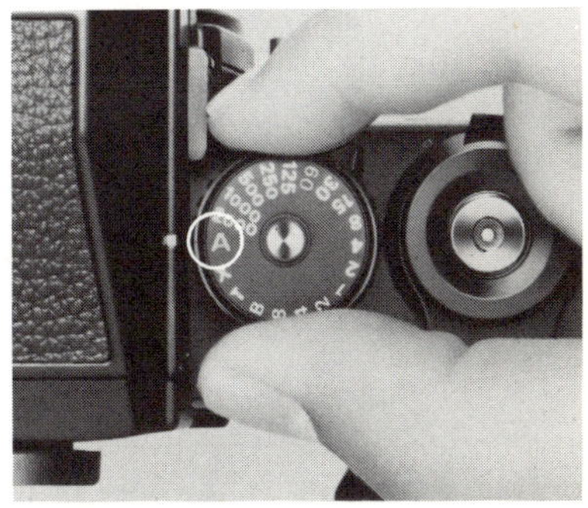

Setting the shutter speed. On Photomic finders (left), use scale on base of column. On all other Nikons, rotate dial until number on dial aligns with index mark (FM, center), or set at "A" with automatic models (F3, right).

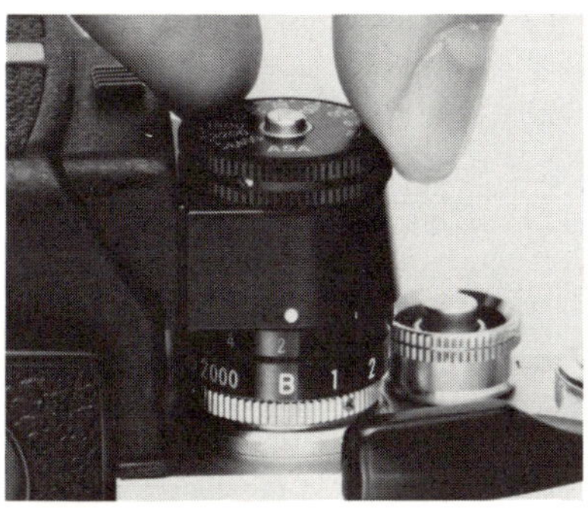

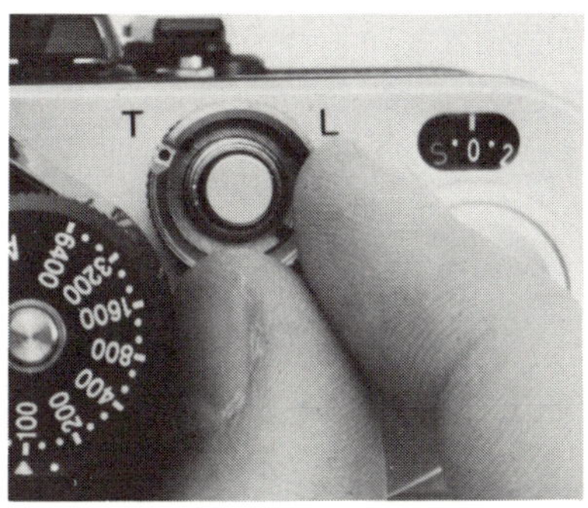

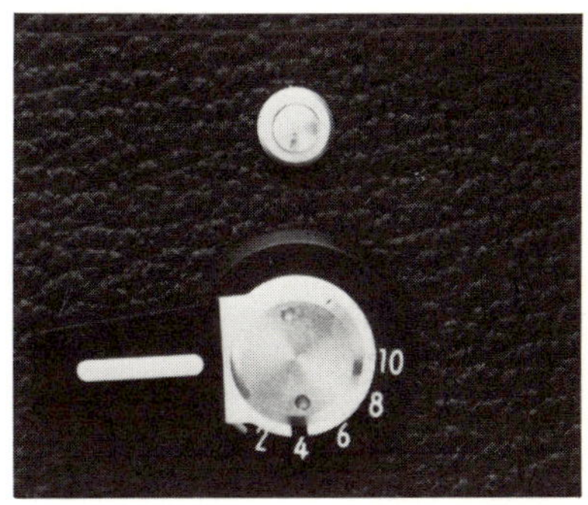

Long shutter speeds on F2. Set dial at "B"; turn fingerguard to "T"; then set self-timer to desired speed.

Press shutter-release gently, or use a cable release.

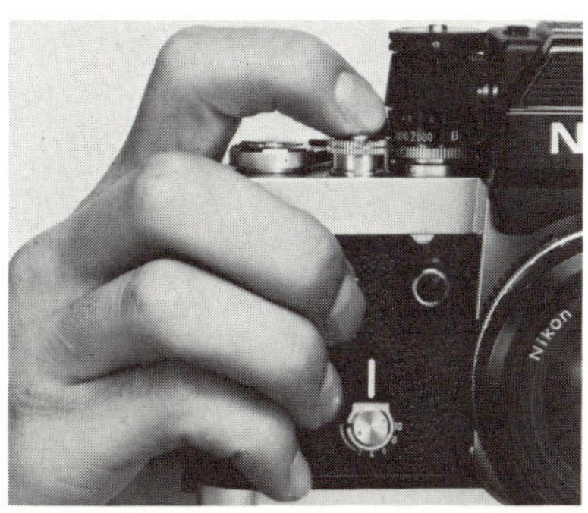

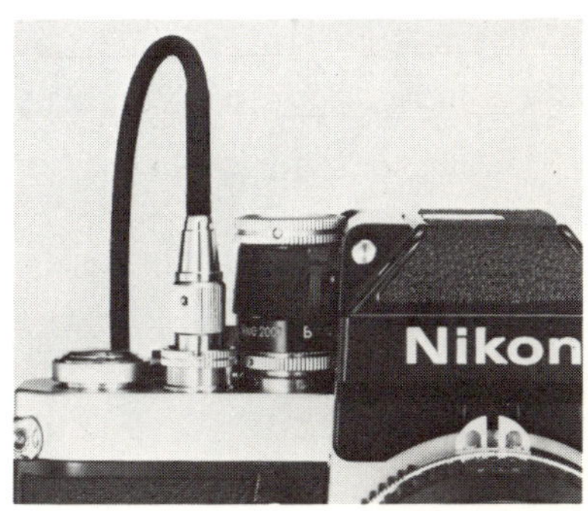

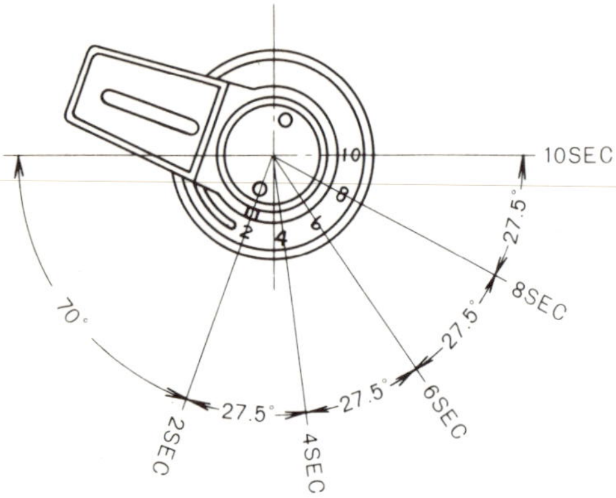

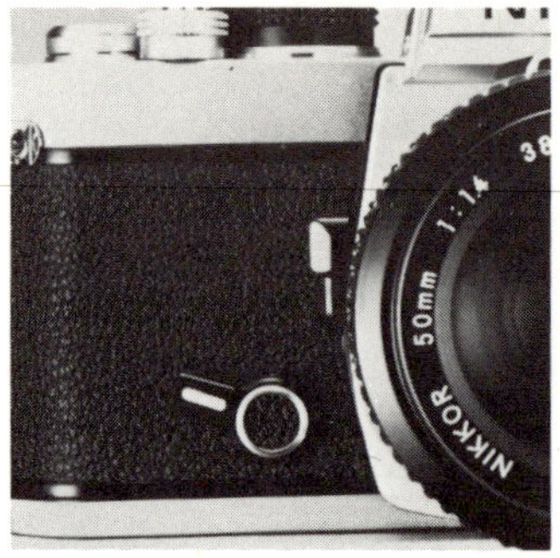

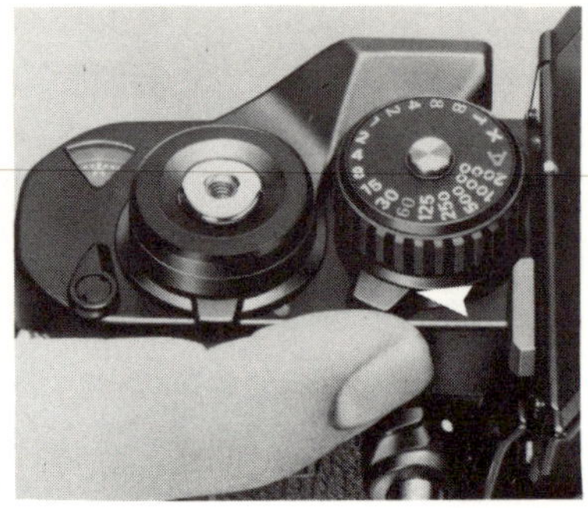

Self-timers for Nikon F2, F (left), other models (center). On F3 only (right), lever on shutter-speed dial activates timer; blinking LED indicates that it is in use.

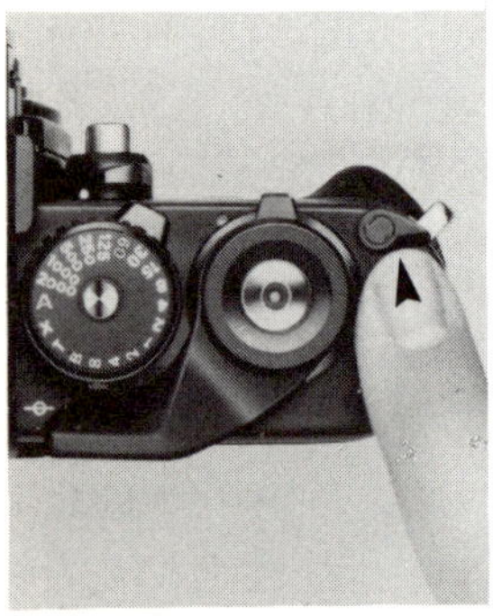

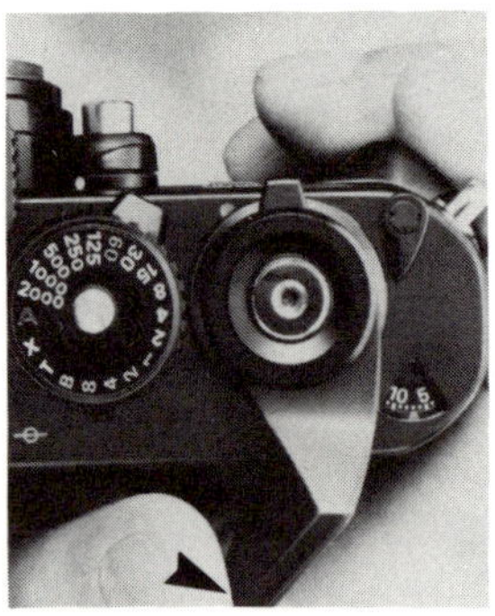

Multi-exposure lever on Nikon F3 makes perfectly aligned multiple exposures. Just push it forward after taking the first exposure and wind the film advance; the shutter will cock, but the film (and frame counter) will remain still. The lever flips back as you wind. Multiple-exposure controls on the FE and FM work the same way.

Any Nikon reflex makes multiple exposures easy. This triple exposure of amusement park signs was exposed for the lights only, letting the dark backgrounds merge. Each exposure: 1/30 sec. at *f*/2.8 on Plus-X, with the 50 mm Nikkor.

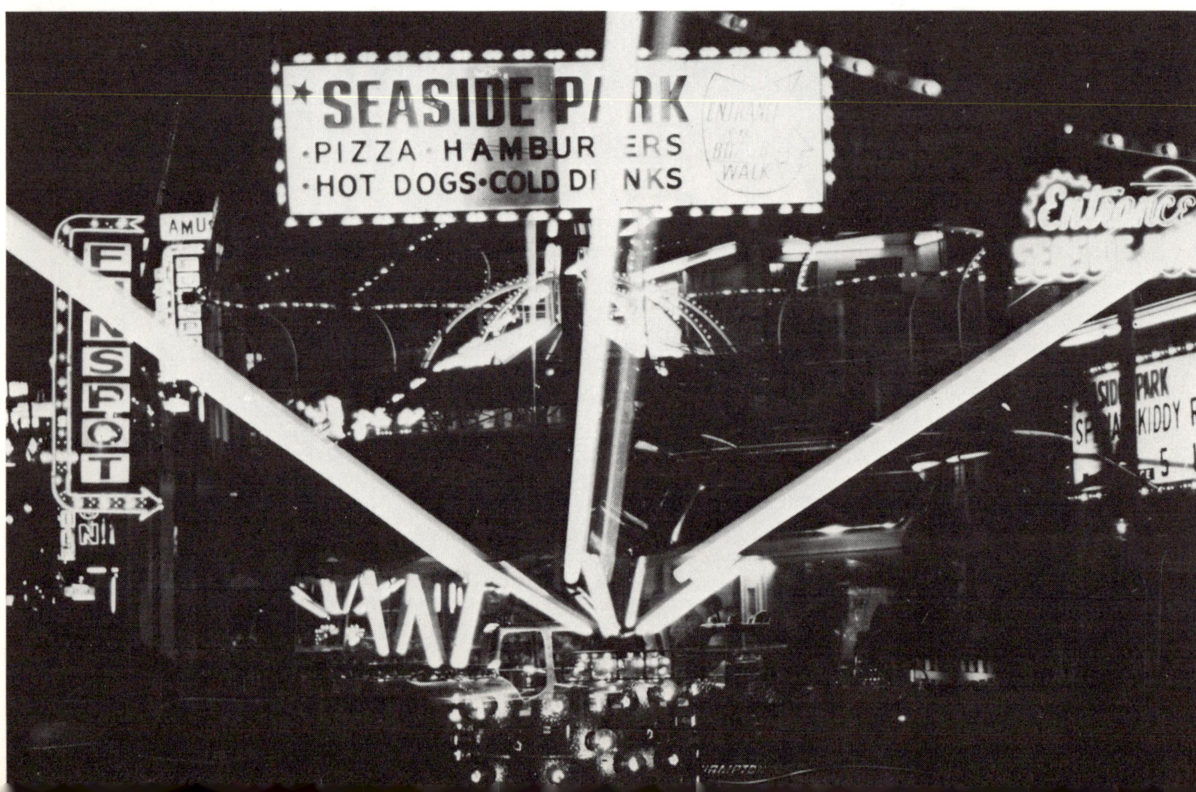

Cock the lever and shoot. The Nikon F3, FE, and FM have a multiple-exposure button or lever. Push it as you wind the film-advance lever, then re-expose. On the Nikon EL2 first take up slack in the film by turning the rewind knob. Make the first exposure. Keeping your finger on the clutch button, cock the lever and shoot. Any setting may be changed on any camera between exposures.

LENS INTERCHANGE

Changing lenses on a Nikon SLR is swift, sure, and has grown increasingly simple. In all cases, the same sturdy Nikon bayonet lensmount has been used continuously since the Nikon F was introduced in 1959. Therefore any Nikkor lens will fit any Nikon SLR the same way. The only differences in procedure involve coupling the various lenses to the various meters. Any AI or Auto-Nikkor will automatically couple to the automatic-diaphragm pin. In every case, this is the basic operation:

Press in the lens-release button. This is on the front of the camera, to the right of the lensmount. Hold the camera in your right hand and grip the lens with your left. Push in the button with your right thumb.

Twist the lens. Holding the button in, twist the lens by the milled grip ring *clockwise* as far as it goes (about 60°), then lift it out.

Mount the new lens. Insert the new lens into the mount so that the index mark on the milled ring aligns with the dot on the camera body. Turn the lens *counterclockwise* until it clicks and locks into place.

These steps are all that is required on the *Nikon F3*, *F2A*, and *F2AS Photomics*, the *Nikon FM*, *FE*, *EM*, and *EL2*. The coupling ridge of an AI-Nikkor will insure automatic indexing to the camera meter (as well as the auto-diaphragm). With non-AI-Nikkors, lock up the meter-coupling pin first, except on the EM.

With the *Nikon F2*, *F2S*, and *F2Sb Photomics*, you must also index the lens (Auto-Nikkor) with the meter, after mounting: Simply twist the aperture ring all the way to the minimum aperture—the largest *f*-number—then all the way in the opposite direction. The maximum aperture of the lens should then appear in the indicator window of the finder.

With the *Nikon Photomic FTN* on the camera, *center* the coupling pin *before* mounting the lens, and set the lens at *f*/16. After mounting, close the aperture down all the way, then turn it all the way in the opposite direction. The maximum aperture should appear on the red index on the front of the finder.

With the *Nikon F Photomic, T, and TN,* push the coupling pin to the *right*, and set the lens at *f*/16. Then continue as above. Remember to reset the meter for the new maximum aperture.

VIEWFINDER INTERCHANGE

Changing finders on the *Nikon F3* has been made simpler than ever. *To remove the finder*, slide the finder-release levers toward the back of the camera and lift the finder out. *To mount a finder*, simply hold the release levers back and press the finder into place. Release the levers.

Changing finders on the *Nikon F2* or *F* is slightly more complicated. The two cameras work the same way (although the finders are *not* interchangeable between Nikon F and F2 models).

To remove a viewfinder. Push the finder-release button on the back of the camera with your finger or a coin. If the finder on the camera is a Photomic model, depress (or rotate) the finder-release lever of the viewfinder, as well. (The earliest Photomics and non-Photomic finders have no release lever.) Then simply lift out the finder.

To mount a finder with no lens on the camera. Simply position the new viewfinder over the receptacle. Then gently press it down until the two clamps click into place. (With the Nikon Photomic FTN *only*, it is necessary to center the pin and squeeze the finder-release lever as you settle the finder into place.) Once any Photomic finder is seated, rotate its shutter-speed dial left and right until it engages the camera shutter-speed dial and the two rotate together.

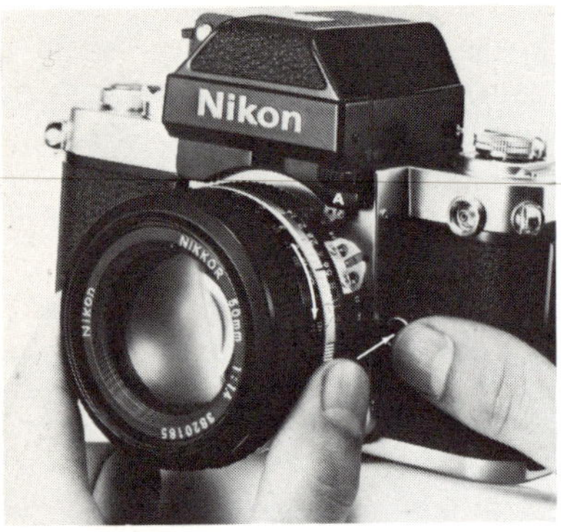

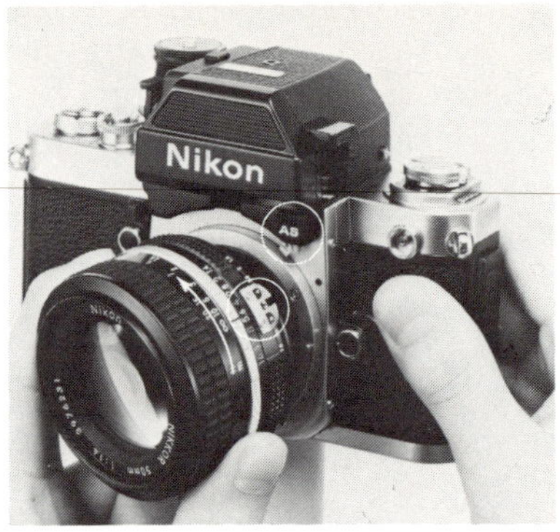

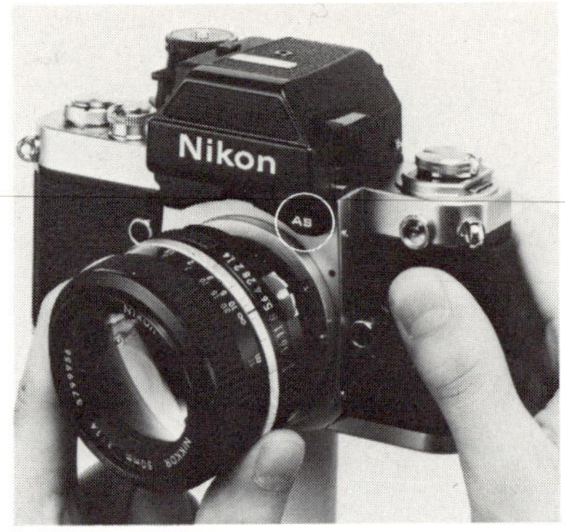

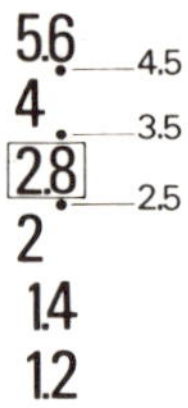

To remove lens, push in lens-release button, rotate lens clockwise (above, left). To insert AI lens, just reverse procedure (center). To insert Auto-Nikkor on newest cameras, lock up meter-coupling lever first (right). On older Photomics, see that maximum aperture of lens shows in window (left).

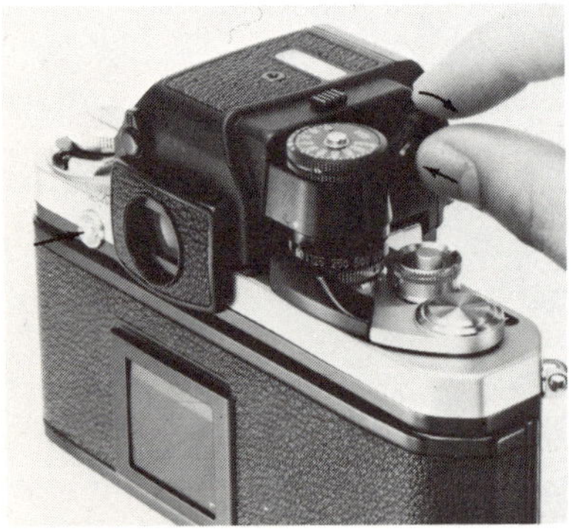

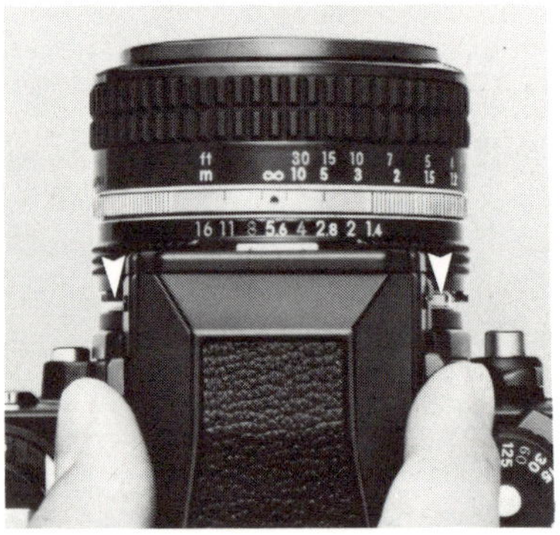

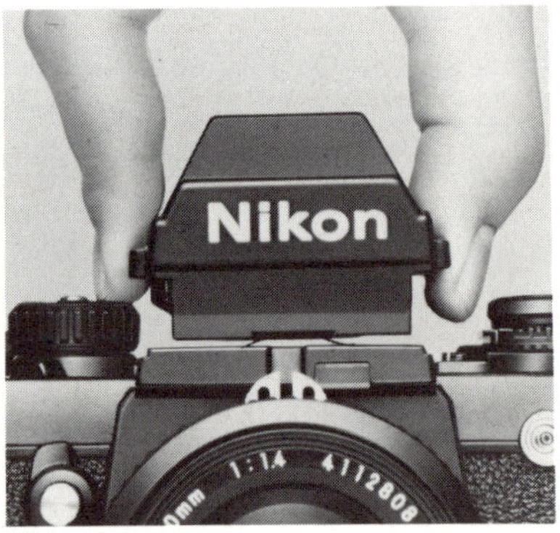

To remove finder on F or F2 (left), push in release button on camera and lever on finder. On F3 (center), slide release levers back. With either model, lift finder straight up (right). To replace, press finder down into position until it catches. See text for more detail.

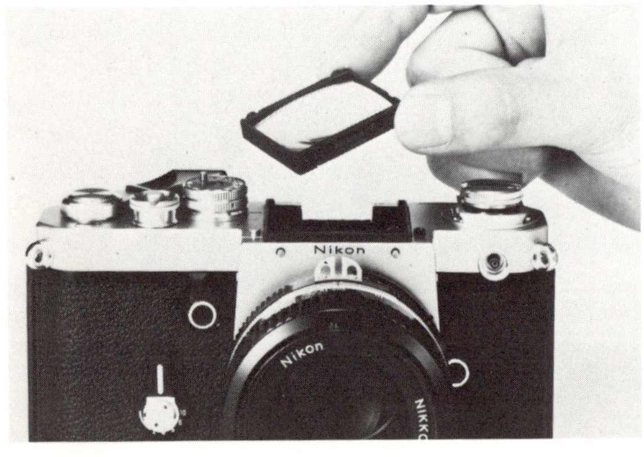

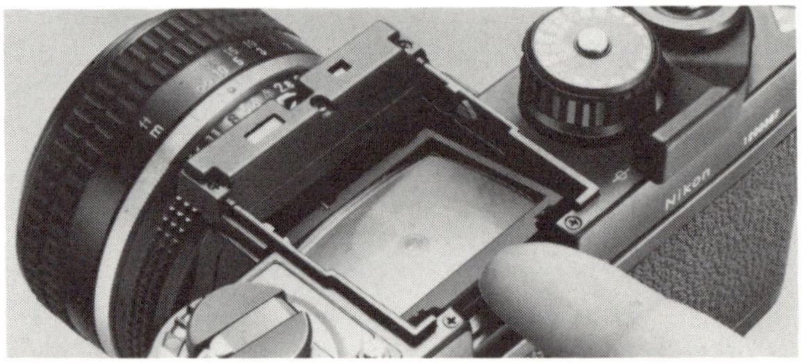

To remove or insert screen on Nikon F or F2 (left), push release button again, then let screen drop out. On F3 (above) merely slip your nail under rear edge of screen and lift it out. Insert new screen front edge first.

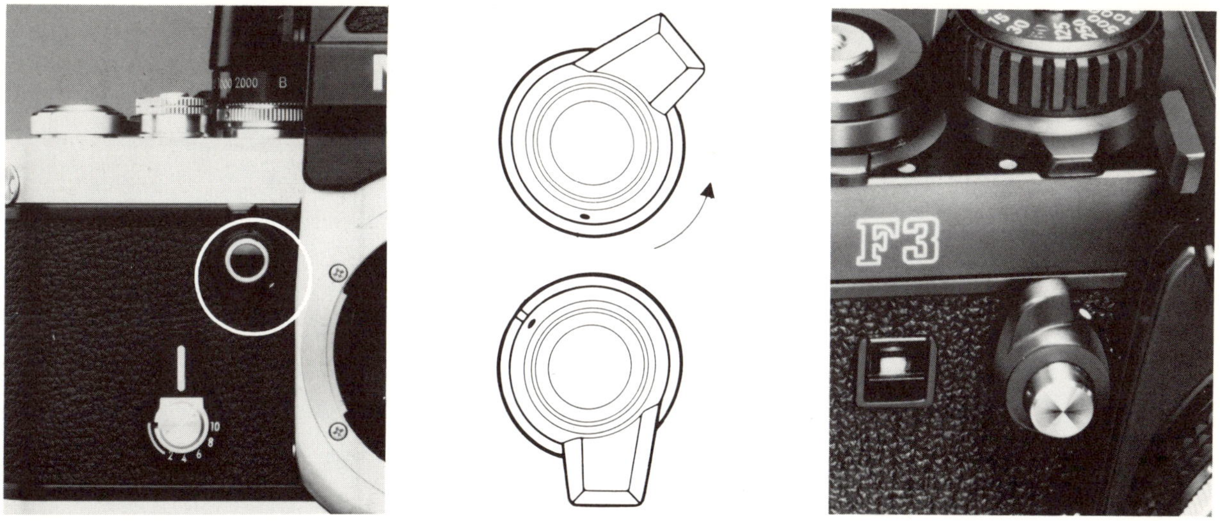

Mirror lockup. On Nikon F2 (left and center), rotate lever around preview button until dot is opposite line. On F3 (right), *push in* preview button and rotate lever.

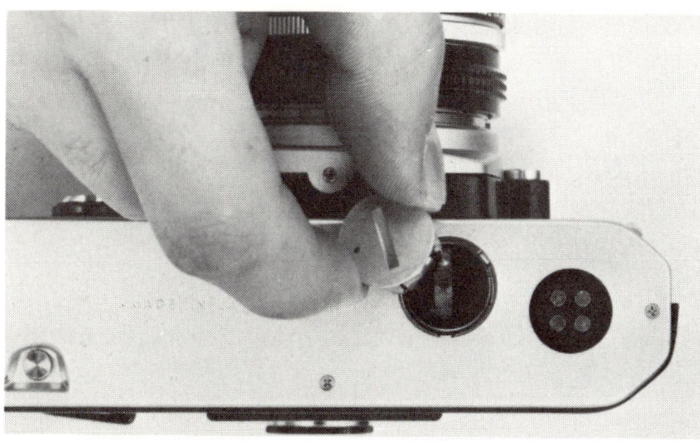

Battery replacement. On all current Nikons, battery chamber is in camera baseplate. Unscrew lid and replace batteries.

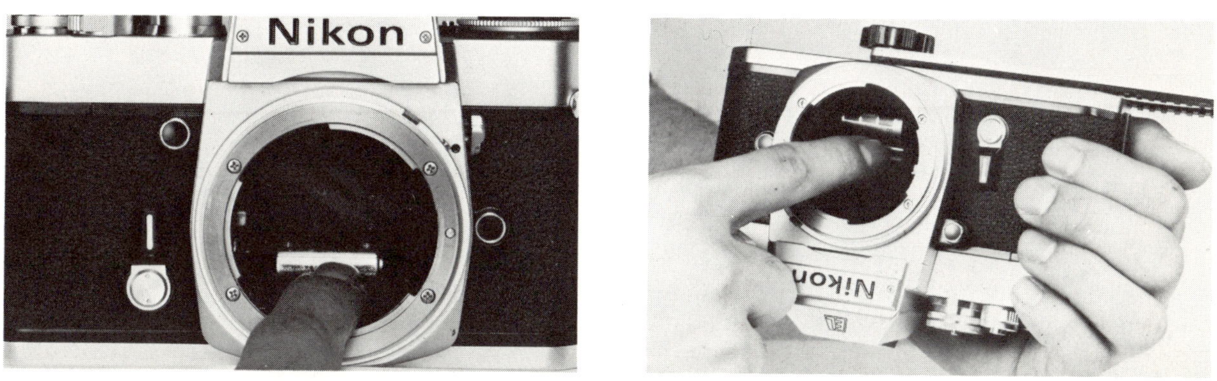

On EL2 , battery is in internal chamber, under mirror. Follow instructions in text.

To mount a finder with a lens on the camera. With a non-Photomic finder, the procedure is the same as above. With any Photomic finder, set the lens aperture to *f*/5.6 or larger (with the latest Photomics, open it all the way), and center the coupling pin (if there is one) on the finder. Proceed as explained above, and also rotate the aperture ring all the way left and right to be certain it is properly engaged.

SCREEN INTERCHANGE

To change the focusing screen, remove the viewfinder as described above. On the *Nikon F3*, lift out the old screen by hooking a fingernail under its rear edge and lifting up. Insert a new screen by *gently* sliding the front (slotted) edge under the pin and pushing the rear edge down. On the *Nikon F2 or F*, turn the camera upside down and press the finder-release button a second time; the screen will drop out. Place the new screen over the receptacle, flat slide down, press the release button, and drop the screen into place.

MIRROR LOCKUP

The mirror of certain Nikon reflexes can be locked up (1) to accommodate lenses that extend deeply into the camera body and (2) to insure completely vibrationless shots for macro and close-up photography. On the Nikon F3, the lever is around the depth of field button. Push the button in and rotate the lever downward until it stops. On the Nikon F2, turn the lock-up lever—above the self-timer—downward until the white dot is opposite the white line. On the Nikon F, the lock-up button is on the left of the lensmount; rotate it upward. On the EL2, the lock-up lever is on the right of the lensmount; rotate it upward.

REPLACING BATTERIES

Except for the battery in the Nikon EL2, the batteries in the other Nikon cameras or finders are of the long-lasting button type—either mercury or silver oxide. They should last one or two years, but don't wait for them to die; replace them regularly. Unscrew the battery-chamber cover, place the correct batteries in, "+" side out, and replace the cover. The Photomic finders for the Nikon F take two 1.3V mercury batteries: Mallory PX-13, PX-625, or their equivalent. The Nikon F3, F2, FE, FM, and EM take two 1.5V silver-oxide Mallory MS-76 batteries, or their equivalent. The EL2 has a special 6V Type 544 battery in an internal chamber. Remove the lens, lock up the mirror, and release the battery-chamber lid, while holding the camera upside down. The old battery will drop out. Put in a new one, making sure to align the "+" and "−" ends as shown on the lid. Shut the lid and lower the mirror.

MOTORS AND AUTO-WINDERS

The full extent of motorized operation for the various Nikon reflexes is beyond the scope of this book. Suffice it to say that every Nikon SLR has its own motor-drive units or auto-winder (described in Chapter 4, "Accessories"), and that these permit the Nikon photographer to shoot faster than is possible manually, since all units advance the film by themselves; to take pictures from a remote position; and to take sequences of pictures, either very *slow*, by means of timing devices, or very fast, using the motors themselves, up to 6 fps.

Although the Nikon F must be adapted to accept its motor-drive units, the Nikon F3, F2, FE, FM, EM, and EL2 can be attached to their units with no modification whatever. The Nikon F3 takes the MD-4 motordrive; the F2 is matched to the MD-1, MD-2, or MD-3; the FM and FE models share the MD-12 or MD-11; the EM has its own MD-E; and the EL2 can be attached to the Auto Winder AW-1. Each of these units has its own power supply.

CHAPTER 3

Lenses

The "normal" lens that comes with your camera is the most useful all-around lens there is. It is very sharp, very fast (by the standards of a few years past, any of the current lenses is tack sharp and blazing fast), and very easy to use. The scene it takes in (its "angle of view") is just about right for most photographic purposes; the perspective it usually records is pleasing to the eye. With all these features, it would appear that the normal lens would fill every photographic need; and in fact, it fills 75 percent of those needs. It is the remaining 25 percent that makes for varied, creative, and expanding photographic horizons.

After you have been taking pictures or making pictures—there's a difference—awhile, you will begin to find that the normal lens cannot do a number of things you want it to: It cannot fill the frame of your picture with the detail you want, or perhaps it will not get in the entirety of a broad panorama you wish to record. There are usually alternatives: You can back up or close in, change your angle of view, or use various attachments; but not always. There is something about the spatial relationships between objects that can be bent just so far. The camera, unlike your eye, does not compensate for closeness, nor does it concentrate on detail. Sophisticated though it may be, it stares dumbly ahead, recording whatever is before it. The perspective of the scene, dependent upon distances and positions, changes dramatically, and the picture is quite different from what you thought it would be. These circumstances call for different lenses, which are described below.

LENS CHARACTERISTICS

All lenses, whether telephoto or wide-angle, are subject to the same laws and act in the same ways. Thus, what is true for the "fisheye" is also true for the telephoto. Before one decides which lenses to add to his or her battery, one must know how they work and how they differ.

All photographic lenses are compounds of simple lenses, with the object of getting light from the subject to the film plane, or "focal plane." The various elements are designed to cancel out aberrations in the others and deliver an image of predetermined size and brightness to the film. The size of that image is determined by the placement of the elements, and it is the prime attribute of lens focal length.

Focal Length

Literally, focal length is the distance from the optical center of the lens to the film plane. It is the distance at which a lens focused on infinity will bring the points of light together to form an image.

The size of this image varies directly with the focal length: for a given film size, *the longer the focal length, the larger the image*. Conversely, *the shorter the focal length, the smaller the image*. However, if the film size remains the same (in this case, 1″ × 1½″), *less* of the larger image will be recorded with the lens of long focal length, and *more* of the scene will be recorded with the shorter lens. The larger lens thus magnifies a part of the image, apparently "closing in" on it—thus the term "telephoto,"* whereas the shorter lens takes in more than the normal angle of view—thus the term "wide-angle."

Besides image size, focal length affects two other vital aspects of the picture—*depth of field* and *apparent perspective*.

Depth of Field

Earlier, depth of field was defined as the zone of sharp focus, which may be seen through the viewfinder when the lens is stopped down. This phenomenon should be examined further.

Depth of field varies inversely with focal length. In other words, the longer the lens, the less the depth of field *at any given distance*. The shorter the lens, the greater the depth of field. Thus, one of the primary uses of the telephoto lens is to isolate a subject by throwing all distracting elements, such as backgrounds, *out* of focus. The wide-angle lens, on the other hand, is often used principally for its *great* depth of field, when foreground-to-infinity sharpness is desired.

Depth of field varies directly with distance. The nearer the subject focused upon, the less the depth of field; the farther, the greater the depth of field, for any lens *at any given aperture*. Every lens of the same focal length has the same depth of field at any given aperture/distance combination; thus, it is possible to construct depth-of-field tables and depth-of-field scales on any lens.

Depth of field varies inversely with aperture. The larger the lens opening, the smaller the depth of field; the smaller the aperture, the greater the depth. Thus, when photographers "stop down," they usually do so to increase their zone of sharp focus. When they open up, they frequently are trying to throw something out of focus.

Depth of field is a phenomenon closely interrelated with other lens characteristics and still other photographic considerations. But all photographic phenomena are interrelated; this interdependence of functions is nowhere more apparent than in a discussion of perspective.

Perspective

It has been stated that lens focal length affects apparent perspective. The "apparent" is crucial. It is very hard to convince people of this fact, but *only camera-to-subject distance affects actual perspective*. A tele lens "flattens" perspective, while a wide-angle "distorts" perspective, but these effects are in actuality functions of distance. By varying the image size, the length of the lens lets you capture unusual views of subjects at certain distances, so the perspective seems "abnormal."

For example, at great distances, objects seem to be closer to one another than they really are. It is hard to distinguish a man a mile away from us from his car, which may be 10 feet behind him. If the man and the car were only 50 yards away, the 10-foot separation would become obvious, but the long lens, for all its image magnification, is no better able to make the distinction at a mile than are the unaided eye and the normal lens. It just records the scene larger. If you look at photos of a distant object taken from the same place by a normal and a telephoto lens, you will see that if the "normal" picture is enlarged to the same size as the telephoto, *it will be the same*, line for line and angle for angle. It will be a worse picture for the extra magnification, and that is one of the chief reasons for using tele lenses. At the same image magnification, the perspective of any pictures taken from the same distance will be the same. The reason the telephoto picture looks "flat" is that you are not used to seeing a blown-up, "nearby" view of a distant scene.

---

*Strictly speaking, a telephoto is a *particular kind* of long-focus, lens, but here we will use the term to mean any longer-than-normal lens.

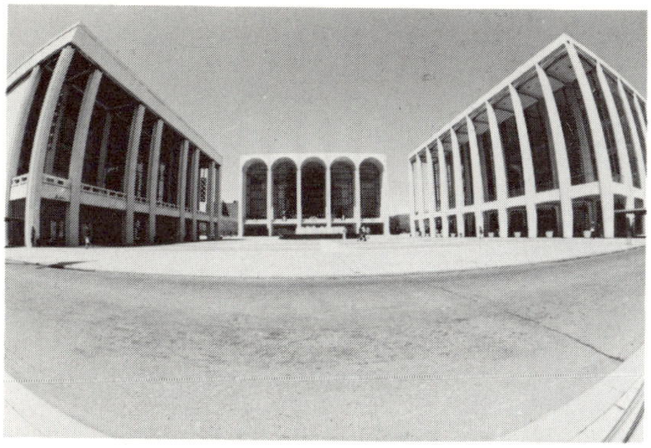

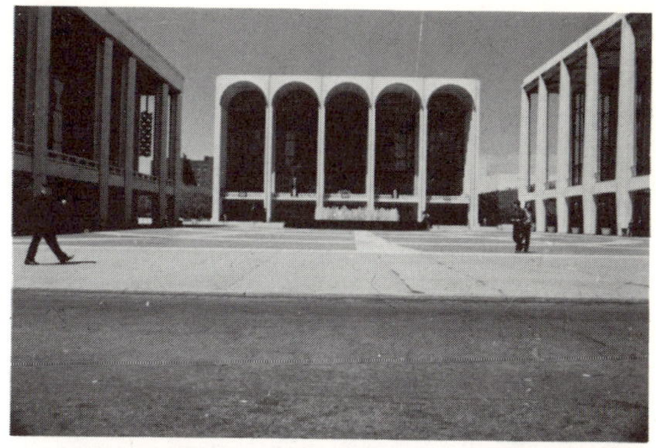

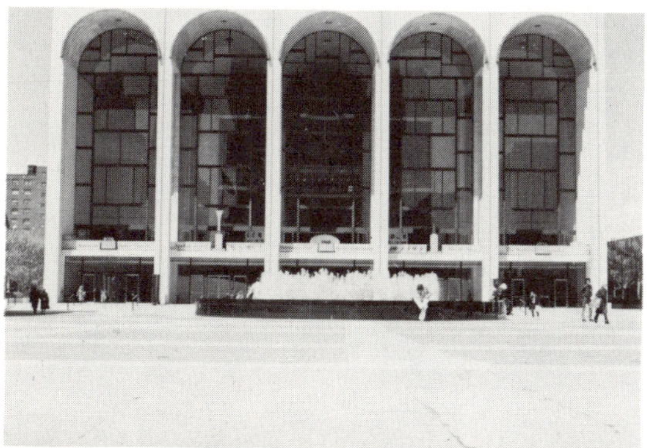

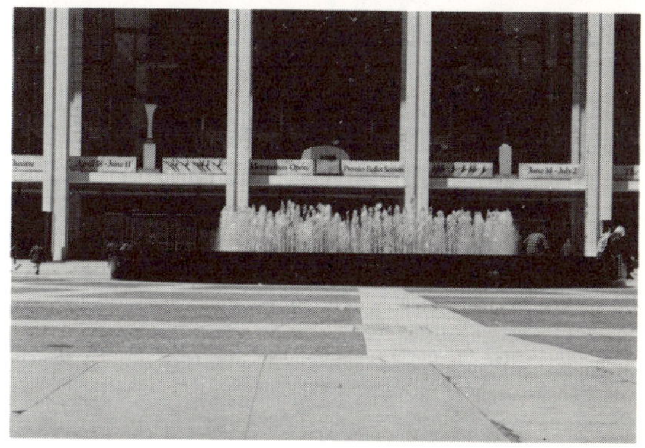

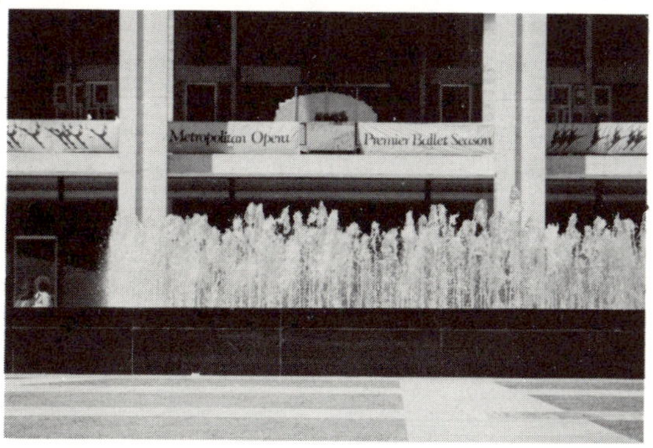

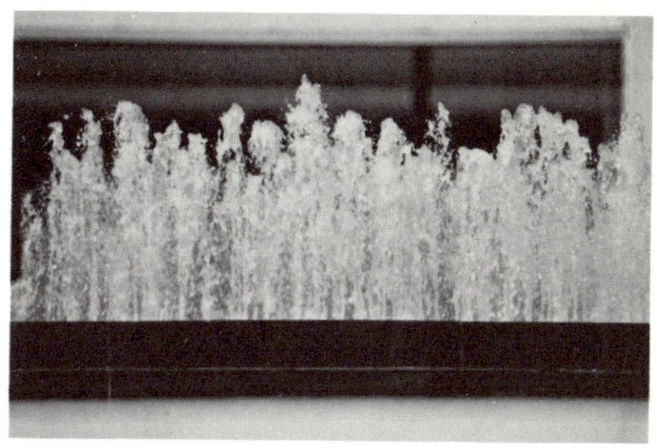

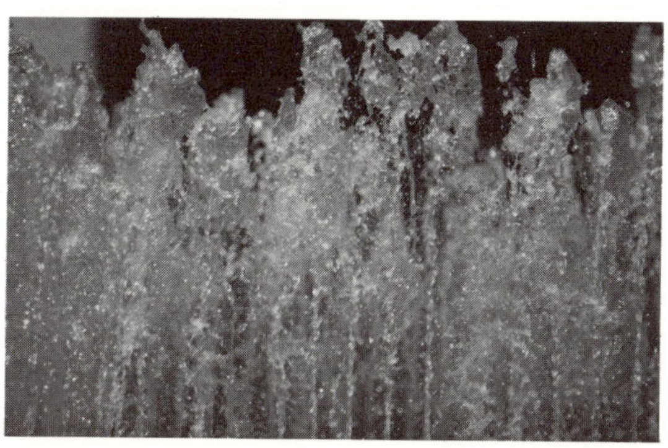

Focal length and image size. The court and fountain of Lincoln Center, New York, taken from the same position with Nikkors of the following focal lengths: 16 mm, 28 mm, 50 mm, 100 mm, 200 mm, 500 mm, and 1000 mm. As the focal length increases, so does the size of the image, but the amount of the image recorded—the "coverage"—decreases. All taken on Plus-X with a yellow filter, 1/125 sec. at *f*/8.

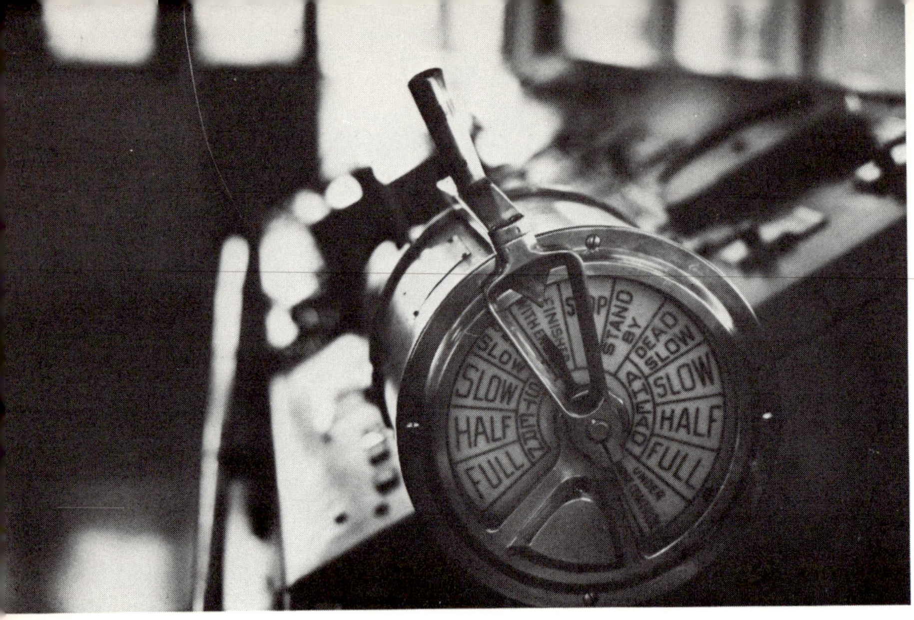

Shallow depth of field. Here a wide aperture (*f*/2.5), a long lens (105 mm), and a close focusing distance (about 5 feet), all combine to limit depth of field and center attention on the ship's control.

Great depth of field. The opposite conditions prevail in this scene, creating sharp rendition from foreground to background: small aperture (*f*/16), shorter lens (35 mm), and greater focusing distance (about 30 feet).

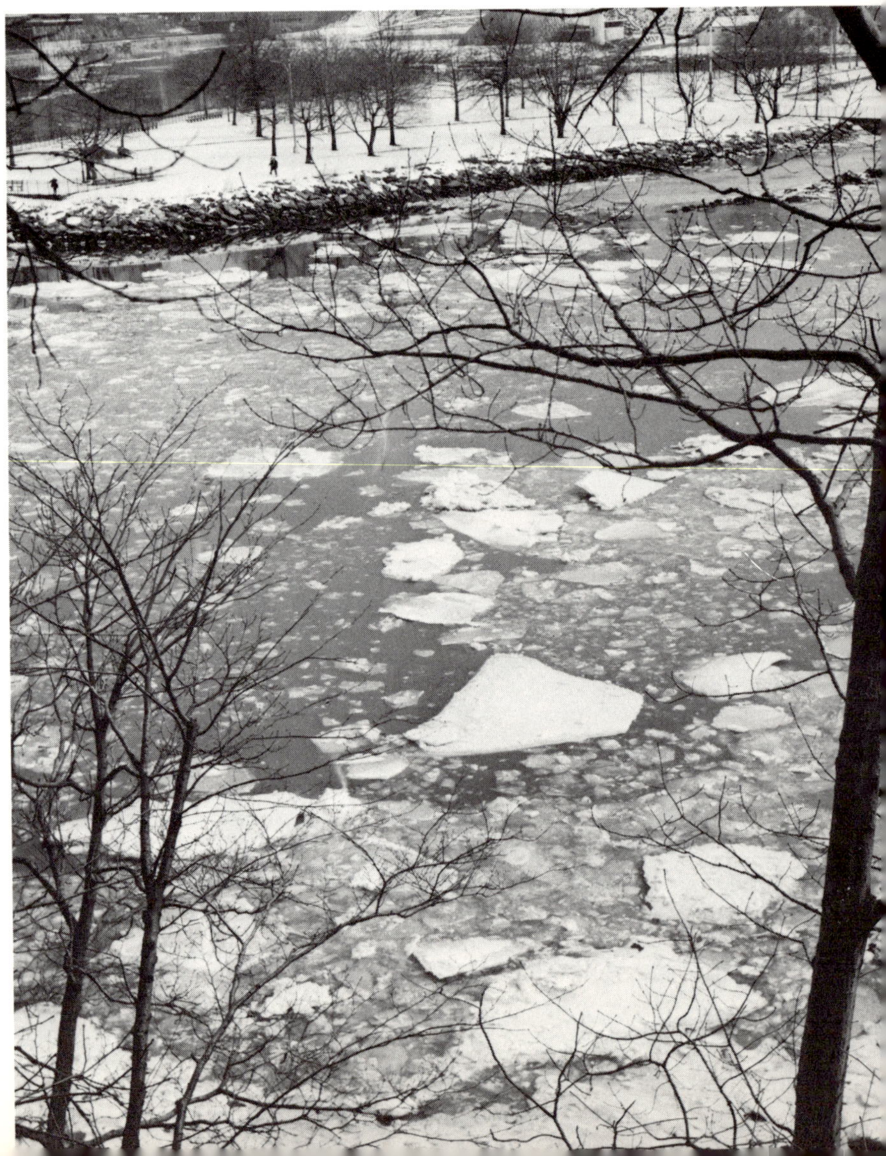

The wide-angle lens has the opposite effect. It takes in more of a scene than a normal or telephoto lens at any particular distance. Although many wide-angle lenses actually *do* distort the edges of the image (the "barrel" effect of fisheye lenses is an extreme case in point), the less obvious but more common distortion results from the wide-angle's ability to render very near foreground objects very sharp. The visual rule that applies here is: *Nearby objects look larger.* At the "normal" or telephoto distances, objects appear smaller and more to the same scale; but the nearer they are to the viewer, the more their relative nearness matters. To look at the face of a person "in perspective" one must back away from him or her. Imagine staring at this person from a distance of one foot! His nose, nearer to you than the rest of his face by an inch or more, would loom hugely all "out of proportion." This is what the wide-angle lens allows. By getting in more and "larger" foreground objects than one is used to seeing at a given distance, it seems to stretch space, producing an abnormal perspective. But the wide-angle, like the telephoto, only allows you to take greater advantage of camera-to-subject distances; it creates no "perspective" of its own.

Aperture

As may be inferred from what has gone before, aperture is a lens characteristic, and it is one of the most fundamental. Simply stated, it is the opening in the lens through which light passes, and nothing more. The widest opening a lens permits is its "maximum aperture" or "lens speed."

Aperture is measured in "*f*-numbers," or "*f*-stops," and since "*f*" represents "focal length," one can see how they are related: An *f*-stop is a ratio of the focal length to the lens diameter. If a 50 mm (two-inch) lens has a maximum diameter of 25 mm (one inch), then its maximum aperture is $2 \div 1 = 2$, or *f*/2. (Perhaps an easier way to remember this is to think of the *f*-number as the lower part of a fraction of the focal length; thus, *f*/2 = ½ the focal length, *f*/8 = ⅛ the focal length, etc.)

It is apparent that *the wider the opening* (and the *smaller* the number—½ being larger than ¼), *the more light will be admitted* and the "faster" the lens will be; an *f*/2 lens admits far more light than an *f*/8 lens. *All* lenses at *f*/2 admit the same amount of light; the longer focal-length lenses make the light go farther, but are wider, to compensate.

The faster the lens, the more prized it is, as a rule. The more light it admits, the easier it is to take pictures in poor, low-level light. Furthermore, since the photographer views and focuses through the lens, the faster lens gives a brighter and clearer image. A lens of *f*/1.4 maximum aperture is much easier to focus than one of *f*/5.6, say, both because the image is brighter and because the depth of field is less, so sharp focus is easier to see.

Aperture may be adjusted downward on most lenses; the series of *f*-stops is calculated to admit half the light of the previous stop (or twice the light, going up the scale). The full range of stops is *f*/1, 1.4, 2, 2.8, 4, 5.6, 8, 11, 16, 22, 32, 45, etc., but no one lens can incorporate all these; the usual range for normal lenses is *f*/1.4 (or *f*/2) to about *f*/16. Some intermediary stops that may appear are just that—intermediary (or fractional) stops.

Aperture affects the depth of field, as noted. Along with focal length and distance, it determines what will be in or out of focus. At any given point of focus, some of the scene before, and more behind, the point will be in focus too. This depth may be carefully controlled by stopping down or opening up the lens. The faster the lens, the more it may be opened, and the more selective focus can be. The reason all lenses are not "fast" is that with the longer focal lengths, increased aperture means vastly increased bulk and weight. The wider apertures are also not as necessary outdoors, where most longer lenses are used. Moderate apertures suffice, and such lenses are much less expensive. A fuller discussion of aperture in relation to exposure and composition will be found in Chapter 6, "Basic Photography."

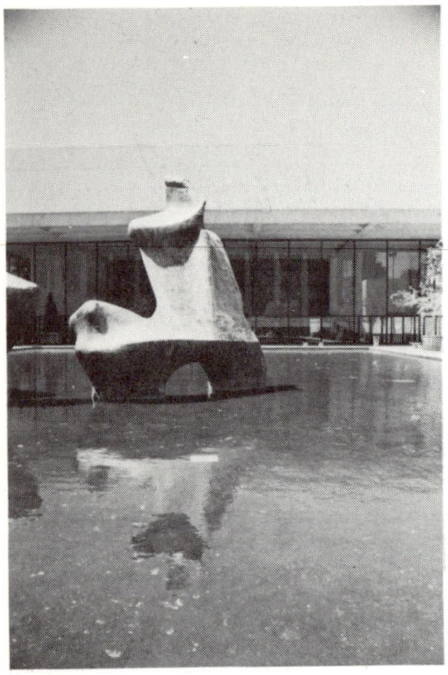
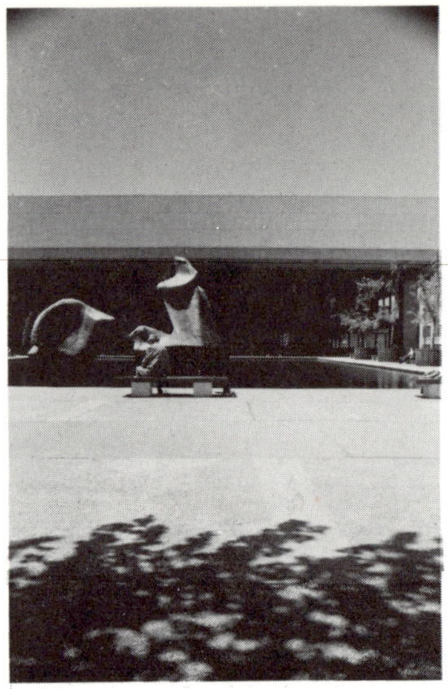
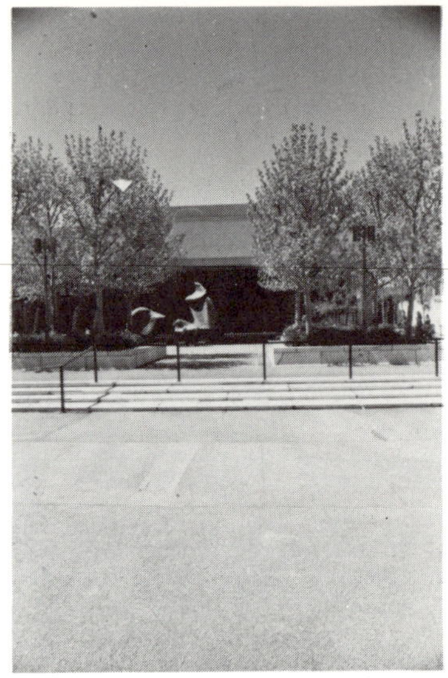
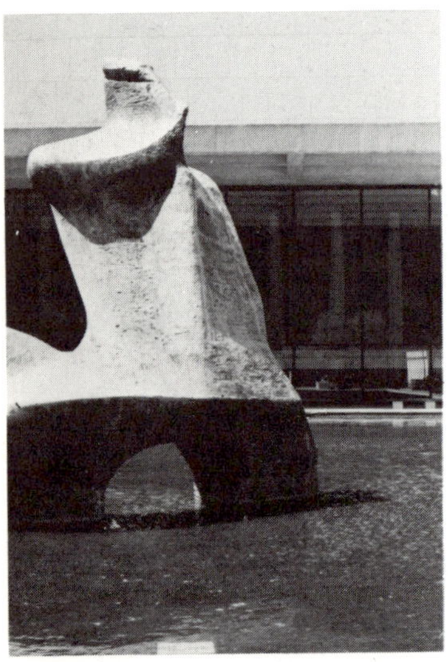
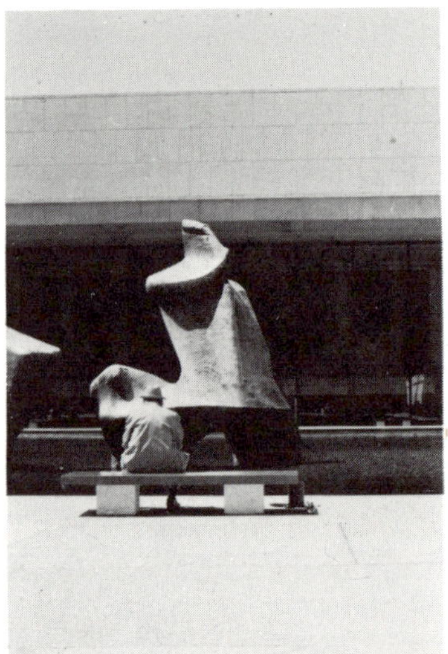
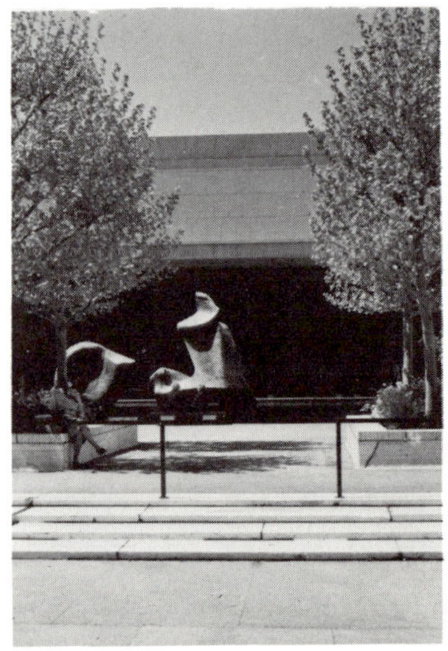
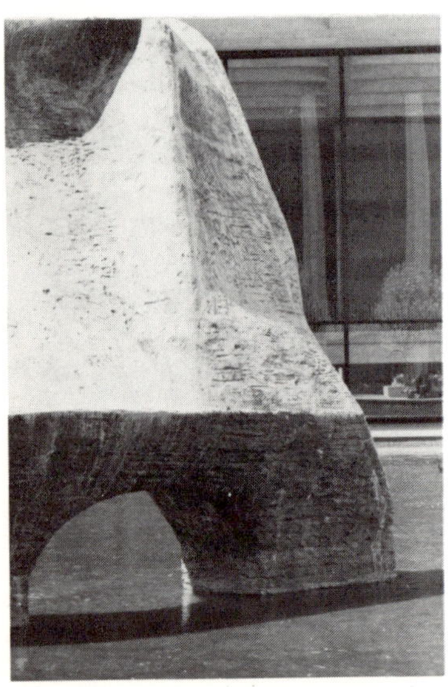
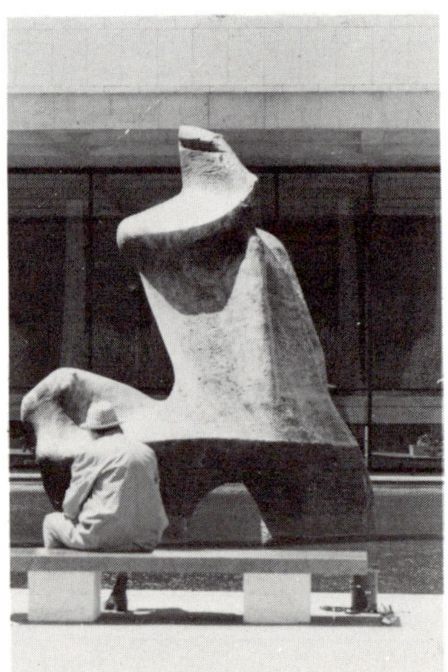
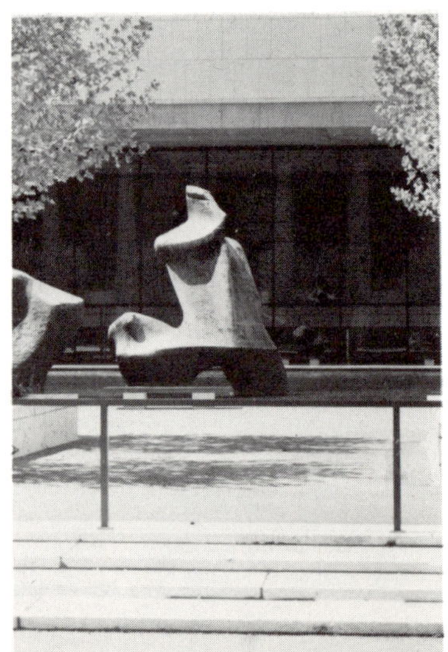

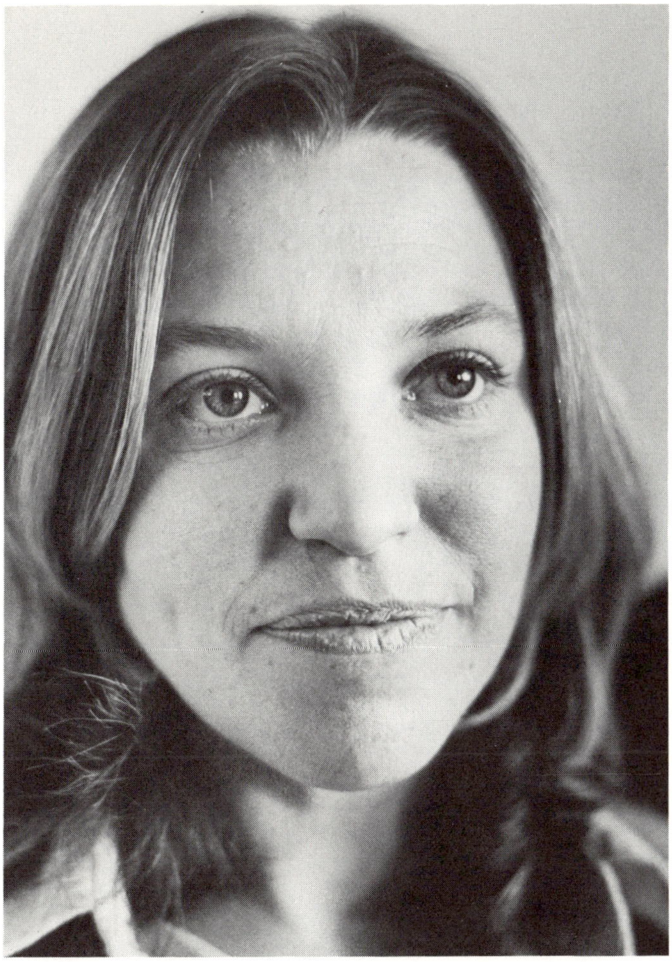

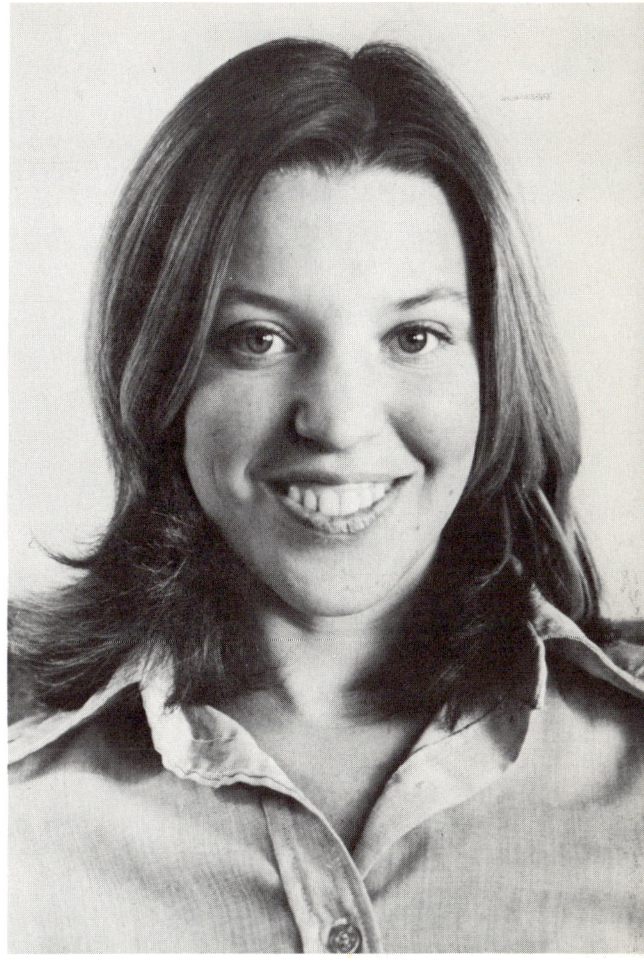

Perspective in portraits. *Do not get too close* to a portrait subject: Perspective effects will enlarge the nose, jaw, and forehead, producing an unpleasant effect, to say the least. Back off, and use a longer lens to get the larger image you want. The first picture of the girl was taken at 2 feet with the 50 mm Nikkor; the second, at 6 feet with the 105 mm. Much prettier, isn't it?

Focal length, distance, and perspective. Reading the pictures on the opposite page *horizontally,* the distance increases: left column, 20 feet; middle, 40 feet; right, 60 feet. Reading them *vertically,* the focal length increases: top row, 28 mm; middle, 50 mm; bottom, 105 mm. Note that for any distance, changing focal length alone does not alter perspective, only size. Changing distance does alter perspective, and changing both accentuates the effect. Moore's "Reclining Figure" at Lincoln Center, taken at 1/500 sec. at *f*/8, on Tri-X, through a medium yellow filter.

WIDE-ANGLE LENSES

Any lens of less than normal focal length qualifies as a wide-angle. They range from an extreme of 6–16 mm or so focal length (the so-called fisheye lenses) to the more moderate (and useful) 24–35 mm category. As their focal length decreases, their wide-angle characteristics increase—greater angle of view, greater depth of field, and greater apparent distortion.

Your own photographic habits should determine which you will buy. Do you need great depth of field? (It eliminates the need for critical focusing.) Do you have insufficient space in which to shoot? (The wide-angle seems to "create" space by getting more into the picture.) Do you dislike distortion? (Better stay away from the extreme lenses.) Do you love it? (Get a fisheye.)

In general, the moderate wide-angle lenses are used much as the normal lenses are, where a slightly enlarged field of view and depth of field are required. In the instance of architectural photography, where the camera may be brought nearer the building than with the normal lens without tilting the camera upward (which causes parallel lines to converge), it may even "correct" distortion. It is a most useful lens for recording interiors, large groups, or individuals in relation to their environments.

The more extreme wide-angle lenses may be used in much the same way, with more of everything. They are notable for enormous fields of view, the ability to resolve objects from a few inches away to infinity, and for deliberately distorted effects.

TELEPHOTO LENSES

Moderate Telephotos

Often called the "portrait lens," the moderate telephoto, of up to 105 mm in focal length, is the author's favorite. It offers a wealth of possibilities second only to the normal lens. Fast and light in weight, it is easy to hand-hold, yet it gives a magnification twice that of the 50 mm lens. It thus brings distant objects twice as "near." Because it usually can be focused close by, it can be used to frame a nearby subject fully and isolate it.

For these reasons, it makes an ideal lens for head-and-shoulder portraits, since at a distance of five to seven feet it eliminates all backgrounds, fills the picture with the subject, and maintains the proper perspective to keep facial features at their most pleasing. (To obtain so large an image with the normal lens would require closing in to three or four feet with the attendant distortion; to retain proper perspective would bring in too much of the surrounding scene as well as shrinking the subject.)

At the same time, the moderate telephoto is an excellent lens to use at sporting events you can get fairly close to. Its angle of view, usually 20°–30°, is large enough to follow the action, yet small enough to isolate the critical moments. Its high speed lets you use it in low-level light with the slower color films, a most useful advantage. To get nearer subjects for candid photos, to separate details from busy surroundings, to maintain a natural-appearing perspective, the moderate telephoto is a splendid performer.

Long Telephotos—the Big Guns

In this range fall some of photography's most spectacular optics, from about 135 mm focal length to 1000 mm or more. These fairly specialized lenses require special handling, though as time goes by they are becoming easier to use and consequently more popular. Their very critical angle of view (from about 18° with a 135 mm lens to 3° or less with lenses of 1000 mm or greater focal length) let them "grab" distant details out of a mass, and their extremely shallow depth of field permits the photographer to throw all but a few inches of a scene out of focus.

These lenses have no equal for sports or special-events photography. With intelligent use, they make first-rate portrait lenses (especially for

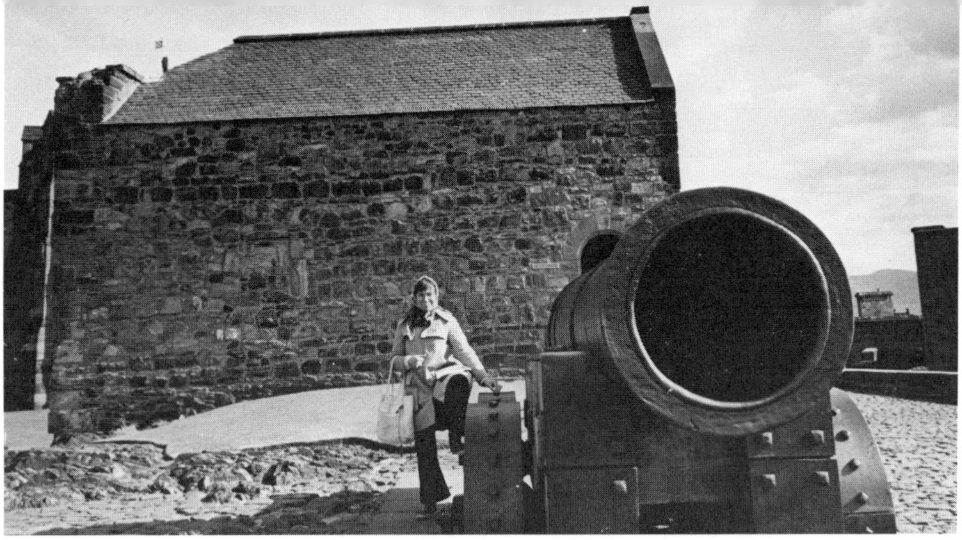

Moderate wide-angle. This view of the battlements of Edinburgh Castle, Scotland, has most of the typical wide-angle features: broad angle of view, great depth of field, and apparent distortion of the nearby gun muzzle. Hold the picture up close, however, and the various parts fall "into perspective." Taken with the 28 mm Nikkor on Plus-X, medium yellow filter, 1/125 sec. at *f*/11.

Extreme wide-angle. The 16 mm Fisheye-Nikkor fills the full frame with startling, distorted effects through a 170-degree angle of view, as in this incredibly sharp front-to-back view of the Lincoln Center fountain, courtyard, and buildings beyond. Taken through the lens's built-in yellow filter on Tri-X, 1/500 sec. at *f*/8.

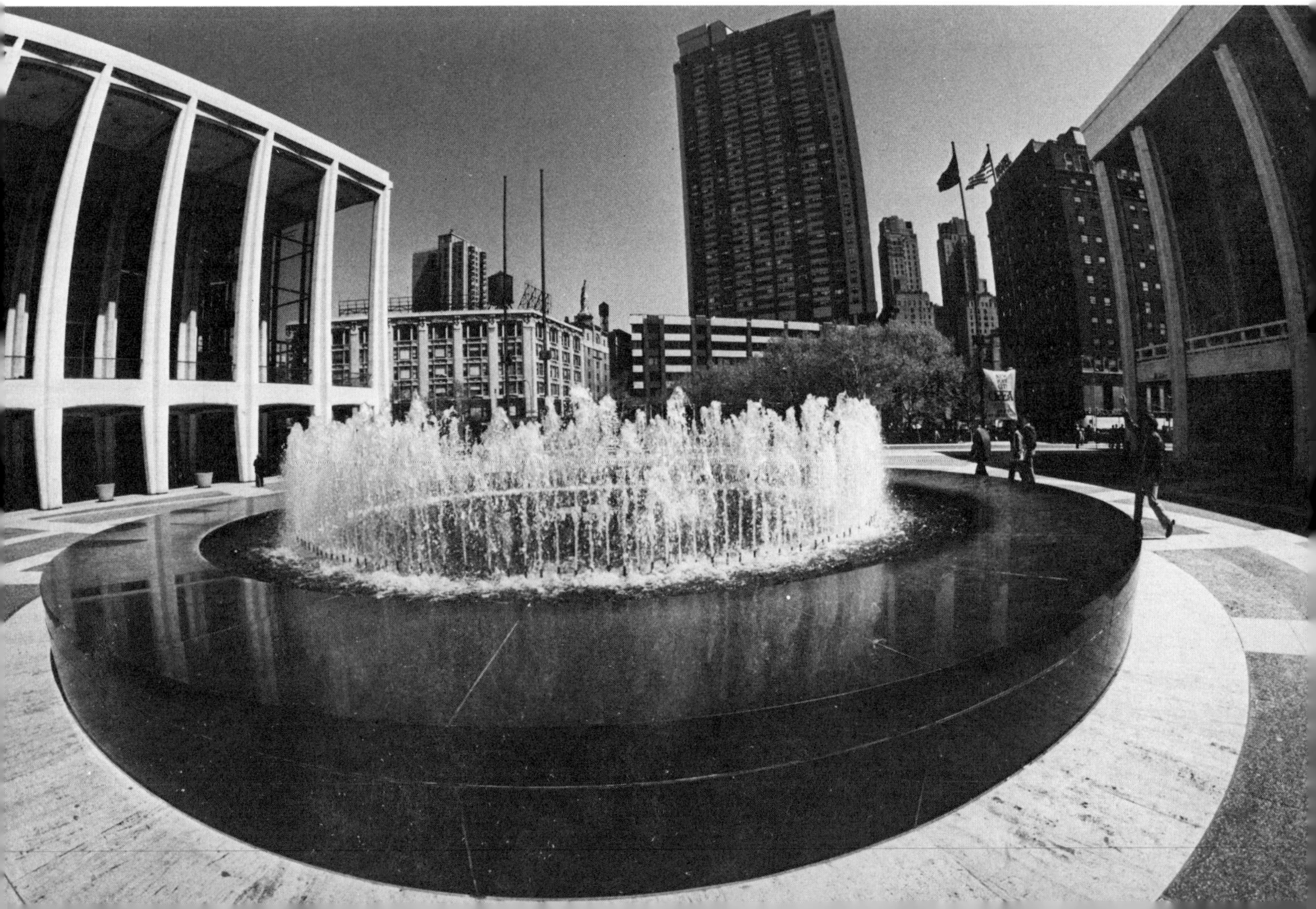

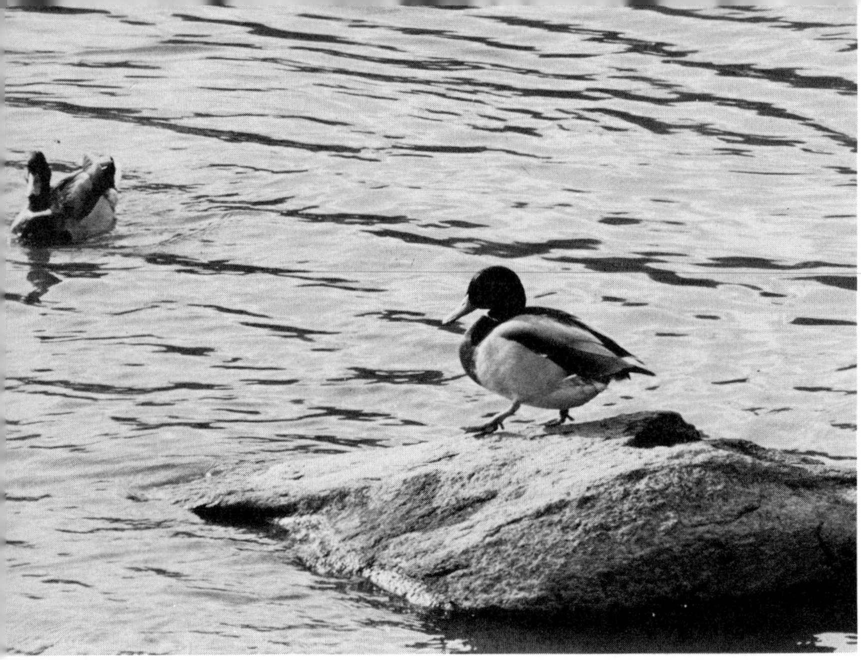

Telephoto for subject isolation. These ducks, more than 50 feet away, are brought in sharp by the 200 mm Nikkor, which "crops out" extraneous fore- and background. Plus-X, exposed 1/250 sec. at *f*/11, retains texture in the rock and water.

Long telephoto compression. The graphic effect of these buildings being "pancaked" is due to distance, not the 300 mm Nikkor. Each building is one block farther away than the last, but the nearest is 5 blocks (about ¼ mile) from the camera. The low structure in the foreground looms disproportionately large. Tri-X, exposed 1/500 sec. at *f*/8.

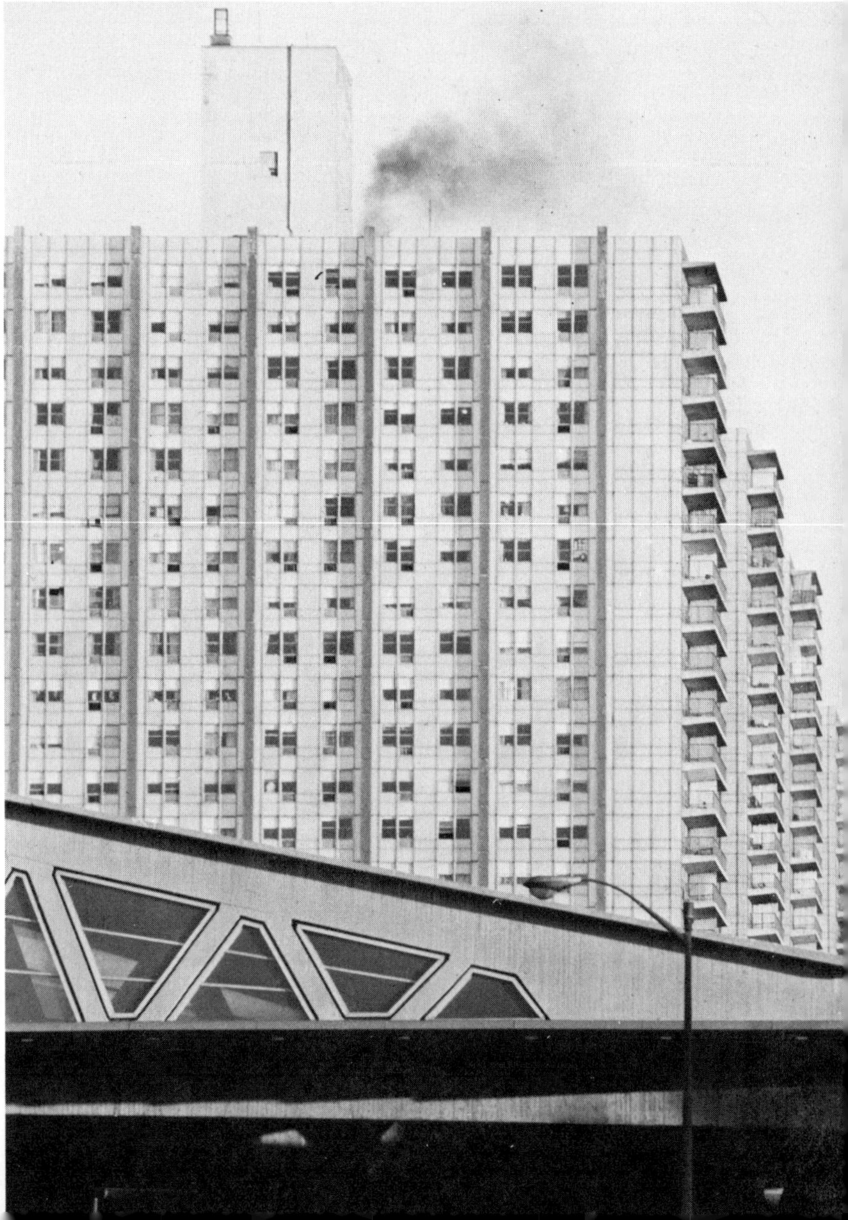

candid portraits of unsuspecting persons in a crowd). The curious flattening-out of perspective, characteristic of these long lenses, is today synonymous with sports and reportage photography.

Special attention is necessary when one uses a lens of over 135 mm. Almost no camera-shake at all is tolerable; as the image is magnified, so are the results of camera movement. Solid support is needed for the camera and lens at any shutter speed; a tripod and cable release are mandatory with all slower speeds, and the longer the lens, the higher the acceptable speed will be. Although faster films (and therefore faster shutter speeds) allow the lenses to be hand-held, it is difficult to do so since they are heavy. They are also relatively slow, and because of their limited depth of field you must focus them very precisely.

But with all these disadvantages, unless you have seen a bird in a tree five times "life-size"; or watched a pass receiver come down with the ball at the moment you squeeze the shutter; or extracted one haunting face from a crowd of hundreds—you have not truly experienced single-lens-reflex photography.

NIKKOR LENSES

The superb qualities of the normal Nikkor lenses applies to the following lenses as well. Many optical innovations were introduced in the Nikkors: among them the close-range correction system—called the "floating-element" system—for large-aperture wide-angle lenses of the retrofocus type; and "Integrated Coating" (IC), a multilayer coating for individual lens elements, to enhance light transmission, image contrast, and color fidelity, while at the same time reducing image-degrading flare caused by internal reflections. Nearly all Nikkor lenses have this coating.

A more recent development carries the idea of image improvement to new lengths: the development by Nikon of a new type of optical glass—extra-low dispersion (ED) glass. In larger telephoto lenses, "chromatic aberration," the tendency for light of different colors to come to focus at different points and thus degrade the image—be it color or black-and-white—is accentuated. ED glass solves this problem, ending lack of sharpness and "color fringing" so effectively that most ED lenses do not need special focusing indexes for infrared focusing. ED glass is also combined with new internal-focusing (IF) construction, which reduces the size of the lens considerably and permits easier and closer focusing with a very bright image. Lenses designated "IF-ED" are the most advanced of their type.

Nikkor lenses will be grouped here by type. Observe that most lenses in the wide-angle and telephoto ranges are designated "AI." These are, of course, the latest automatic aperture-indexing Nikkors, for the most recent Nikons. Older Auto-Nikkors with the same (or nearly the same) specifications are essentially identical optically. Both types offer full-aperture metering. Several lenses in the different types—especially extreme telephoto and special-purpose lenses—are not AI or Auto-Nikkors. Some do not couple to the meter and must be metered in the stop-down mode; others have manual diaphragms, or fixed apertures. They are, nevertheless, perfectly good lenses, suited to their specific tasks. The new Series E lenses, for the Nikon EM, are listed separately, at the end. Many older Nikkor lenses, which have since been discontinued, can be used on any Nikon SLR, in the same manner as the lenses listed here. All Nikkors since 1959 have used the same Nikon bayonet mount.

Fisheye-Nikkor Lenses

Nikon's unparalleled range of fisheye lenses includes a full-frame, rectangular-image lens, one of orthographic projection, and several that produce the now-familiar circular image of equidistant projection, with its curved lines and distortion

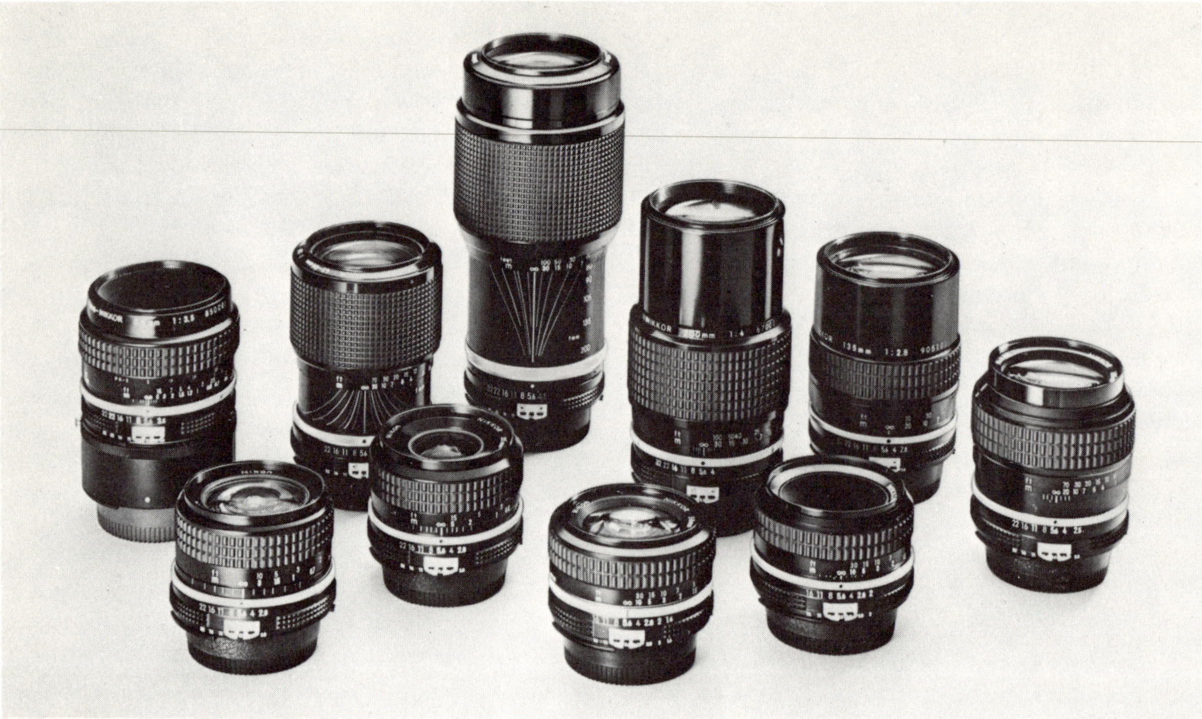

Some of the more than 50 Nikkor lenses. These are the latest AI-Nikkors.

of spatial relationship. Some require the 160° Fisheye Viewfinder.

6 mm f/2.8 AI Fisheye-Nikkor. The most dramatic, the fastest, and the widest-angled of all true fisheye lenses—a full 40° wider than the standard fisheye—this giant lens is a fully meter-coupled, auto-diaphragm AI lens that uses the Nikon's viewing system, and produces a circular, equidistant image. The lens has 12 elements; its angle of view is 220°; it focuses to 11.8 inches; and it stops down to *f*/22. The lens has five built-in filters, is 6.7 inches long, and weighs 11.5 lb.

8 mm f/2.8 AI Fisheye-Nikkor. A basic, fast fisheye of 180° equidistant projection formula, the 8 mm fisheye produces the familiar circular image down to very near focusing distances, employing the camera's viewing and metering systems. It has ten elements; its angle of view is 180°; it focuses to 11.8 inches; and it stops down to *f*/22. The lens has five built-in filters, is 5.5 inches long, and weighs 35.3 oz.

10 mm f/5.6 OP Fisheye-Nikkor. This special-purpose lens gives a circular image of orthographic projection (with uniform brightness over the whole image) and remarkable distortion. The lens does not couple to the camera's viewing or metering system; the mirror must be locked up, and the Fisheye Viewfinder used. It has nine elements; its angle of view is 180°; its focus is fixed; and it stops down to *f*/22. The lens has six built-in filters, is 4.1 inches long, and weighs 14.1 oz.

16 mm f/2.8 AI Fisheye-Nikkor. Filling the entire film format with a rectangular (but not rectilinear) image, this new 16 mm fisheye was designed to produce startling photographic effects. It couples to the Nikon viewing and metering systems, with an auto-diaphragm and standard focusing mount. Number of elements: 8. Angle of view: 180°. Focuses to 1 foot (.3 m). Stops down to *f*/22. Filter: four built-in filters. The lens is 2.6 in. (66 mm) long and weighs 10.9 oz. (310 g).

Wide-Angle Nikkor Lenses

Nikon has more wide-angles than anyone: from a near-fisheye 13 mm *f*/5.6 to a blazingly fast 35 mm *f*/1.4 lens that is often used in the same way as a normal lens. There is a lens for every purpose. All have automatic diaphragms and couple to the meter.

13 mm f/5.6 AI-Nikkor. The widest-angled of all standard Nikkor lenses, this lens has more than 2½ times the coverage of the 50 mm lens, enormous depth of field, and fills the full frame. Its "floating element" design gives the sharpest possible image, even at the closest distances. It has 16 elements; its angle of view is 118°; it focuses to 11.8 inches; and it stops down to *f*/22. The lens takes special behind-the-lens filters, is 4 inches long, and weighs 43.7 oz.

15 mm f/3.5 AI-Nikkor. A new, super-fast, super-wide-angle, the 15 mm Nikkor is 1½ stops faster than the 13 mm, nearly as wide, yet far more compact. It also uses "floating" elements for contrast and sharpness, and has an integral scalloped lens hood and four turret-mount filters. Number of elements: 14. Angle of view: 110°. Focuses to 1 foot (.3 m). Stops down to *f*/22. Built-in filters. The lens is 3.7 inches (94 mm) long and weighs 22.3 oz (630 g).

18 mm f/4 AI-Nikkor. A full stop faster than the 13 mm and the 15 mm, this lens is a panoramic ultra-wide-angle with very even illumination and sharpness, yet much reduced bulk. It has 13 elements; its angle of view is 100°; it focuses to 11.8 inches; it stops down to *f*/22; and its filter size is Series 9. The lens is 2.3 inches long and weighs 11.1 oz.

20 mm f/3.5 AI-Nikkor. This thoroughly redesigned, "basic" ultra-wide-angle lens is also ultra-compact, takes standard 52 mm filters, and is highly corrected to eliminate aberrations and to insure image sharpness. Number of elements: 11. Angle of view: 94°. Focuses to 1 foot (.3 m). Stops down to *f*/22. Filter size: 52 mm. The lens is 1.9 inches (50.5 mm) long and weighs 8.3 oz (235 g).

24 mm f/2 AI-Nikkor. A brand-new, blazing fast, medium-wide-angle lens, between the ultra and moderate wide-angle lenses, this one uses "floating element" design for better close-up sharpness. It uses standard filters; it has 11 elements; its angle of view is 84°; it focuses to 11.8 inches; it stops down to *f*/22; and its filter size is 52 mm. The lens is 2.4 inches long and weighs 10.8 oz.

24 mm f/2.8 AI-Nikkor. This fairly fast, medium-wide-angle lens permits optimum image quality at close distances by means of "floating" rear elements, which move as the lens focuses. It has nine elements; its angle of view is 84°; it focuses to 11.8 inches; it stops down to *f*/22; and its filter size is 52 mm. The lens is 2.2 inches long and weighs 9.5 oz.

28 mm f/2 AI-Nikkor. This is another super-fast, moderate-wide-angle design, employing "floating" rear elements and multi-layer coatings on all glass/air surfaces to improve image rendition by reducing flare. It has nine elements; its angle of view is 74°; it focuses to 11.8 inches; it stops down to *f*/22; and its filter size is 52 mm. The lens is 2.7 inches long and weighs 12.5 oz.

28 mm f/2.8 AI-Nikkor. A new design, the 28 mm *f*/2.8 offers all the quality of the lens above in a slower, but much more compact design. This focal length is rapidly becoming the "standard" wide-angle. It has seven elements; its angle of view is 74°; it focuses to 11.8 inches; it stops down to *f*/22; its filter size is 52 mm. The lens is 2.1 inches long and weighs 8.5 oz.

28 mm f/3.5 AI-Nikkor. A slightly slower and less expensive version of the above lens, this lens has also been recently redesigned to improve sharpness. It has six elements; its angle of view is 74°; it focuses to 11.8 inches; it stops down to *f*/22; and its filter size is 52 mm. The lens is 2.2 inches long and weighs 8.5 oz.

35 mm f/1.4 AI-Nikkor. The fastest and sharpest wide-angle lens there is, this one utilizes both "floating" rear elements and multi-layer coatings to obtain maximum definition at all apertures and distances. It has nine elements; its angle of view is 62°; it focuses to 11.8 inches; it stops down to *f*/16; and its filter size is 52 mm. The lens is 2.9 inches long and weighs 14.4 oz.

35 mm f/2 AI-Nikkor. For years the most popular wide-angle Nikkor, the *f*/2 is still a versatile, sharp lens in this most widely used focal length. It has eight elements; its angle of view is 62°; it focuses to 11.8 inches; it stops down to *f*/22; and its filter size is 52 mm. The lens is 2.4 inches long and weighs 9.9 oz.

35 mm f/2.8 AI-Nikkor. A very compact version of this most useful format, this lens is widely used as a normal lens. It has six elements; its angle of view of 62°; it focuses to 11.8 inches; it stops down to *f*/22; and its filter size is 52 mm. The lens is 2.1 inches long and weighs 8.5 oz.

Telephoto Nikkor Lenses

These are the "regular" telephotos, from 85 mm to 300 mm, which cover most ordinary telephoto applications, up to the extremely long focal lengths and special glass types. All are auto (AI) lenses that couple to the Nikon meter.

85 mm f/1.4 AI-Nikkor. This fastest of all Nikkors, above normal focal length, allows candid portraiture at lighting levels formerly restricted to 50 mm lenses only. It is a full stop faster than the *f*/2 and is the first "floating-element" telephoto, giving very sharp definition at the closest distances. Number of elements: 7. Angle of view: 28°30′. Focuses to 3 feet (.85 m). Stops down to *f*/16. Filter size: 72 mm. The lens is 2.9 inches (72.5 mm) long and weighs 21.4 oz (605 g).

85 mm f/2 AI-Nikkor. This very fast Nikkor is an ideal portrait lens. It has been recently recomputed to focus closer than ever. Number of elements: 5. Angle of view: 28°30′. Focuses to 33.5 inches (.85 m). Stops down to *f*/22. Filter size: 52 mm. The lens is 2.4 inches (61 mm) long and weighs 10.9 oz (310 g).

105 mm f/1.8 AI-Nikkor. The first all-new reformulation of the popular "portrait" lens, the *f*/1.8 is also a stop faster than its partner, but only a bit larger, and focuses as close. It is an excellent available-light lens. Number of elements: 5. Angle of view: 23°20′. Focuses to 3.3 feet (1 m). Stops down to *f*/22. Filter size: 62 mm. The lens is 3.5 inches (88.5 mm) long and weighs 20.5 oz (580 g).

105 mm f/2.5 AI-Nikkor. This lens is a longtime favorite version of the fast, light, moderate telephoto of so many applications. It is slightly longer than the 85 mm, for slightly larger images. It has five elements; its angle of view is 23°20′; it focuses to 39.4 inches; it stops down to *f*/32; and its filter size is 52 mm. The lens is 3.1 inches long and weighs 15.3 oz.

135 mm f/2 AI-Nikkor. This is a new, extremely fast version of this most popular tele length for general work. It fills the full frame with a head shot at about six feet. Its high speed is useful for action photography; it has six elements; its angle of view is 18°; it focuses to 51.2 inches; it stops down to *f*/22; and its filter size is 72 mm. The lens is 4.1 inches long and weighs 30.3 oz.

135 mm f/2.8 AI-Nikkor. One stop slower than the preceding lens, but half the weight, this tele has long proved to be a rugged and versatile lens for action and available-light shooting. It has five elements; its angle of view is 18°; it focuses to 51.2 inches; it stops down to *f*/32; and its filter size is 52 mm. The lens is 3.6 inches long and weighs 15.2 oz.

135 mm f/3.5 AI-Nikkor. Slightly slower than the preceding lens, this version is yet smaller and lighter, and ideal for travel, as an all-around telephoto. It has four elements; its angle of view is 18°; it focuses to 51.2 inches; it stops down to *f*/32; and its filter size is 52 mm. The lens is 3.5 inches long and weighs 14.1 oz.

180 mm f/2.8 AI-Nikkor. Probably the maximum combination of focal length and speed possible for hand-held photography, this is among the fastest of the long Nikkors. It has five elements; its angle of view is 13°40′; it focuses to 70.9 inches; it stops down to *f*/32; and its filter size is 72 mm. The lens is 5.6 inches long and weighs 29.3 oz.

180 mm f/2.8 AI-Nikkor ED. A new, ED-glass version of the very fast and long 180 mm Nikkor, the ED lens improves on the latter's sharpness and color rendition. It has a built-in lens hood. Number of elements: 5. Angle of view: 13°40′. Focuses to 5.9 feet (1.8 m). Stops down to *f*/32. Filter size: 72 mm. The lens is 5.4 inches (138 mm) long and weighs 29.3 oz (830 g).

200 mm f/4 AI-Nikkor. An excellent telephoto, with extended "reach" and speed necessary for action photography or portraiture, this is a lightweight alternative to the 180 mm. It has five elements; its angle of view is 12°20′; it focuses to 78.7 inches; it stops down to *f*/32; and its filter size is 52 mm. The lens is 5 inches long and weighs 19 oz.

300 mm f/4.5 AI-Nikkor. This is a longer action lens, fast and light for its length, with a built-in tripod socket for greater stability. It has six elements; its angle of view is 8°10′; it focuses to 13 feet; it stops down to *f*/22; and its filter size is 72 mm. The lens is 8 inches long and weighs 40.2 oz.

ED-Nikkor Telephoto Lenses

The following lenses, from 300 mm to 1200 mm, are all-glass lenses using Nikon's extra-low dispersion (ED) glass, described earlier. They are not the only ED-Nikkors, but this group was especially computed for the purpose, and each mounts directly on the camera. All are AI lenses and have new internal-focusing (IF) construction. They are easily distinguished by a gold ring around the barrel.

300 mm f/2.8 AI-Nikkor IF-ED. The fastest of all really long Nikkor lenses, the 300 ED-Nikkor gets really astounding speed for its length. Number of elements: 6. Angle of view: 8°10′. Focuses to 13 feet (4 m). Stops down to *f*/32. Filter size: 39 mm (slip-on). The lens is 9.9 inches (249 mm) long and weighs 5.5 lb (2500 g).

300 mm f/4.5 AI-Nikkor IF-ED. Virtually the same lens physically as the 300 mm *f*/4.5 non-ED lens, this lens uses ED glass for much better image sharpness; it needs no infrared correction; and it permits full-aperture metering. Number of elements: 6. Angle of view: 8°10′. Focuses to 8.2 feet (2.5 m). Stops down to *f*/22. Filter size: 72 mm. The lens is 7.9 inches (200 mm) long and weighs 2.2 lb (990 g).

400 mm f/3.5 AI Nikkor IF-ED. This is one of the IF (internal-focusing) lenses that combine all the latest design advances, including ED glass, to get maximum speed and image quality in ultra-telephotos that mount to the Nikon's viewing and full-aperture metering systems directly. It uses slip-in filters. Number of elements: 8. Angle of view: 6°10′. Focuses to 14.7 feet (4.5 m). Stops down to *f*/22. Filter size 39 mm (behind the lens). The lens is 11.9 inches (304 mm) long and weighs 6.2 lb (2800 g).

400 mm f/5.6 AI-Nikkor IF-ED. This first ED lens made by Nikon is remarkably compact for this focal length, and very sharp. It takes standard filters and has its own rotating tripod socket. Its image is 8× that of a normal lens. Number of elements: 5. Angle of view: 6°10′. Focuses to 13 feet (4 m). Stops down to *f*/32. Filter size: 72 mm. The lens is 10.3 inches (262 mm) long and weighs 2.7 lb (1200 g).

600 mm f/5.6 AI-Nikkor IF-ED. This amazing lens uses internal focusing and ED glass to get very high speed and great image crispness into a compact design that couples fully to all camera systems. It uses slip-in filters. Number of elements: 7. Angle of view: 4°10′. Focuses to 18 feet (5.5 m). Stops down to *f*/22. Filter size: 39 mm (behind the lens). The lens is 15 inches (382 mm) long and weighs 5.9 lb (2700 g).

800 mm f/8 AI-Nikkor IF-ED. This ultra-telephoto is the sharpest in its length, thanks to ED glass. Its image is 16× that of a normal lens. Number of elements: 9. Angle of view: 3°. Focuses to 32.8 feet (10 m). Stops down to *f*/32. Filter size: 39 mm (slip-in). The lens is 18.1 inches (460 mm) long and weighs 7.2 lb (3300 g).

1200 mm f/11 AI-Nikkor IF-ED. The longest standard lens that mounts directly on the camera, the 1200 mm is a true telephoto, only 579 mm in actual length. It employs both internal focusing and ED glass for compact design and a sharp image, one 24× that of the normal lens. Number of elements: 9. Angle of view: 2°. Focuses to 46 feet (14 m). Stops down to *f*/32. Filter size: 39 mm (slip-in). The lens is 22.7 inches (569 mm) long and weighs 8.6 lb (3900 g).

Reflex-Nikkor Lenses

To answer the problem of increasing size in all-glass (refracting) lenses in the extreme focal lengths, the *catadioptric* lens was developed. Similar to astronomical telescopes, these lens-and-mirror optics "fold" the light path, bouncing it back and forth, and are therefore considerably shorter and lighter than equivalent all-glass lenses would be. Because they have no diaphragms (and so cannot be stopped down), they are not as absolutely sharp as a refracting lens, but in the ultra-telephoto range they are *much* more convenient.

500 mm f/8 Reflex-Nikkor. This amazingly compact catadioptric lens is less than ⅓ its focal length in physical length (142 mm), and weighs about as much as a fast 135 mm lens. It can be hand-held; it focuses very close; and the camera can be rotated for vertical or horizontal format. Its screw-in rear filters adjust exposure. It has five elements; its angle of view is 5°, it focuses to 13 feet; it has a fixed diaphragm; and its filter size is 39 mm (behind the lens). The lens is 5.6 inches long and weighs 2.2 lb.

1000 mm f/11 Reflex-Nikkor. This is another very compact "cat," similar in design to the 500 mm. It is too long to hand-hold, but is portable enough to carry anywhere. The same 39 mm filters as are used with the 500 mm fit into the rotating filter wheel, to control exposure. It has five elements; its angle of view is 2°30′; it focuses to 25 feet; and it has a fixed diaphragm. The lens has a built-in filter wheel, is 9.5 inches long, and weighs 4.2 lb.

2000 mm f/11 Reflex-Nikkor. This is the longest lens for 35 mm photography in the world! Its image is 40× that of a 50 mm lens. It requires the Nikon AY-1 Mounting Platform, and can be used for astrophotography. It has five elements; its angle of view is 1°10′; it focuses to 59.1 feet; and it has a fixed diaphragm. The lens has four built-in filters, is 23.5 inches long, and weighs 38.6 lb.

Zoom-Nikkor Lenses

The zoom lenses combine several focal lengths in one lens. Their focal length is variable, and they can change the image magnification of a particular scene, while keeping the same focus and aperture. Most Zoom-Nikkors are in the telephoto range, but some newer ones are in the normal and wide-angle range. Except for the longest zooms, these lenses couple to the meter and are now AI Nikkors; two even use ED glass.

25-50 mm f/4 AI Zoom-Nikkor. A wide-to-normal zoom with one of the shortest focal lengths made, the 25-50 gives the photographer of interiors nearly infinite range, with apertures that permit available-light shooting. Number of elements: 11. Angles of view: 80°40′–47°50′. Focuses to 2 feet (.6 m). Stops down to *f*/22. Filter size: 72 mm. The lens is 4.4 inches (112 mm) long and weighs 21.2 oz (600 g).

35–70 mm f/3.5 AI Zoom-Nikkor. This is a brand-new zoom of moderate-wide-angle to moderate-telephoto range. It is a fast all-purpose lens, with macro provisions. It has ten elements; its angle of view is 62°–34°20′; it focuses to 39.4 inches; it stops down to *f*/22; and its filter size is 72 mm. The lens is 4 inches long and weighs 19.4 oz.

43–86 mm f/3.5 AI Zoom-Nikkor. This is the most popular and versatile of all Nikkor zooms. Its single zoom/focus control makes for instantaneous operation with the eye at the finder. It has a standard filter size; 11 elements; its angle of view is 53°–28°30′; it focuses to 47.2 inches; it stops down to *f*/22; and its filter size is 52 mm. The lens is 3.4 inches long and weighs 15.9 oz.

50-300 mm f/4.5 AI Zoom-Nikkor ED. A reformulation of the first zoom lens with a 6:1 zoom ratio, the current model incorporates ED glass to sharpen its images and reduce its weight from the previous version. A standout favorite among sports and nature photographers who need normal-to-extreme-telephoto lengths for tripod work (lens has its own rotating tripod collar). Number of elements: 15. Angles of view: 46°–8°10′. Focuses to 8.2 feet (2.5 m). Stops down to *f*/32. Filter size: 95 mm. The lens is 9.7 inches (247 mm) long and weighs 4.9 lb (2200 g).

80–200 mm f/4.5 AI Zoom-Nikkor. This hand-holdable, medium-telephoto 2.5:1 zoom is light and fast. The sharpest zoom known, it takes a standard filter size. It has single zoom/focus control; 15 elements; its angle of view is 30°10′–12°20′; it focuses to 5.9 feet; it stops down to *f*/32; and its filter size is 52 mm. The lens is 6.4 inches long and weighs 28.9 oz.

180–600 mm f/8 ED Zoom-Nikkor. This new, ED-assisted ultra-telephoto zoom is light for its reach. It has an auto-diaphragm, but no meter coupling, so the lens must be used in stop-down mode. It has single focus/zoom control, and a rotating collar with a tripod socket; 18 elements; its angle of view is 13°40′–4°10′; it focuses to 8.2 feet; it stops down to *f*/32; and its filter size is 95 mm. The lens is 15.9 inches long and weighs 7.6 lb.

200–600 mm f/9.5 Zoom-Nikkor. Somewhat slower, but much lighter than the previous lens, this zoom can be used with a close-up attachment, down to 7.5 feet. It has stop-down metering; single focus/zoom control, with a rotating collar with a tripod socket; 19 elements; its angle of view is 12°20′–4°10′; it focuses to 13 feet; it stops down to *f*/32; and its filter size is Series 9. The lens is 15 inches long and weighs 5.3 lb.

360–1200 mm f/11 ED Zoom-Nikkor. This is the longest zoom of all, with ED glass to insure crisp images. It is the perfect lens for nature, sports, and surveillance. It has stop-down metering; single focus/zoom control, with a rotating collar with a tripod socket; 20 elements; its angle of view is 6°50′–2°; it focuses to 19.7 feet; it stops down to *f*/32; and its filter size is 122 mm. The lens is 27.7 inches long and weighs 15.7 lb.

Special Nikkor Lenses

In this category are some of the most unusual optics made by Nikon, including micro lenses, the perspective-control Nikkors, and other lenses for specific technical purposes.

55 mm f/2.8 Micro-Nikkor. This ultra close-up lens used alone can produce 1:2 magnification; its automatic extension ring produces 1:1 (life-size) magnification. Usable with teleconverter or bellows to obtain greater magnifications, it has six elements; its angle of view is 43°; it focuses to 10 inches; it stops down to f/32; and its filter size is 52 mm. The lens weighs 10.24 oz.

105 mm f/4 AI Micro-Nikkor. This is a longer focal-length macro lens, which allows greater space between lens and subject, for more pleasing perspective effects. It also obtains a 1:2 image alone or 1:1 (life-size) with its own extension ring. It has five elements; its angle of view is 23°20′; it focuses to 18.5 inches; it stops down to *f*/32; and its filter size is 52 mm. The lens is 4.1 inches long and weighs 17.6 oz.

200 mm f/4 AI Micro-Nikkor IF. The first "macro" lens in this focal length, the 200 mm Micro-Nikkor lets the photographer shoot close-up work from greater distances than ever. Number of elements: 9. Angle of view: 12°20′. Focuses to 2.3 feet (.71 m). Stops down to *f*/32. Filter size: 52 mm. The lens is 7.1 inches (180 mm) long and weighs 22.6 oz (640 g).

28 mm f/3.5 PC-Nikkor. One of two perspective-control lenses that shift, up to 11 mm, off-axis, to correct perspective distortion while keeping the film plane parallel to the subject; it can be rotated 360°. Its manual aperture requires stop-down metering. Number of elements: 9. Angle of view: 74°. Focuses to 1 foot (.3 m). Stops down to *f*/22. Filter size: 72 mm. The lens is 2.7 inches (69 mm) long and weighs 13.4 oz (380 g).

35 mm f/2.8 PC-Nikkor. This faster, smaller perspective-control lens shares 11 mm maximum optical shift with the wider 28 mm PC-Nikkor. It can be rotated 360°, and can be used as a regular-purpose wide-angle lens. It also has a manual diaphragm. Number of elements: 7. Angle of view: 62°. Focuses to 1 foot (.3 m). Stops down to *f*/32. Filter size: 52 mm. The lens is 2.6 inches (66 mm) long and weighs 11.3 oz. (320 g).

58 mm f/1.2 Noct AI-Nikkor. This is a brand-new ultra-high-speed lens in the normal focal-length range, with special application in nighttime photography. It has seven elements; its angle of view is 40°50′; it focuses to 19.7 inches; it stops down to *f*/16; and its filter size is 52 mm. The lens is 2.5 inches long and weighs 17.1 oz.

120 mm f/4 Medical-Nikkor IF. This new Medical-Nikkor brings to the Medical-Nikkor close-up system many of the latest advances in electronics, auto-flash, and data imprinting, in a smaller package, for all technical work. Alone, the lens yields magnifications of 1/11× to 1:1; with its attachment lens, from .8× to 2×. Its built-in xenon ringlight flash and coupled diaphragm automatically give the proper exposure. Reproduction ratios may be imprinted on the film with each shot. The lens also has a focusing lamp and a flash ready-light. Number of elements: 9. Angle of view: 20°30′. Focuses to 10.2 inches (.26 m). Stops down to *f*/32. Filter size: 49 mm. The lens is 5.6 inches (142 mm) long and weighs 32.5 oz (920 g).

200 mm f/5.6 Medical-Nikkor. A highly specialized lens, the Medical-Nikkor was originally used for medical and dental work, but now finds application in industrial and scientific photography. Its self-contained close-up system uses additive components to give a 3:1 image ratio; its built-in ringlight flash gives shadowless illumination. It has four elements; its angle of view is 12°20′; it focuses to 13.2 inches; it stops down to *f*/45; and its filter size is 38 mm. The lens is 7 inches long and weighs 24.7 oz.

Nikon Series E Lenses

The compact lenses introduced for the Nikon EM are slightly different from the standard Nikkor line. They are lightweight, of simpler construction, and less expensive than the Nikkors; but they are optically excellent. They permit AI and ADR with *any* current Nikon, but since they have no meter *prong*, they must be used in the stopped-down mode with older models.

28 mm f/2.8 Nikon Series E. Now the "standard" wide-angle focal length, the Series E 28 mm is the smallest such made. Number of elements: 5. Angle of view: 74°. Focuses to 1 foot (.3 m). Stops down to *f*/22. Filter size: 52 mm. The lens is 1.7 inches (45 mm) long and weighs 5.3 oz (150 g).

35 mm f/2.5 Nikon Series E. Built on the same mold as the 28 mm; provides moderate wide-angle view. Number of elements: 5. Angle of view: 62°. Focuses to 1 foot (.3 m). Stops down to *f*/22. Filter size: 52 mm. The lens is 1.7 inches (45 mm) long and weighs 5.3 oz (150 g).

50 mm f/1.8 Nikon Series E. The standard Series E lens; it comes with the Nikon EM. Number of elements: 6. Angle of view: 46°. Focuses to 2 feet (.6 m). Stops down to *f*/22. Filter size: 52 mm. The lens is 1.3 inches (33 mm) long and weighs 4.8 oz (135 g).

100 mm f/2.8 Nikon Series E. The perfect "portrait" telephoto, virtually pocket size. Number of elements: 4. Angle of view: 24°20′. Focuses to 3.3 feet (1 m). Stops down to *f*/22. Filter size: 52 mm. The lens is 2.3 inches (58 mm) long and weighs 7.9 oz (225 g).

75-150 mm f/3.5 Zoom Nikon Series E. A remarkable, lightweight zoom, with 2:1 ratio. Number of elements: 12. Angle of view: 31°41′—17°. Focuses to 3.3 feet (1 m). Stops down to *f*/32. Filter size: 52 mm. The lens is 4.9 inches (125 mm) long and weighs 18.3 oz (520 g).

Teleconverters

Nikon has introduced three coated optical teleconverters, to extend the focal length of almost any AI-Nikkor. The TC-200 doubles the length of the 500 mm Reflex-Nikkor and any other lens up to 200 mm; the TC-300 does the same for lenses 300 mm and up; the TC-14 increases the focal length 1.4×.

Tele-Nikkor Lenses (require focusing mount)

Prior to the development of compact IF-ED lenses, Nikon produced seven short-mount lenses, from 400 mm to 1200 mm, that required a separate focusing mount to be attached to the camera (the *Standard Focusing Unit* or later *Focusing Unit AU-1*). All lenses worked with either mount automatically, except the 1200 mm lenses, which were manual, and all had to be stopped down for metering. In addition to the two lenses still available, the series consisted of a 600 mm *f*/5.6 ED, an 800 mm *f*/8, an 800 mm *f*/8 ED, a 1200 mm *f*/11, and a 1200 mm *f*/11 ED Tele-Nikkor.

400 mm f/4.5 Tele-Nikkor. The shortest but also the fastest of the focusing-mount Nikkors, the 400 mm provides an image 8× that of the normal lens. It focuses quite close, and is ideal for nature photography.

600 mm f/5.6 Tele-Nikkor. With an image size 12× that of the normal lens, and excellent speed for its size, this is an excellent lens for nature or sports photography.

CHAPTER 4

Nikon Accessories

The truly huge number of accessories made for the various Nikon cameras are intended to increase the versatility of each camera to a true "system" status, and they succeed. From the modest lens-hood to the most elaborate flash or motor-drive unit, these accessories widen the opportunities of every Nikon photographer who wishes to improve and extend his or her efforts into new areas.

Limitations of space force this listing to be perfunctory, but additional information may be obtained from your local camera store or from Nikon, Inc. Each accessory purchased new comes with complete operating instructions.

NIKON FLASH UNITS

The use of flash is detailed in Chapter 6, under "Flash and Electronic Flash." Nikon makes a variety of "SB" automatic flash units. Only the current models are described here, but there have been other units, designed principally for older Nikon cameras, which share many of their characteristics, and which operate similarly. Some of the most notable were the SB-5 (bracket unit); SB-2 and SB-3 (hot shoe units for F2 and standard-shoe models, respectively); and the SB-4 and SB-9 compacts.

Nikon SB-11 Flash Unit. This is a professional bracket-type unit that gives thyristor-governed automatic flash with any Nikon, by means of an accessory sensor (SU-2) and *through-the-lens* direct output control with the Nikon F3, using the SC-12 sensor cord. It actually reads exposures off the shutter curtain, using the camera's meter sensor. In either case, it retains full auto operation with bounce or off-camera flash. A very powerful unit (GN 60 with ASA/ISO 25, GN 120 with ASA/ISO 100, in feet; 18 and 36 in meters, respectively), the SB-11 has an auto range over 3 *f*/stops to distances up to 18 m (60 feet). It is powered by eight AA (penlight) batteries, either alkaline or rechargeable NiCads. On auto, the unit recycles in a fraction of a second; on manual, in eight seconds. The SB-11 has the coverage of a 35 mm lens (28 mm with SW-3 adapter).

Nikon SB-12 Flash Unit. A shoe-mount thyristor unit especially designed for the Nikon F3 only. Like the SB-11, the SB-12 provides through-the-lens output control, using the F3's SPD metering system, and it activates the viewfinder ready-light while at the same time setting the shutter at 1/80 sec. synch speed, automatically. The SB-12 has guide numbers of: GN 40 with ASA/ISO 25, GN 80 with ASA/ISO 100, in feet (GN's 12 and 25, in meters respectively) and is powered by four AA batteries. Its automatic range, varying with the aperture on the lens, extends to 15 m (49 ft); the unit will recycle in 8 seconds (manual), in a frac-

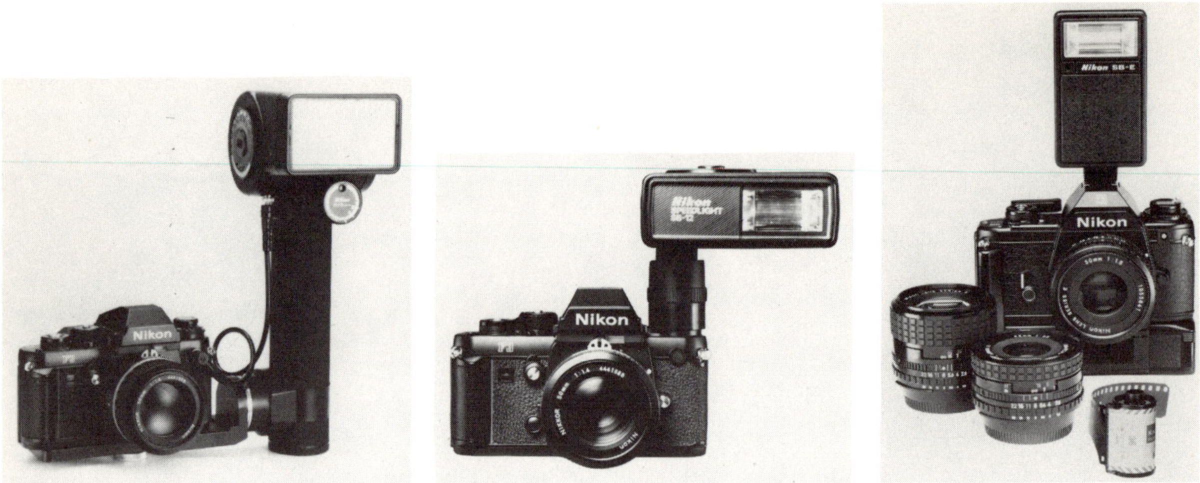

The Nikon thyristor auto electronic flash units (left to right): SB-11, SB-12, and SB-E.

tion of a second on auto, and it has the coverage of a 35 mm lens (28 mm with SW-4 adapter).

Nikon SB-10 Flash Unit. This shoe-mount unit provides the Nikon FE or EM with the "dedicated" thyristor services the previous models give the F3. Like those flashes, the SB-10 automatically sets the shutter and viewfinder displays of the camera it was built for, and like them, it may be used as a "non-dedicated" auto flash with other Nikons. The SB-10 has the same general specifications as the SB-12, with the same guide numbers and power sources. Its automatic range, over 2 *f*/stops, extends to 6 m (20 ft), and it will recycle in 8 seconds (manual) or a split-second (auto). It, too, covers the field of view of a 35 mm lens (28 mm with SW-2 adapter).

Nikon SB-E Flash Unit. Less than five ounces in weight, the SB-E gives the Nikon EM, for which it was designed, or the FE fully "dedicated" thyristor auto flash: that is, it programs the camera's shutter for the proper flash-synch speed, it activates the viewfinder ready and warning signals, and it quenches itself, according to the *f*/stop on the Series E or AI-Nikkor lens. It requires *no* settings or adjustments on the EM; it can be used as an ordinary auto flash on any other Nikon. The SB-E has guide numbers of: GN 28 with ASA/ISO 25, GN 56 with ASA/ISO 100 (GN's 8 and 17, in meters) and is powered by four AAA mini-batteries. The auto-range of the flash, over three lens-set apertures, extends to 6 m (20 ft), and it will recycle in less than one second on auto (nine seconds at manual). It covers the field of a 35 mm lens.

Flash accessories. Nikon has a number of accessories to increase the flexibility of the various SB units. Among them are various synch cords and extension cords; power packs and battery rechargers; flash couplers, to adapt one form of hot shoe to another; the Ready-Light SF-1, for cameras without a ready light; and a Ready-Light Adapter SC-4 for off-camera steady-light operation with the Nikon F2.

CLOSE-UP ACCESSORIES

The world of close-up photography is totally different from the rest of the photographic universe; it deals with exciting new subjects, new methods, new types of pictures, and new tools. Before the advent of SLR photography, it was also incredibly complex. Exposure factors, bellows extensions, and the like, caused many potential investigators of this fascinating area to give up. Now, Nikon through-the-lens viewing and metering make close-up photography, "macro"-photography (or photomacrography), and photomicrography* both accessible and fun. Exposure problems are solved automatically; extension tubes and bellows are used as easily as are Nikkor lenses.

This area is too large and rich to examine fully in a volume this size; besides, it is treated extensively elsewhere. Described here are the accessories Nikon has made available for focusing closer. And closer.

Close-Up Attachment Lenses

The simplest of close-up accessories, these diopter lenses screw into the filter thread on the wide-angle, normal, or shorter tele Nikkors. Available in 52 mm thread mounts, there are three lenses, designated "0," "1," and "2." Lenses 1 and 2 may be used in combination with the normal lens to yield magnifications up to about 1/3× (1:3). Lens 0 may be used in continuous magnification with the 105 mm, 135 mm, and 200 mm Nikkors to yield magnifications up to about 2/3× (2:3). These lenses require no exposure alteration or calculation.

Extension Ring Sets

These devices, which are the next step up in magnification, lead to true photomacrography by extending the lens out from the camera body. They are attached to the camera in the same manner as are lenses; and lenses are attached to them the same way. Several sets exist, in various sizes and combinations, for automatic or manual-diaphragm operation over a wide range of magnifications. The latest models, designed for the AI-Nikkors, are similar to those made for Auto-Nikkors.

E2 Ring. A single ring, 14 mm thick, for any Nikkor from 20 mm up, the E2 provides low magnification in its most compact form. A built-in plunger allows the auto diaphragm of a stopped-down lens to re-open to maximum aperture for viewing and focusing; therefore, it is often used on the end of a bellows attachment. Typical magnifications are 1/3× with the 50 mm lens and 1/4× with the 105 mm.

Auto Extension Ring PN-11. A single ring, 52.5 mm thick, the PN-11 is actually the extension ring for the 105 mm AI Micro-Nikkor (the nearly identical PN-1 is for Auto-Nikkors) but it works with most focal lengths. It provides fixed magnification in a compact form, with auto diaphragm and meter-coupling. With the 50 mm lenses, magnification is slightly above life size. Similar rings in smaller sizes are in the PK sets (below).

Ring Set K. This manual set of five rings—K1–5.8 mm, K2–5.0 mm, K3–5.8 mm, K4–10.0 mm, and K5–20.0 mm—offers a total extension of 46.6 mm. These rings may be used individually, or in nine different combinations. Metering is performed by the stop-down method, and the diaphragm must be operated manually. With the normal 50 mm lens, magnifications of 1:8.9 to 1:1 (life-size) are possible; with the 28 mm lens, nearly 2:1; with the 105 mm lens, about 1:1.7.

Auto Ring Sets PK. These two sets of three rings each include the PK-1, PK-2, and PK-3 (for Auto-Nikkors and corresponding cameras), and the PK-11, PK-12, and PK-13 (for AI-Nikkors and corresponding cameras). They are used singly or in seven different combinations to yield extensions from 8 mm to 49.5 mm. Depending on the model, full-aperture metering and automatic-diaphragm coupling are retained—a *great* convenience in macro work. Magnification ranges are similar to those of manual rings, up to 1.1× with the 50 mm lens.

Bellows Focusing Attachments

Bellows units are far more advanced and versatile than extension rings; they provide continuously variable extension between lens and film, over a far greater range. They accept Nikkors from 20 mm to 300 mm, and can be used on a tripod or with the Nikon Repro-Copy Outfit.

Bellows Attachment PB-6. A new, deluxe unit with a "double-dovetail" rail, the PB-6 gives variable extension from 48 mm to 208 mm alone, and with its exclusive *Extension Bellows PB-6E* more than doubles this range: 83 mm to 438 mm. This yields magnifications with the normal 50 mm lens

---

**Photomacrography*: photography of objects at larger than 1:1 (or life-size) magnification. *Photomicrography:* photography through a microscope.

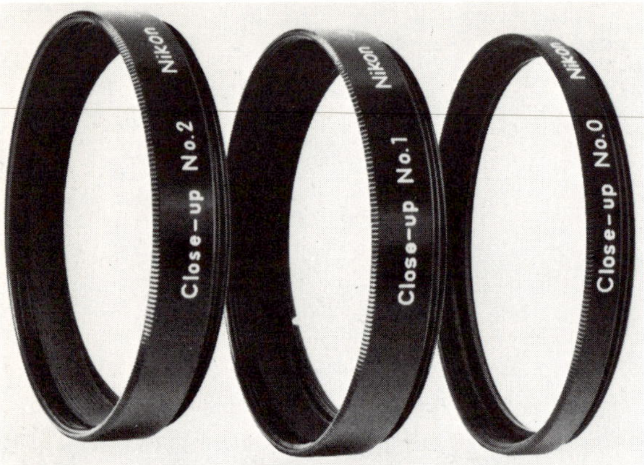

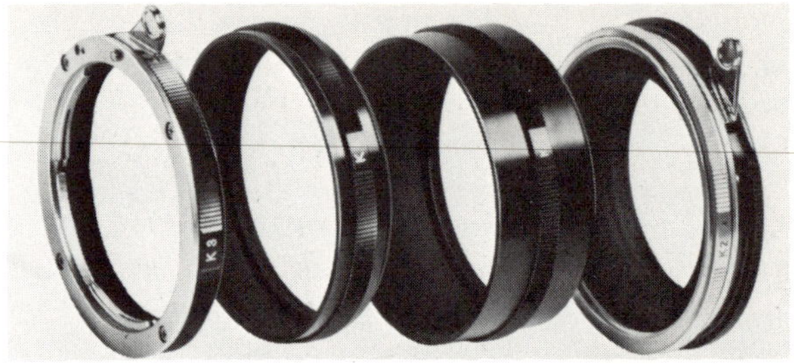

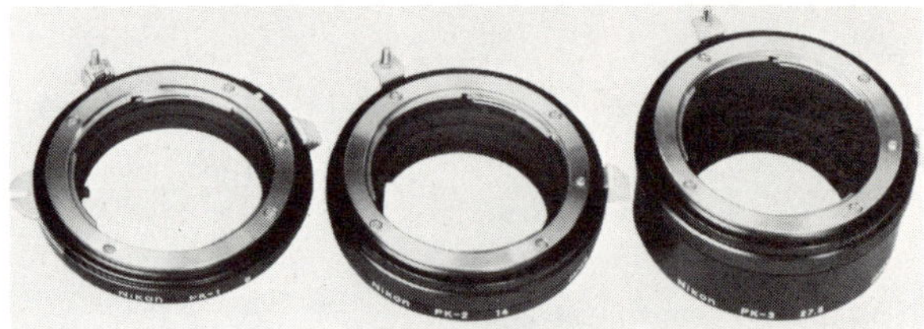

Above, close-up attachment lenses. Above right, manual extension Ring Set K. Right, Auto Ring Set PK.

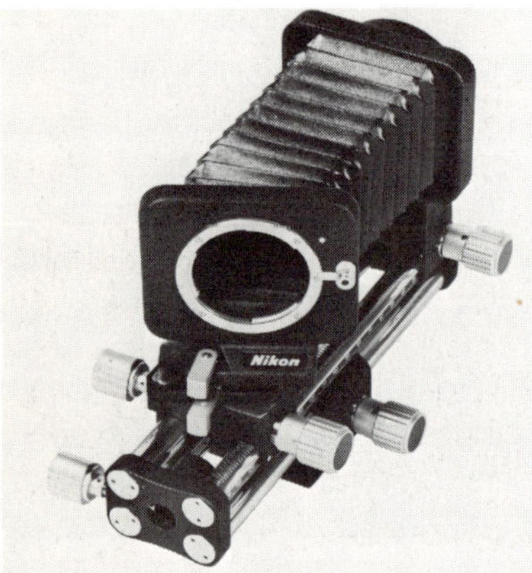

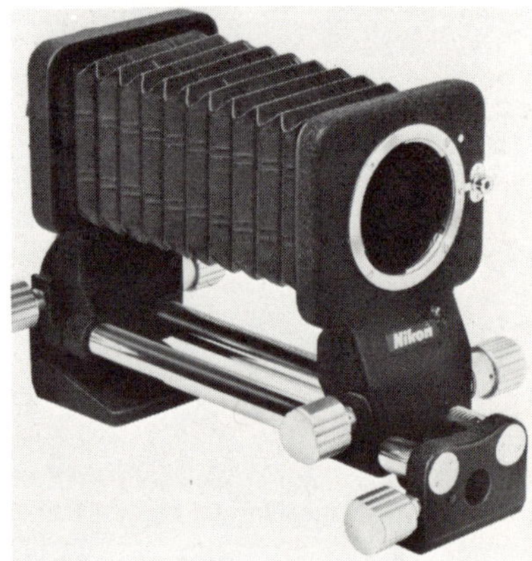

Bellows Attachments PB-4 (left) and PB-5 (right), with their corresponding Slide Copying Adapters, PS-4 (below, left) and PS-5 (below, right).

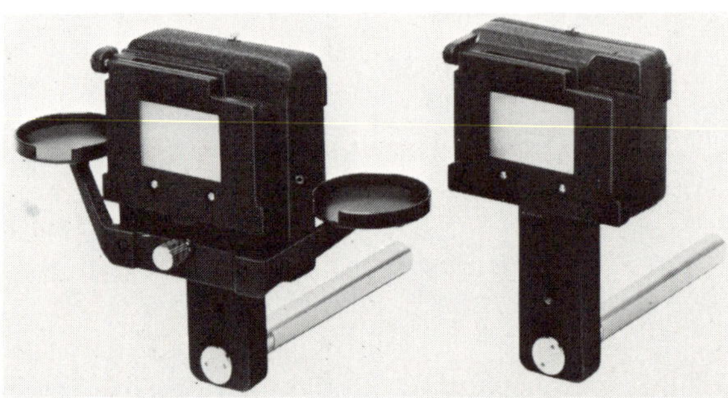

These photographs of the Mexican postage stamp—all reproduced at twice the negative size—were taken with the 55 mm Micro-Nikkor, on Tri-X film in daylight, on a repro-copystand. The aperture was set at *f*/16 (except for the last picture: *f*/11), with the shutter speeds being varied from 1/125 sec. for the lowest magnification to two full seconds for the highest. *A*. Lens alone at 2 feet (1:10). *B*. Lens alone at 9.5 inches (1:2). *C*. Lens plus auto-extension ring, at minimum focus (1:1, life-size). *D*. Lens used on PB-5 Bellows, at 10 cm extension (2:1). *E*. Lens on bellows at 15 cm extension (3:1). *F*. Lens in reversed position on bellows (4.3:1).

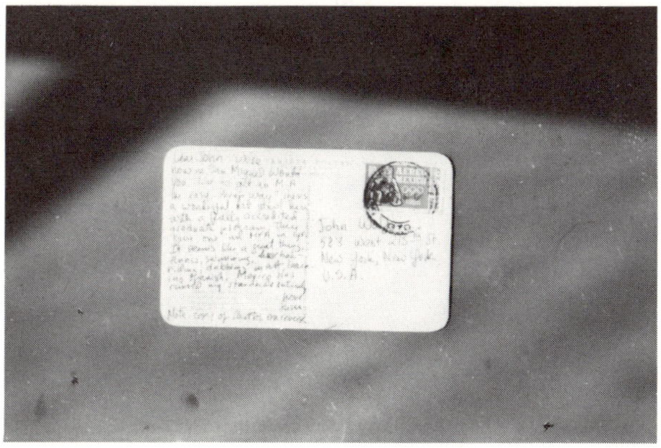

A

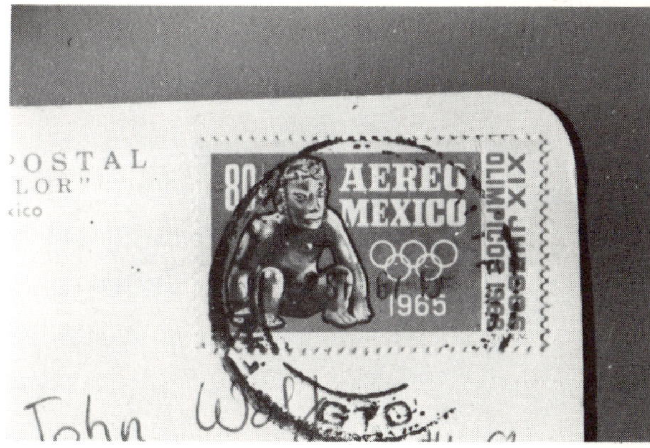
POSTAL
80
AEREO
MEXICO
1965
OLIMPICOS 1968
John

B

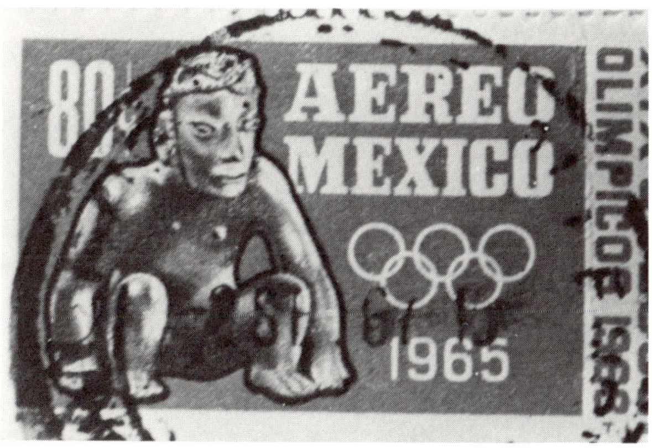
80
AEREO
MEXICO
1965

C

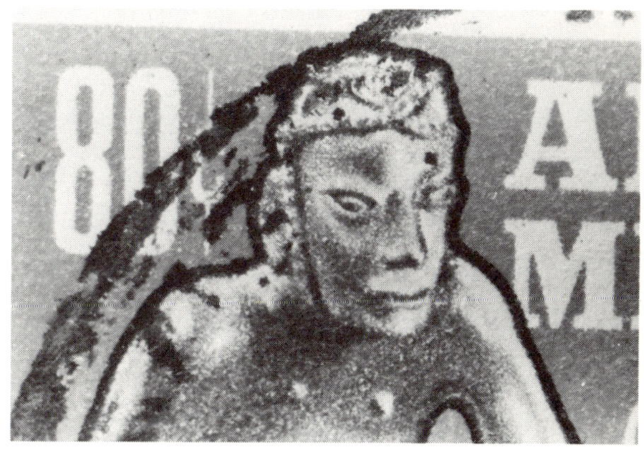
80

D

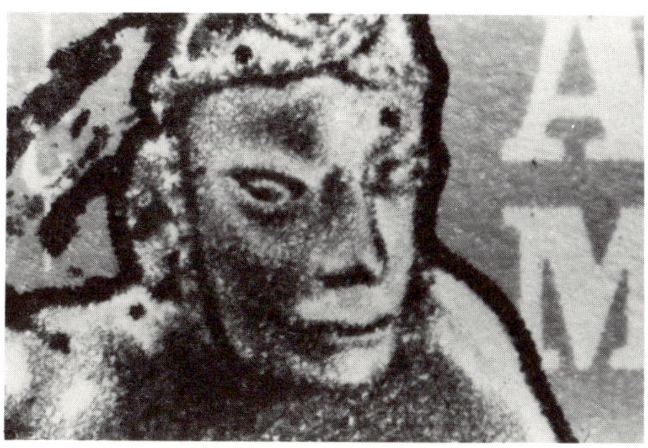

E

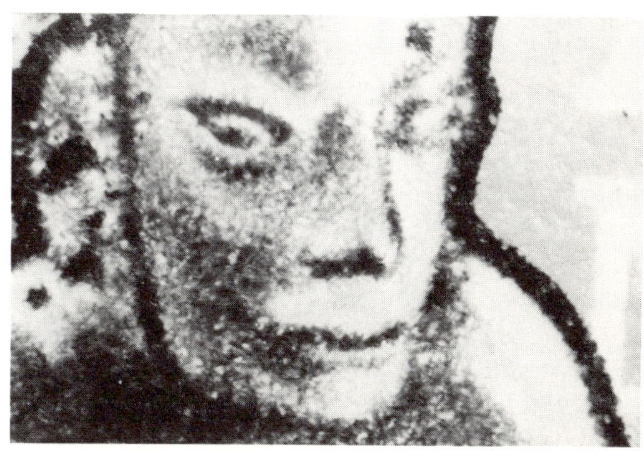

F

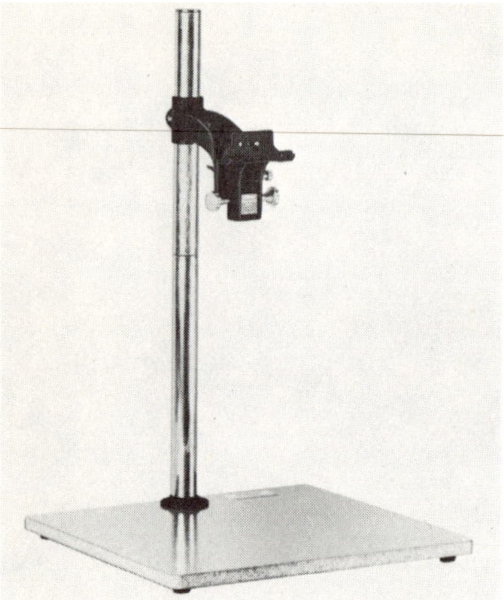

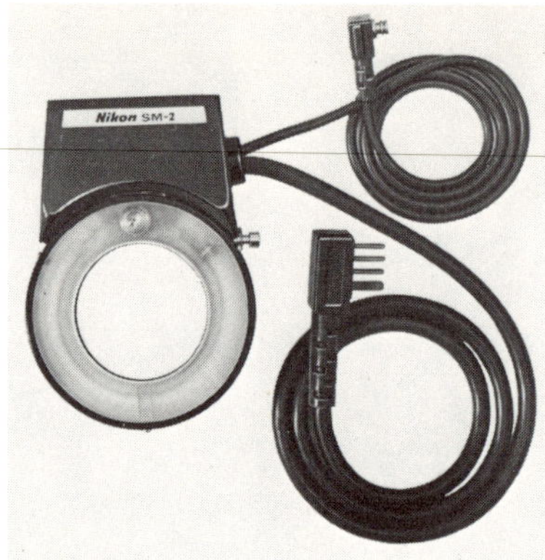

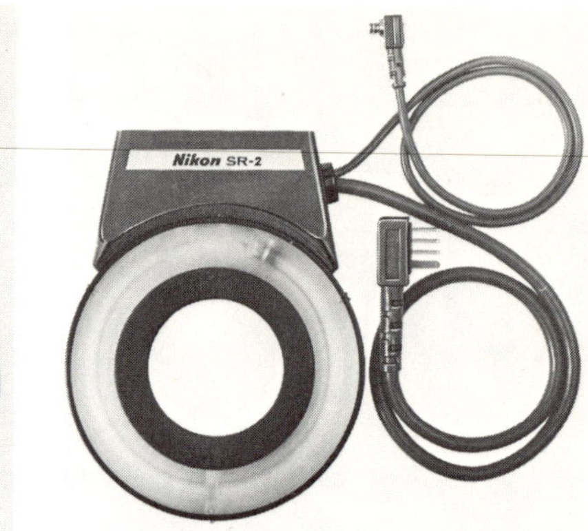

At left, the Repro-Copy Outfit, Model PFB-2, and two ringlight units, the SM-2 (center) and SR-2 (right).

up to 4× (bellows alone) or 8.4× (extension). With a 20 mm Nikkor, the largest magnification is a startling 11× (bellows) or *23 times life size* (extension)! Among the distinguishing features of the PB-6 are: modular construction, with removable lens/camera panels (which permit reversing the lens without an adapter); clip-on attachment, requiring no rings; two-level rail, which lets the camera/bellows/lens assembly be moved for focusing without altering magnification; rotating camera-panel collar, for switching from vertical to horizontal format; semiautomatic diaphragm control without adapter (requires AR-4 or 7 Double Cable Relase); and manual stop-down levers, for depth preview and stop-down metering; and double engraved scales, to facilitate precise measurement of extension.

Bellows Attachments PB-4 and PB-5. These older units work in much the same way as the PB-6, without some of the newer model's features. Both extend to 185 mm. The PB-4, a double-track bellows, features a swinging and shifting lens panel for perspective correction. It has a second set of rails for focusing. The PB-5, a single-track unit, has a rotating camera panel.

Bellows Accessories. Few accessories are required with the PB-6, other than its *Macro Copy Stand PB-6M* and *Slide Copying Adapter PS-6*. Adapters PS-4 and PS-5 are intended for the earlier models, as are a number of adapter and lens-reversing rings, cable releases, and a lens diaphragm-actuating ring.

Repro Copy Outfits

The repro-copy outfits are complete camera-support systems for copying flat objects and photomacrography. Model PFC-2 is an upright column with a sliding mounting arm and a precision cradle, in a wooden storage case that unfolds to become the baseboard. Model PFB-2 is the same, with a rigid baseboard. Deluxe models PF-3 and PF-4 are heavier, with counterbalanced elevation controls and special cradles for Nikons with motor-drive units. On all models, the camera mounts to the cradle by means of the tripod socket. The cradle, which may be locked at eight different positions, at 45° intervals, can itself be adjusted by means of rack-and-pinion fine focusing, and slides up or down the column, locking at any position.

Ringlights

More properly in the flash category, ringlights are circular electronic-flash units for shadowless, close-up photography. The lighting element fits around the lens, like a doughnut. There are two models: the *Macro Ringlight SM-2*, lightweight and compact, is specifically designed for use with Nikkors from 20 mm to 135 mm in reverse position on one of the bellows units. It is to be used at shooting distances of 20 cm or less. The *Ringlight SR-2* is a larger unit, for Nikkors up to 200 mm long, with 52 mm front threads, and is intended for more general flash use. It may be used at shooting distances from 20 cm to 3 m.

IMAGE (REPRODUCTION) RATIOS FOR BELLOWS MODELS PB-6/PB-6E

Relationships of bellows extension, subject field, working distance, and reproduction ratio.

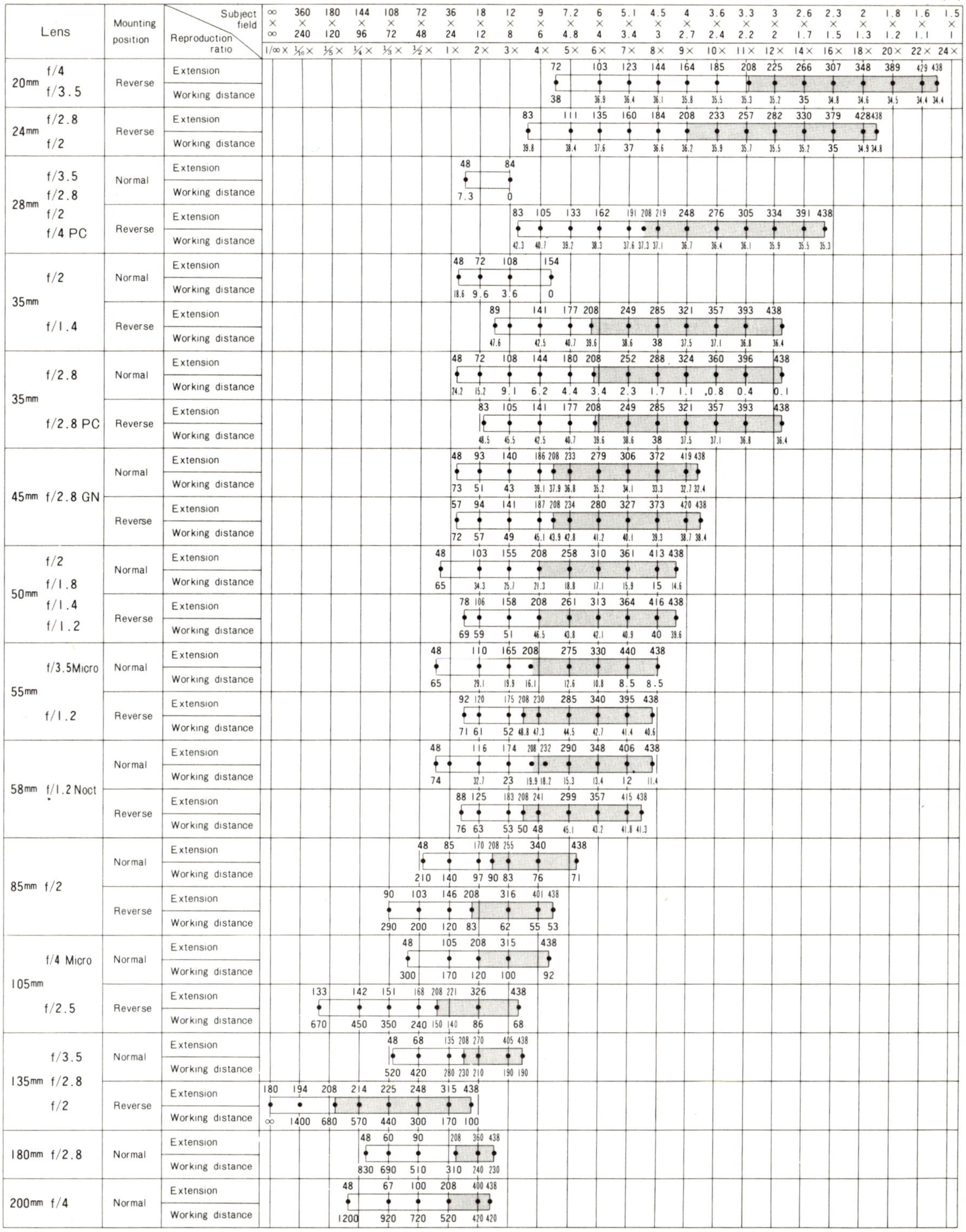

Notes: 1) AI-Nikkor lens is used; with non-AI-Nikkor, the values may be slightly different.
2) Magnifications are those obtained at the infinity setting.
3) If more than one lens is included in each lens column, magnifications apply only to the first lens.
4) The 135mm f/2 and 28mm f/4 PC lenses cannot be used in the reverse position because of the larger size of their attachments.
5) ☐ = with PB-6 alone. ▩ = with PB-6 and PB-6E together.

MAGNIFICATION RANGES OF THE LENSES SUITED FOR CLOSE-UPS

Lens	Close-up Accessories	Lens Mounting	Magnification Range
50mm f/2	Lens alone	Normal	1/9.7X-∞
	Close-up Attachments	Normal	No. 0 1/5.4X-1/27X
			No. 1 1/4.4X-1/13X
			No. 2 1/3.3X-1/6.6X
			Nos. 1 & 2 1/2.7X-1/4.4X
	Extension Ring E2	Normal	1/2.4X-1/3.7X
	Extension Ring Set K	Normal	1.1X-1/8.9X
	*Extension Ring Set PK	Normal	1.1X-1X, 1/1.1X-1/1.2X, 1/1.3X-1/1.5X, 1/1.6X-1/2.3X, 1/2.7X-1/3.7X, 1/3.9X-1/6.5X
	Bellows PB-4, PB-5	Normal	3.6X-1/1.2X
		Reversed	4.4X-1.6X
55mm f/3.5 Micro	Lens alone	Normal	1.2X-∞
	With PK-3	Normal	1X-1/2X
	Bellows PB-4, PB-5	Normal	3.4X-1/1.3X
		Reversed	4.3X-1.7X
105mm f/4 Micro	Lens alone	Normal	1.2X-∞
	With PN-1	Normal	1X-1/2X
	Bellows PB-4, PB-5	Normal	1.8X-1/2.4X
		Reversed	1.6X-1/3.8X
200mm f/5.6 Medical	With or without 6 auxiliary lenses	Normal	3X, 2X, 1.5X, 1X, 2/3X, 1/2X, 1/3X, 1/4X, 1/6X, 1/8X, 1/15X

As indicated earlier, every Nikon reflex now has at least one motor-drive or auto-winder unit specifically designed for it. As a consequence, any Nikon owner may share the pleasures of instantaneous film-wind and rapid-fire sequential shooting. Nikon introduced the first motor-drive unit for 35 mm, and over the years has evolved entire separate systems of motor drives and their accessories. Following are descriptions of some of the current unity.

Motor Drive MD-4

The basic motorized unit for the Nikon F3, the MD-4 produces the fastest framing rate of any standard motor drive made: up to 6 frames per second (fps). It is attached directly to the F3 by screwing it onto the bottom. The unit can be set to give single frame (S) or continuous operation (C) on a single, locking mode selector; in continuous mode, the frame rate is governed by the shutter speed set and by the power source.

The MD-4 is powered by *integral* battery units (which makes it far less bulky than previous units): the *MN-2 NiCad Battery Unit*, which contains fourteen 1.2 V NiCad cells, gives the maximum speed, 6 fps, for up to 80 rolls of 36-exposure film; the standard *MH-3 AA Battery Holder* takes eight 1.5 V alkaline batteries, which can produce a 4 fps rate for 140 rolls of 36-exposure film. An *AC Converter* (MA-4) will run the motor indefinitely at 5.5 fps, off house current.

The MD-4 also features power rewind; an auto-stop provision that shuts the motor off at the end of a roll of film, going forward or rewinding; LED's that signal end-of-film wind, rewind, and battery condition; and an interconnection with the F3's electronics that let the motor batteries power the camera as well.

Nikon has an array of accessories for the MD-4, many of which are compatible with older motor drives. Among the most significant are: *the 250-exposure Magazine Back MF-4*, a bulk-film back with its own operating button and auto-stop control, which operates entirely off the MD-4's batteries; the *NiCad Battery Charger MH-2*; the *Intervalometer MT-1*, a timing device for automatically firing the camera at specific intervals; the *ML-1 Modulite* remote control, which operates the camera remotely, by light signals, up to 200 feet (60 m); the *MW-1 Wireless* radio-remote set, which operates up to 2300 feet (700 m); and various remote cords and tripod adapters.

Motor Drives for Nikon F2

Several units were made for the Nikon F2 cameras, principally the MD-1, MD-2, and compact MD-3. The fastest produced frame rates up to 5 fps, and all took a host of accessories compatible with each other and with the MD-4.

The MD-1 and MD-2 are large units taking external battery packs with either NiCad or (ten) AA alkalines. They, too, can be driven by the MA-4 AC converter. The MD-3 is a much smaller unit (weight: 12.5 oz, or 355 g), which can be operated by any of the power sources above, or its own cordless battery pack, taking eight AA alkalines. The large units have a speed selector, which regulates framing from 1 to 5 fps. They also will take 250- and 750-exposure magazine backs. All three units will operate off the same remote-control devices as the MD-4, and have various battery chargers, cords, and the like.

Motor Drives for Nikon F

Two basic motor drives were supplied for Nikon F cameras. Now discontinued, they may still occasionally be purchased, used. The original unit was the *Model F36*, which took only standard 36-exposure rolls of film. This unit replaced the standard back (and bottom) of the Nikon F in use, and operated off the Cordless Battery Pack or a separate battery-pack unit. The F36 was capable of single frames or continuous exposures up to about 4 fps, depending on shutter speed. The second unit for the Nikon F was the *Electric Motor Drive F250*, an early version of the 250 Magazine Back, except that it was an entire motor-drive unit. This unit had the same capabilities as the F36, except for increased film capacity . Either unit could be operated by remote control, and both had to be fitted to the camera by factory adjustment.

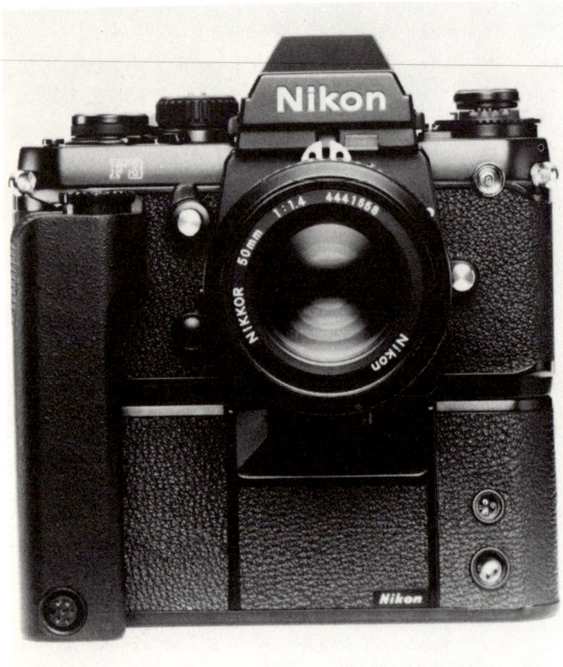

Nikon F3 with the new Motor Drive MD-4, the fastest (6 fps) standard unit made.

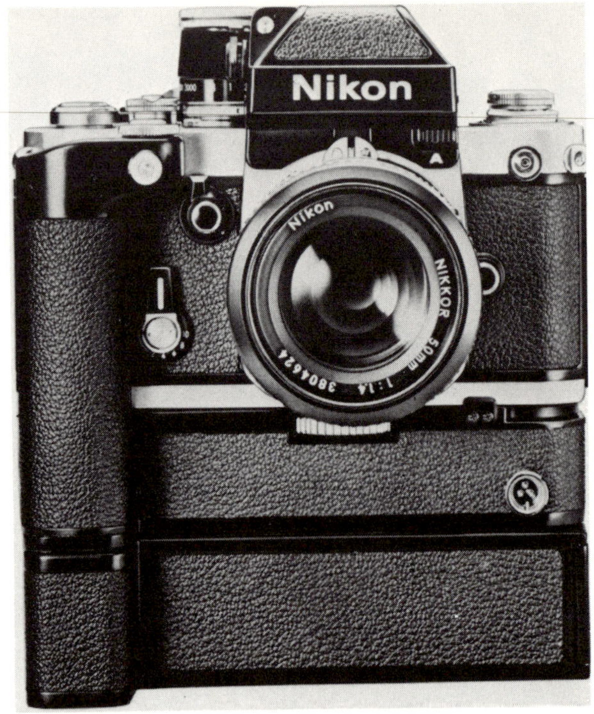

Nikon F2A Photomic mounted on compact Motor Drive MD-3.

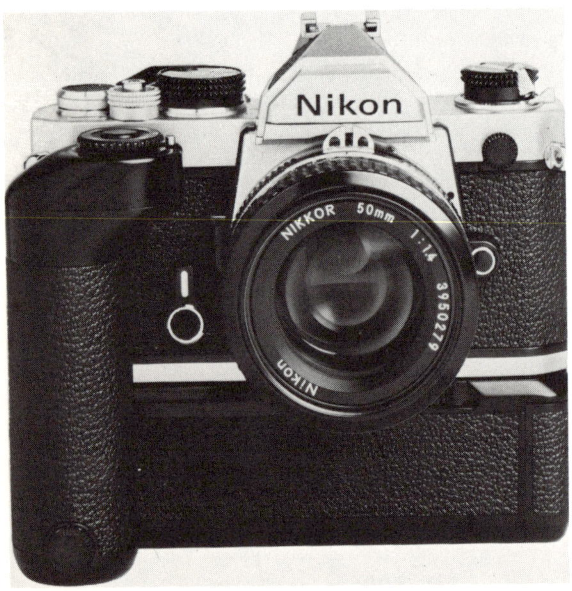

Nikon FE and FM both take their own unit, the Motor Drive MD-12.

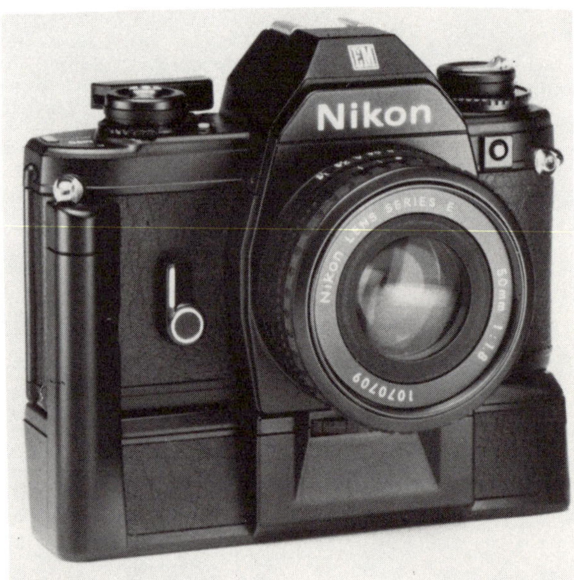

The smallest, lightest motor unit, the MD-E, made for the Nikon EM.

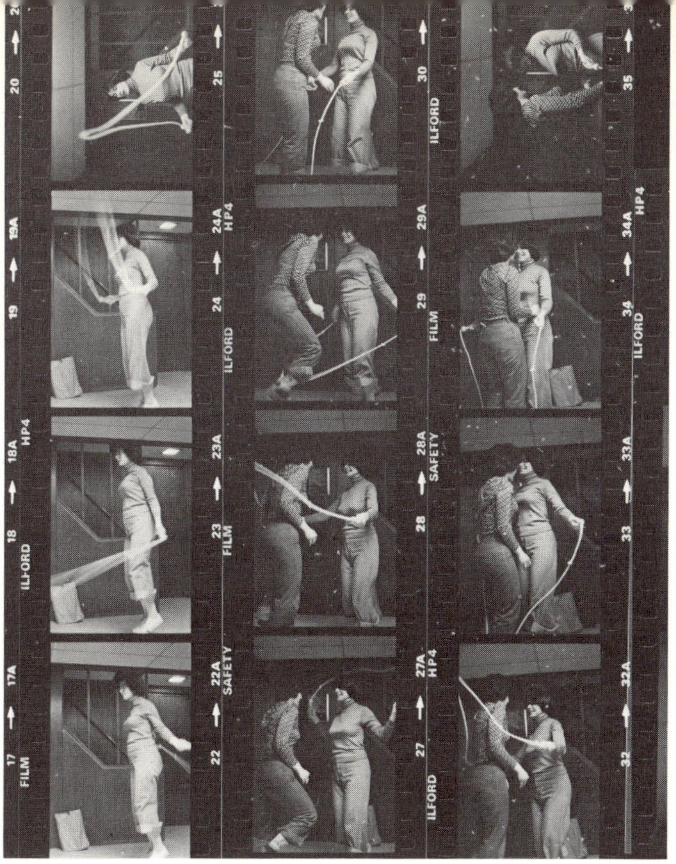

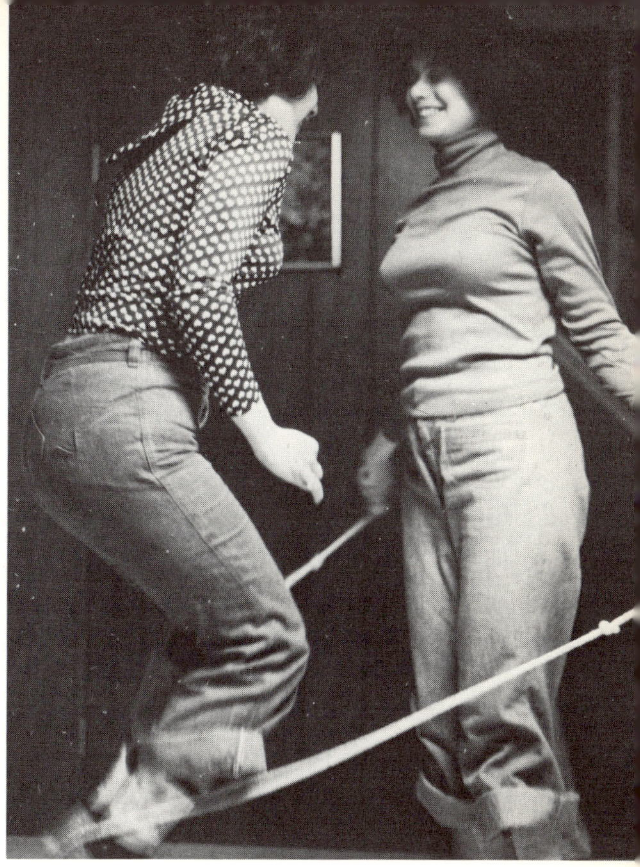

In this motorized sequence of two girls skipping rope, both the framing rate (3.5 fps) and the fast action demanded a shutter speed higher than 1/125, but the dim light, even at *f*/2 on the 50 mm lens, limited it to that speed. Only the many frames exposed gave some assurance of a reasonably sharp picture. Ilford HP4 film.

Motor Drive MD-12

Designed especially for the Nikon FM and FE, the MD-12, like the earlier MD-11, attaches easily to the camera, with no special adjustments. It is capable of single-frame operation, or continuous shooting at speeds up to 3.5 fps (with shutter speeds of 1/125 sec. to 1/1000 sec.). The framing rate adjusts automatically with slower shutter speeds.

The MD-12 operates off eight 1.5V AA batteries housed within the unit. A single set of alkaline batteries will last for about 100 rolls of 36-exposure film. A remote-control socket allows the unit to be fired by such accessories as the Intervalometer MT-1 and the Radio Remote Control Set MW-1. The whole motor-drive unit weighs only 14.4 oz. without batteries.

Motor Drive MD-E

This tiny motorized unit for the Nikon EM (it weighs only 8.2 oz—185 g) lets you shoot at a continuous 2 fps with a minimum of fuss. Attached to the bottom of the camera, the MD-E is instantly ready to fire the shutter in bursts or single frames. Powered by six 1.5 V AAA alkaline mini-batteries, the unit will fire more than 50 rolls of 36-exposure film per set.

EE APERTURE CONTROL ATTACHMENT

The EE Attachment turns the Nikon F2 into a shutter-priority automatic-exposure camera by physically stopping down the lens diaphragm, according to the film speed set on the finder, the shutter speed set by the photographer, and the light entering the lens. There are two models: the DS-2,

Data Back MF-12, for the Nikon FE and FM, records date or time on film frame.

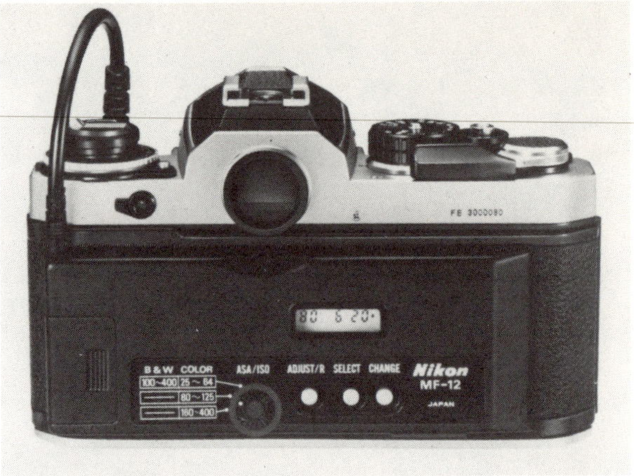

for use with the Nikon F2S and F2Sb Photomic finders, and the DS-12, for use with the newer Nikon F2AS Photomic.

Operated by a small servomotor, the EE Attachment mounts directly onto the F2 accessory shoe; a fastening knob screws into the flash-synch contact, and contacts are made with the Photomic finder. When the attachment is switched to "A" (for Auto), impulses from the finder actuate the servomotor, which rotates a ring around the lens aperture dial until the correct *f*-stop is reached.

The EE Attachment is powered by its own rechargeable NC battery DN-1, which will last three hours of continuous metering, or it can operate off house current, by means of the AC/DC Converter MA-4.

DATA BACK MF-12

For the Nikon FE and FM cameras, Nikon has introduced this special back for imprinting either date (year, month, and day) or time (day, hour, and minute), electronically, on each frame of film. Actually a quartz clock, with an LCD display on the back, the MF-12 will maintain correct time once it is set, so no further resetting is required. It replaces the standard back on the camera, operates off two 1.5 V silver-oxide or two AAA mini-batteries, and will print up to six digits—via LED's on the pressure plate—on the lower right-hand corner of the frame.

MISCELLANEOUS ACCESSORIES

Lenshoods. These are small, but vital items. Made for every lens, they eliminate flare and glare that ruin pictures.

Pistol Grip. Screwed into the tripod socket and attached to the shutter release by means of a cable, the grip gives additional support for long lenses, motor drives, and the like.

Panorama Head. Mounted between camera and tripod, this device permits a full 360° panorama view to be photographed in overlapping segments, with most lenses.

Filters. Nikon makes its own solid glass filters, in a variety of colors and sizes. (See the next chapter for use.)

Nikon also makes various lens and body caps, neckstraps, camera and lens cases, and cable releases.

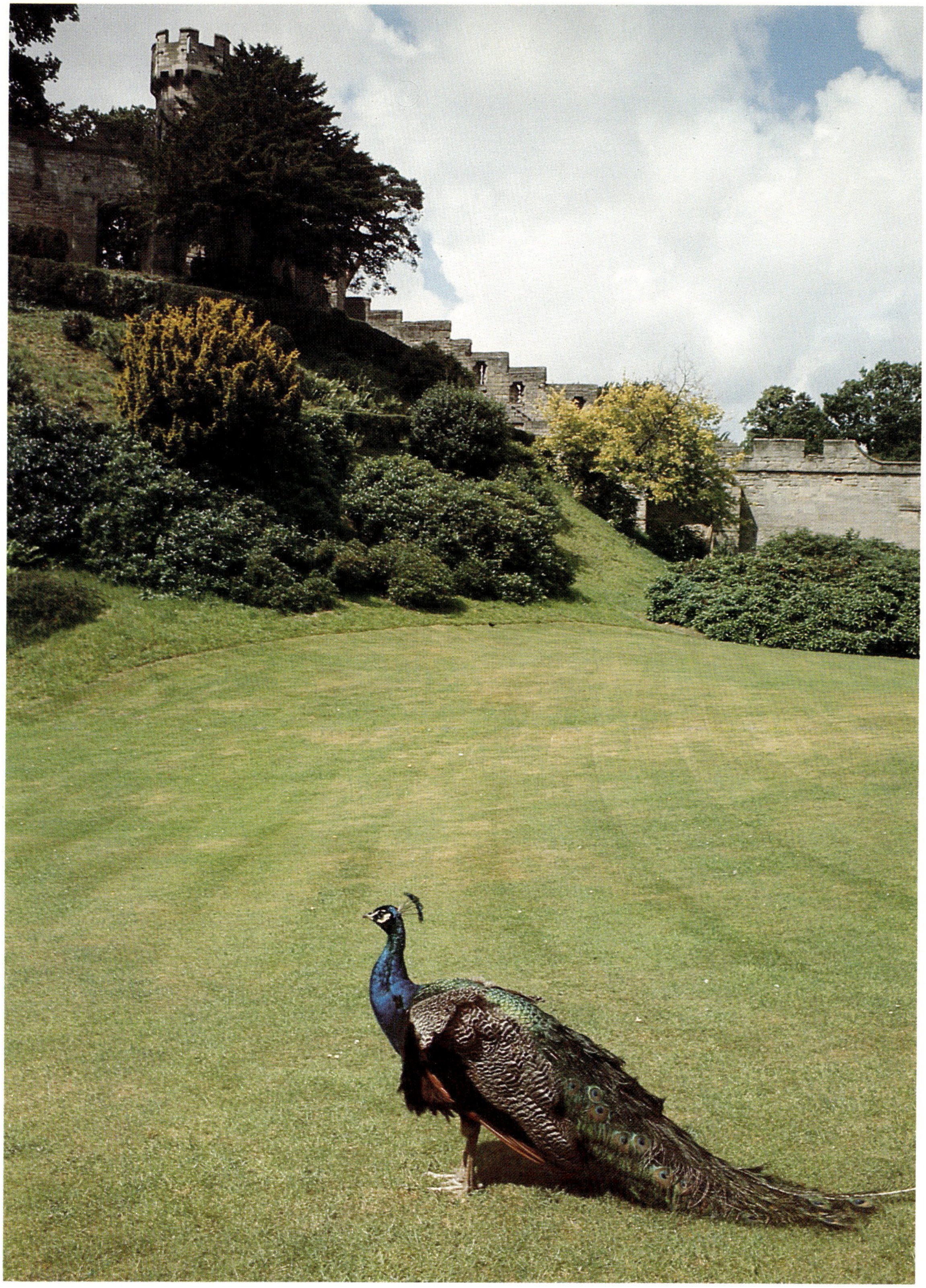

The peacock garden of Warwick Castle, England, in noon summer sunlight offered the ideal color situation—exotic subject matter and perfect shooting conditions. The 28 mm Nikkor was used to emphasize the nearby peacock while keeping the background mound in sharp focus. Ektachrome-X was exposed at 1/125 sec. and *f*/11.

Sometimes the best color pictures are essentially monochrome with very little color in them at all. At right, the soft blues and greens of a hazy day in New York harbor delicately offset the white sails. This picture was taken with the 200 mm Nikkor on Kodachrome 64 at 1/250 sec. and *f*/5.6.

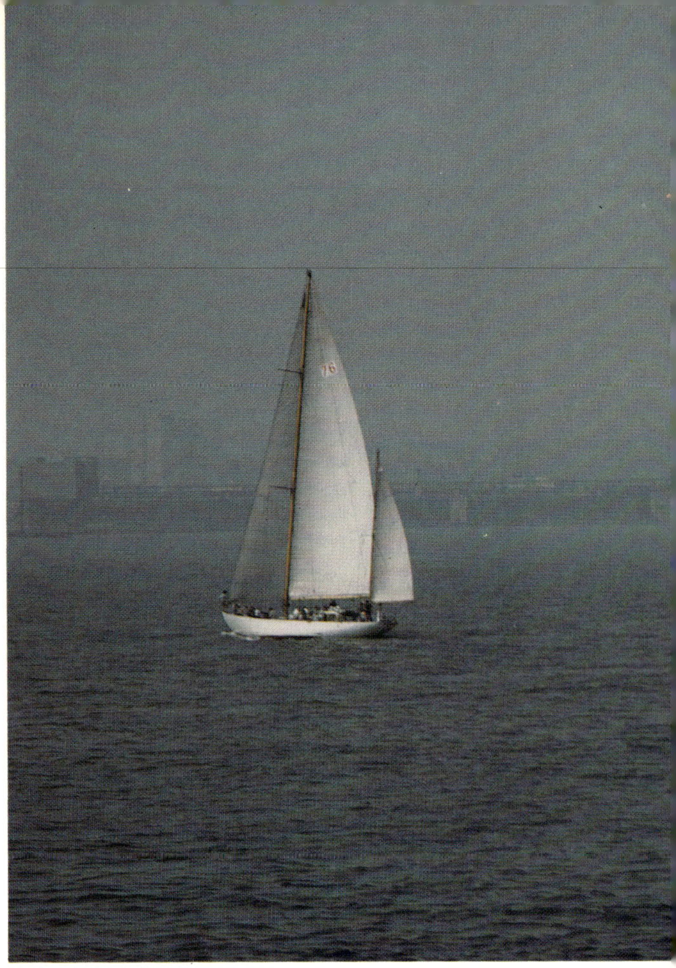

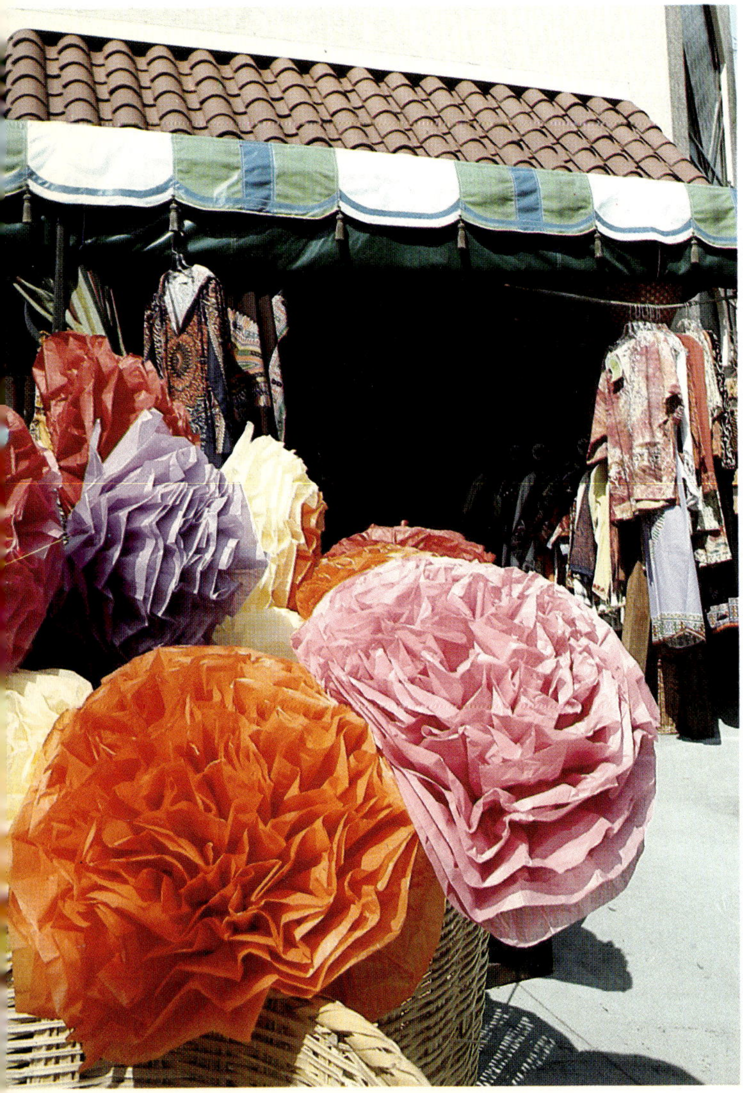

At other times, an explosive burst of bright colors makes the picture, provided there are not too many of them. The paper flowers at left are fully saturated, bright, and contrasty, and are set off by the dark shadow of the stall. The 28 mm Nikkor accentuated the flowers. The shot was exposed on Kodachrome 64 at 1/60 sec. and *f*/16.

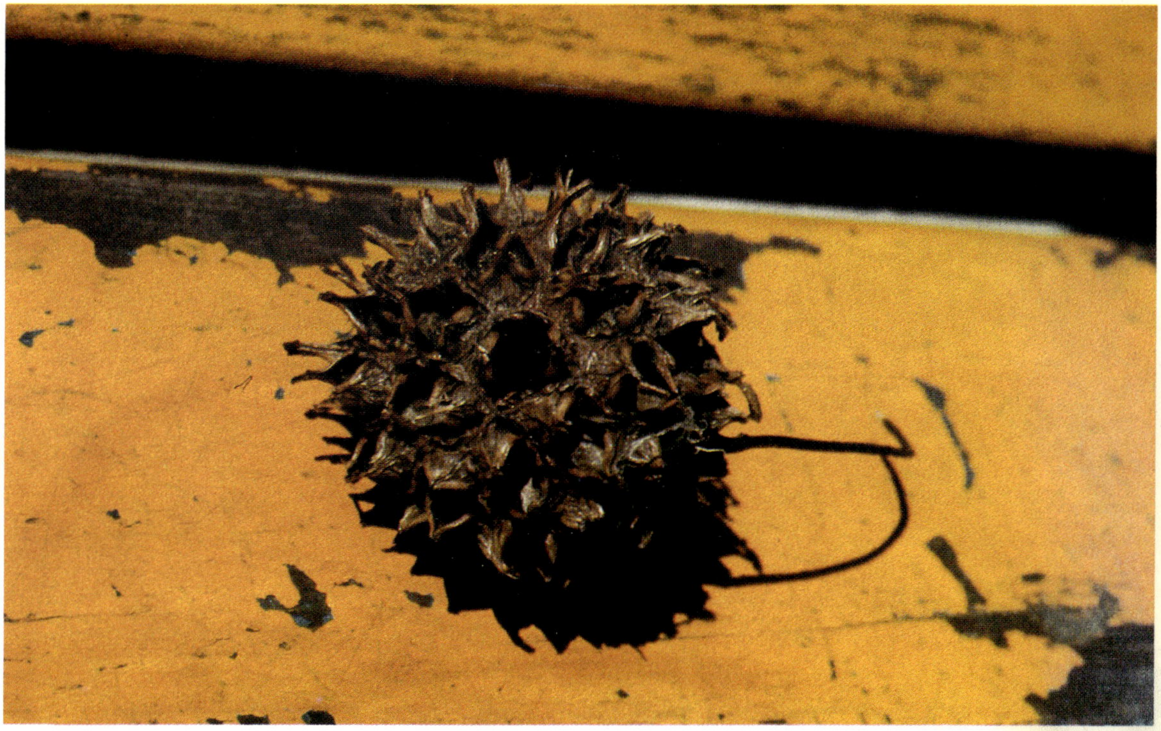

Macro work by daylight often results in soft color and long exposures. The seedpod above was placed on a painted park bench to pep it up and shot with the 55 mm Micro-Nikkor. Bright daylight in regular color work, on the other hand, offers a riot of color, as can be seen below in the shot of a Disneyland scene taken with a 28 mm Nikkor.

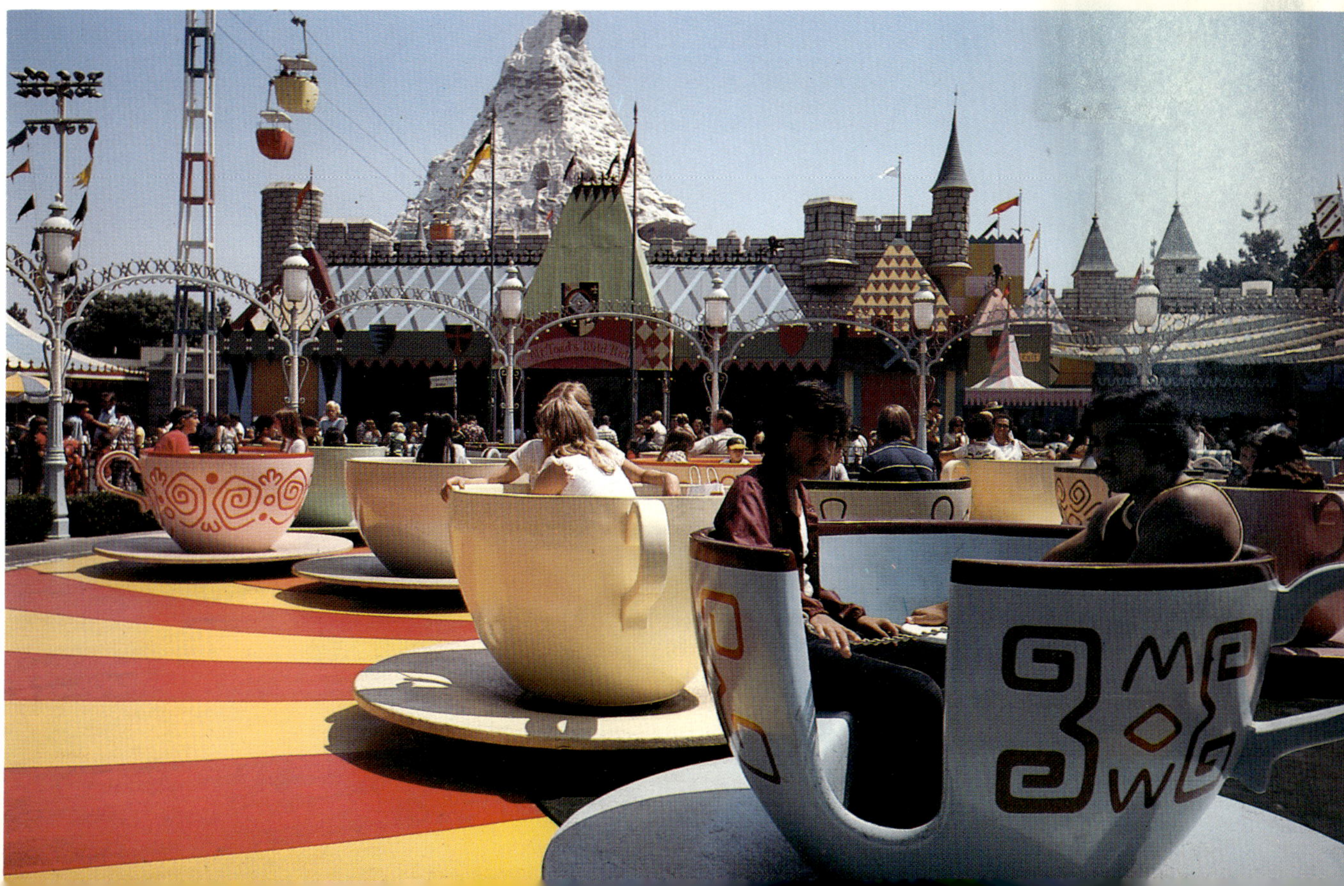

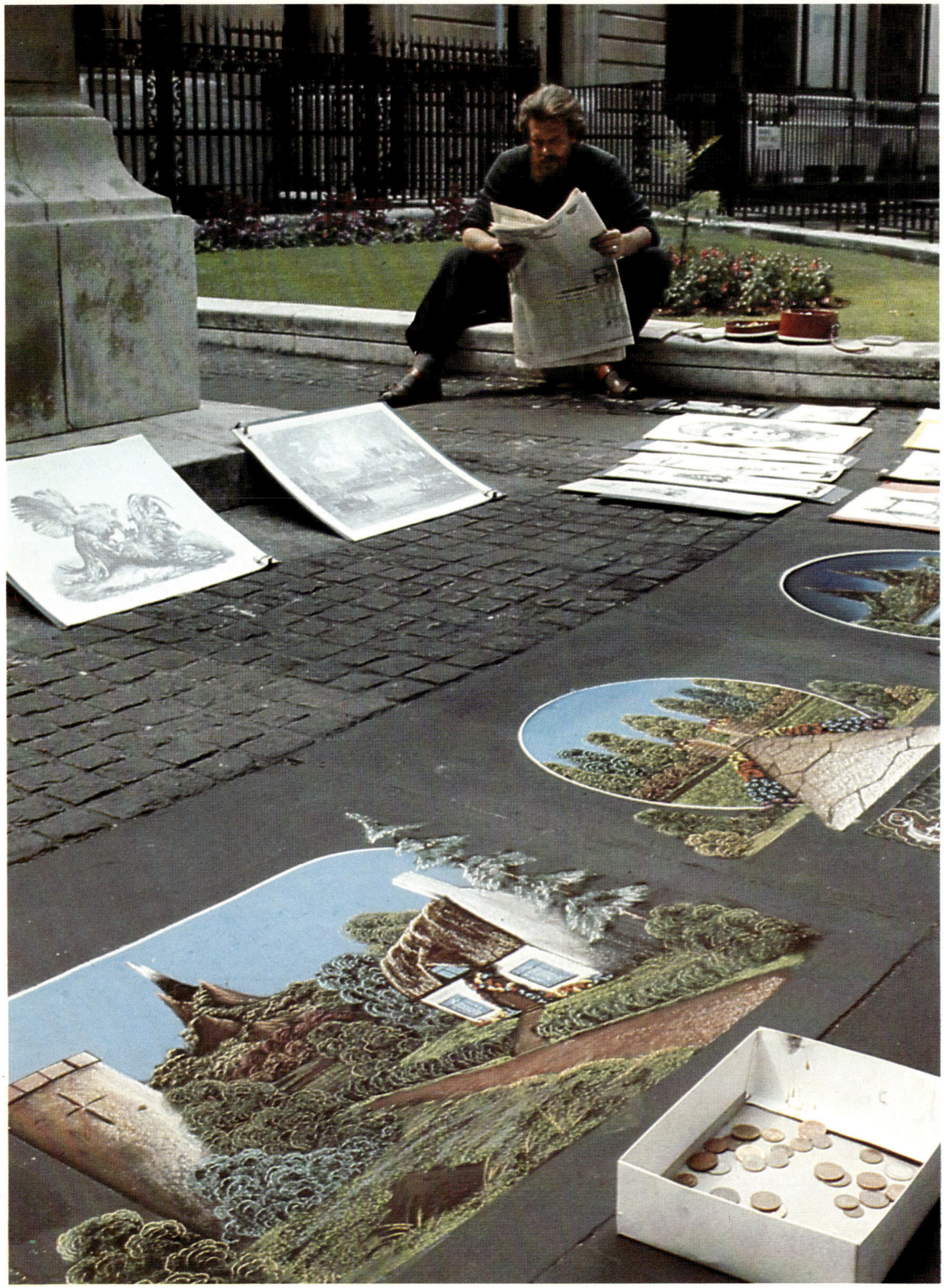

In this photograph of pictures belonging to a London sidewalk artist, the gray, nearly shadowless light accentuates the brilliance of the chalk drawings, contrasting them with the otherwise drab surroundings. This photograph was taken with the 28 mm Nikkor on Ektachrome-X at 1/60 sec. and *f*/11.

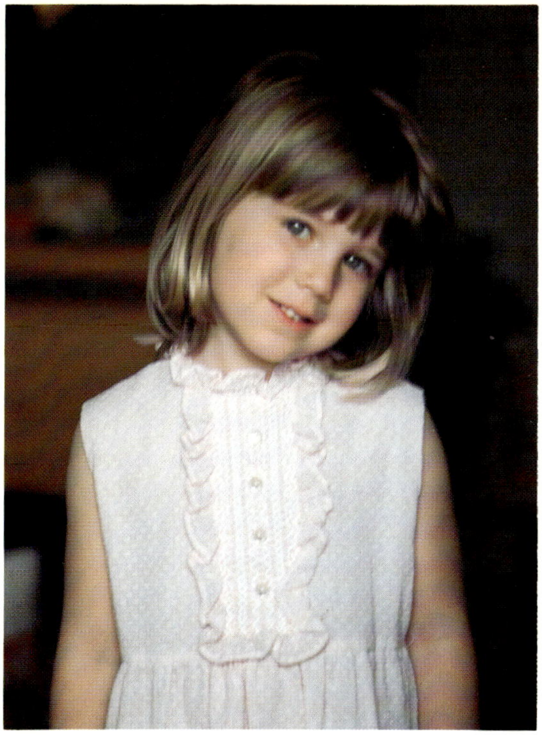

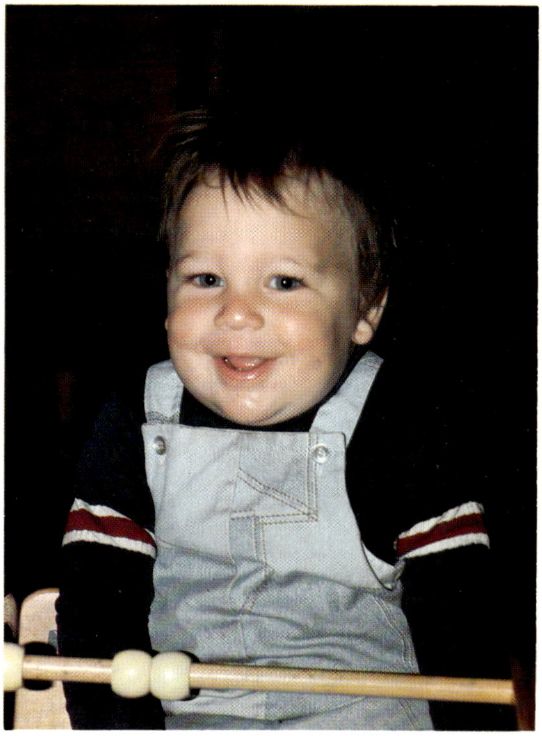

Above, the photograph of the girl, lit by bounced electronic flash, is soft and shadowless, while the one of the boy, lit by direct, on-camera flash, is sharper with brighter colors. Both were shot with the 105 mm Nikkor. Below, the photograph of a tropical flower, taken on an overcast day with the 50 mm Nikkor, has rich, full saturation, and gets its contrast from hue alone. The black-headed gull, which appears separated from its background because of backlighting and shallow depth of field, was shot with the 200 mm Nikkor.

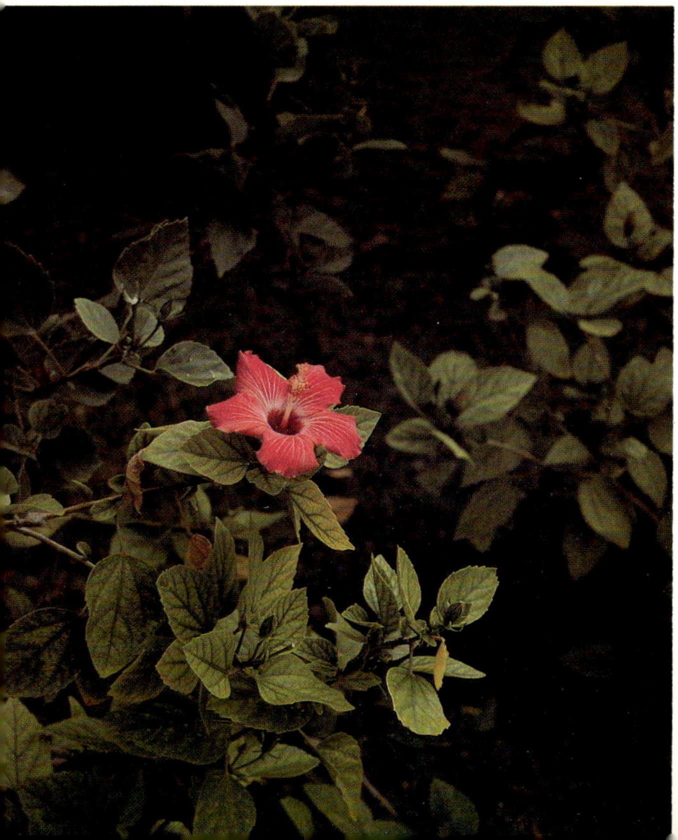

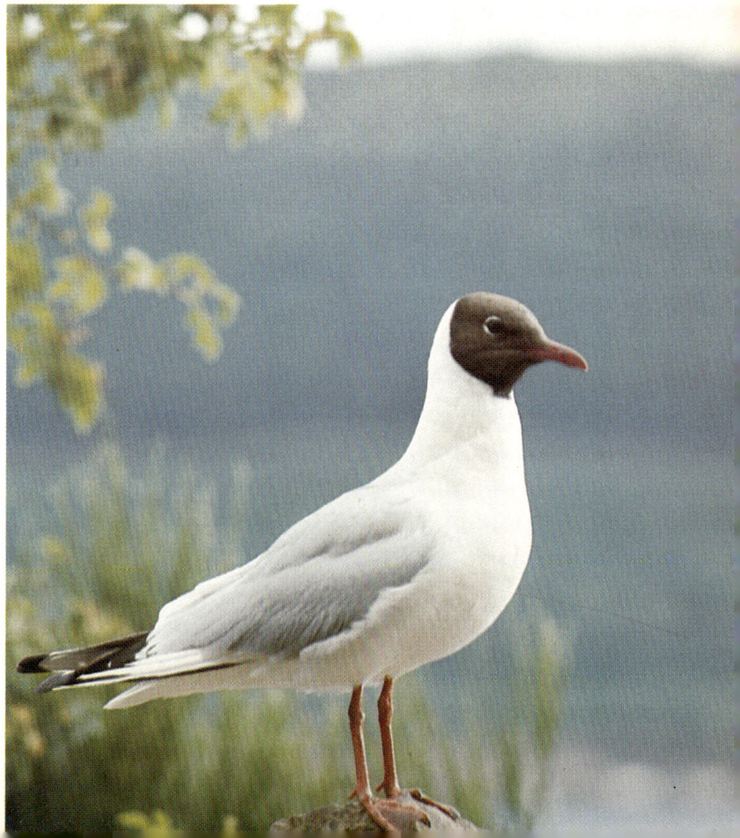

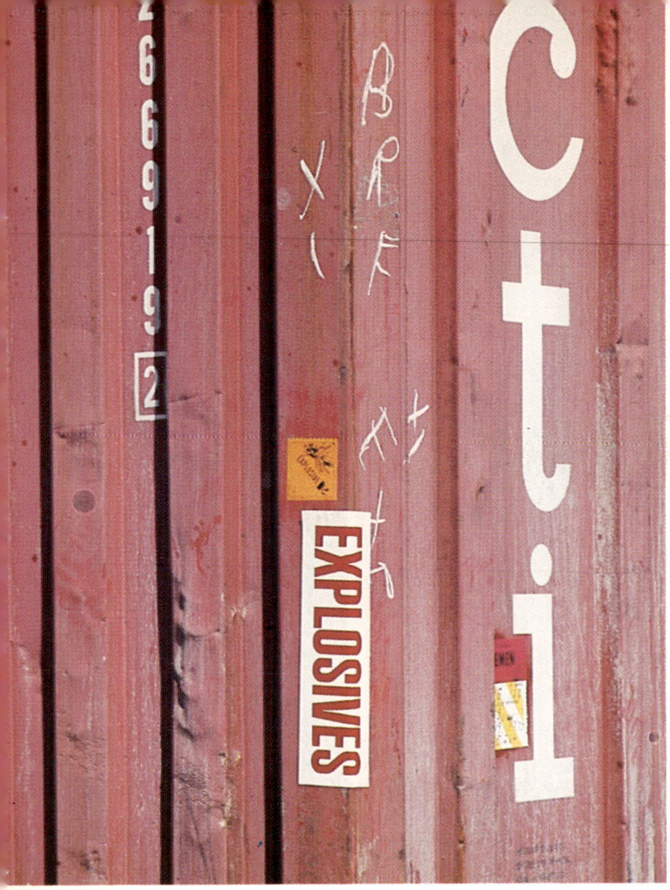

How much of a single color should you use? In pictures like the one at left, all of it. The only arresting thing about the crate of explosives was its red color, which easily distinguished it from hundreds of others stacked on a wharf. So, in lieu of contrast, shadow, or form, the photographer filled the whole frame with hue. The photograph was taken with the 105 mm Nikkor on Agfachrome 64 at 1/125 sec. and *f*/16.

In contrast with the picture above, a "spot" of color transforms the almost black-and-white photograph of a mounted guardsman outside Whitehall, London, into a striking color image. It was shot on Kodachrome 25 with the 43–86 mm Zoom Nikkor at 1/125 sec. and *f*/11.

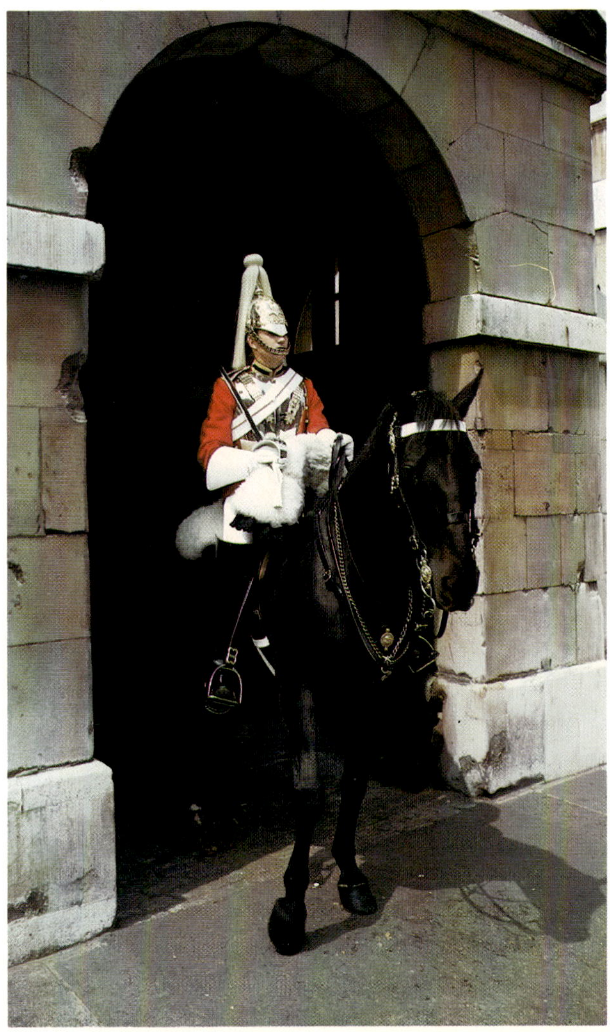

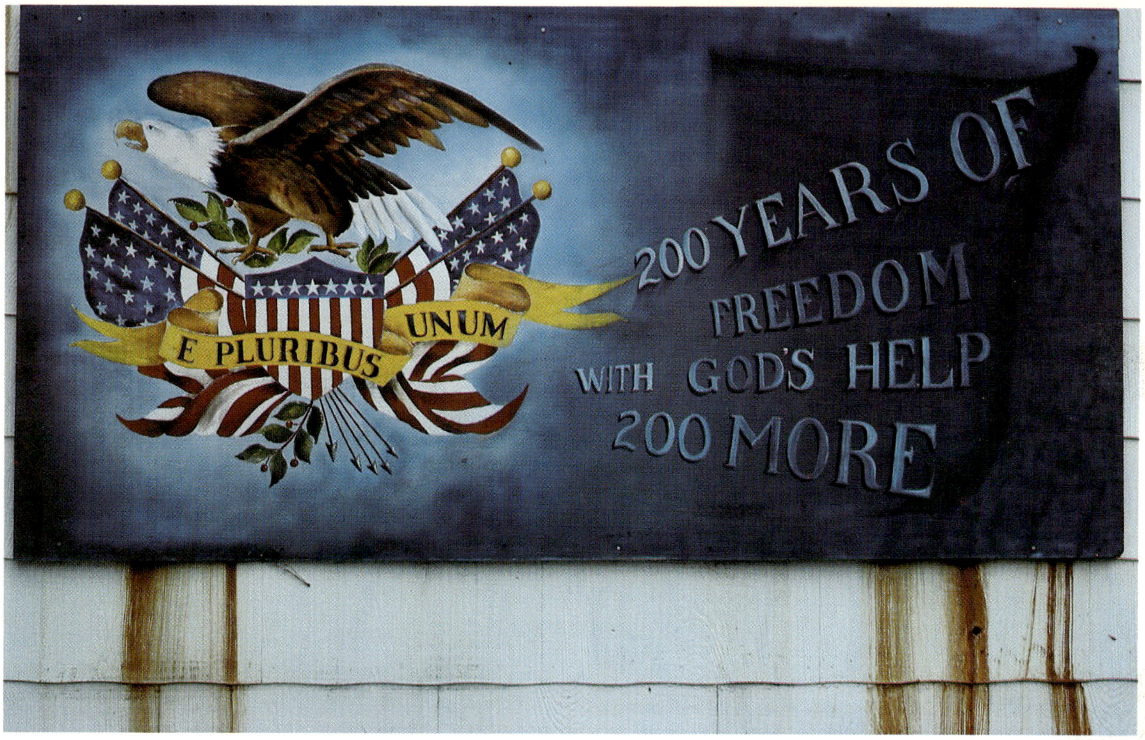

Shown above is another example of dominating color—that of a hand-painted Bicentennial sign on a storefront in Virginia. The deep blue hue was accentuated by slight underexposure on Kodachrome 64. The photograph was taken with the 50 mm Nikkor at 1/60 sec, and *f*/11. Below, the macro shot of Queen Anne's lace is really black-and-white on color film since the flower *is* white, and the background dark. It was photographed in daylight with the 55 mm Micro-Nikkor on bellows at a 1.5:1 reproduction ratio.

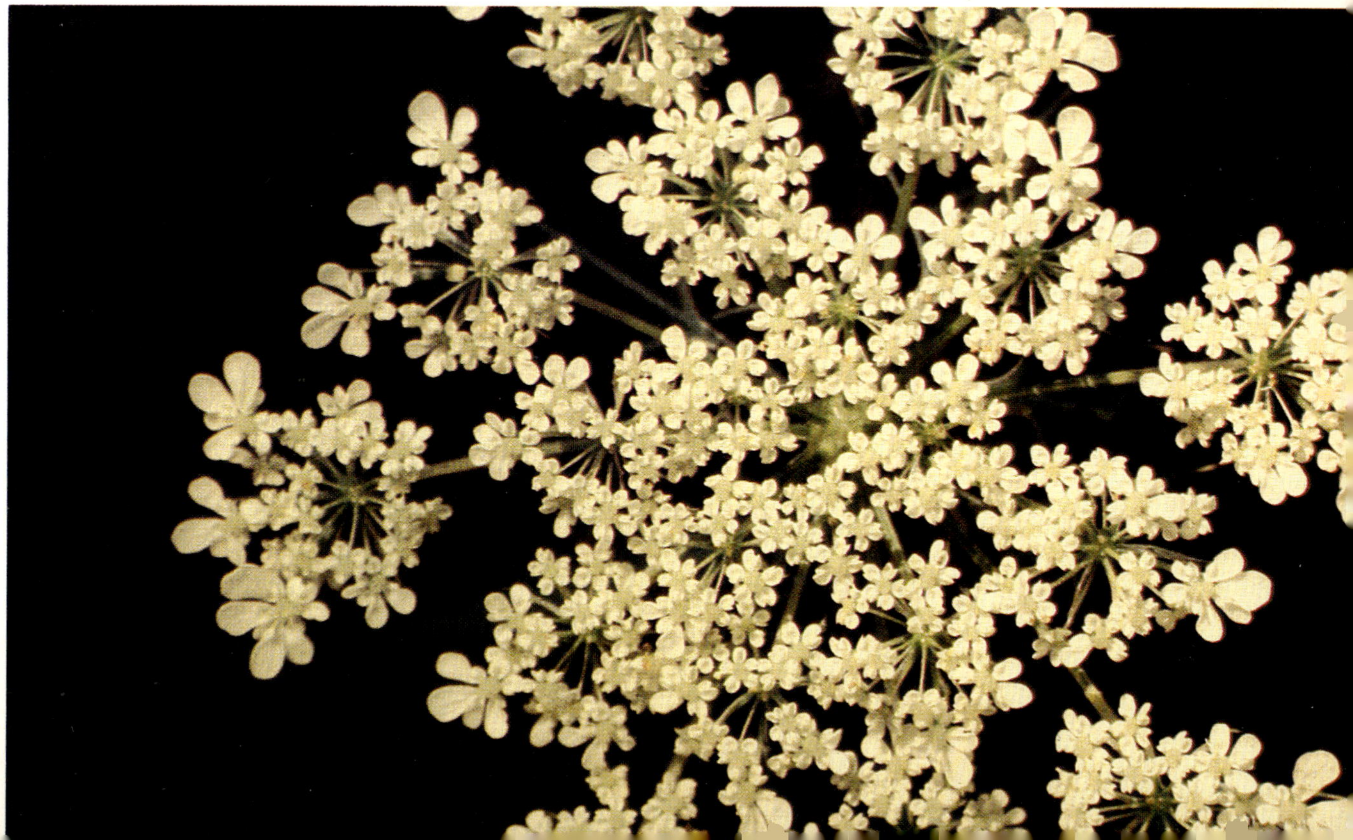

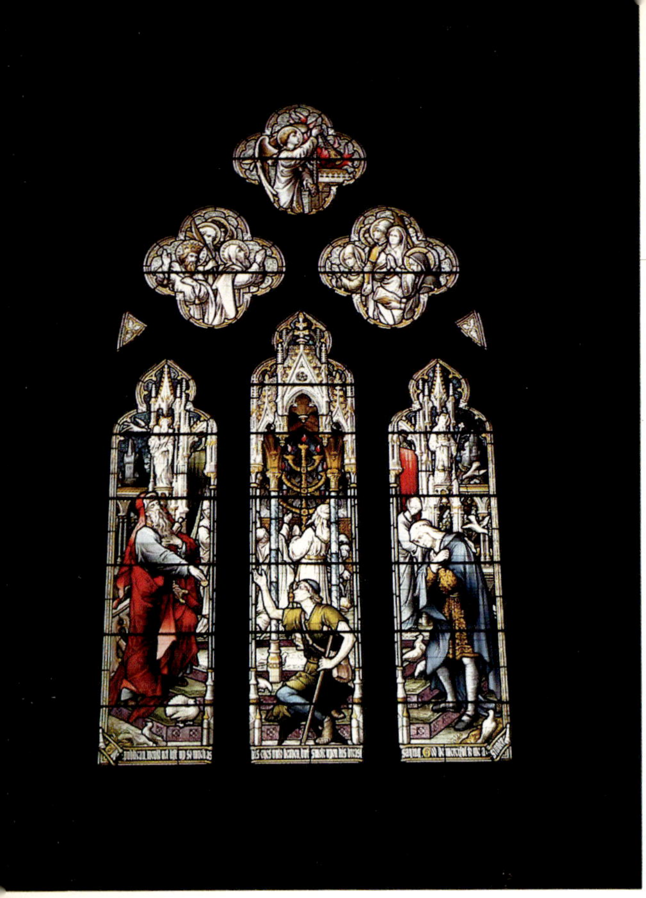

Special lighting situations govern their own exposures, colors, and results. At left, stained-glass windows in Tewkesbury Abbey, in England, required an exposure of 1/30 sec. at *f*/5.6 on Kodachrome 25 to record their transilluminated highlights with the 50 mm Nikkor. Below, the sunset at Big Sur, California, also photographed with the normal lens, but on Ektachrome-X, took an exposure of 1/4 sec, at *f*/11. The choice was to expose for the sun, letting the beach foreground almost silhouette into black.

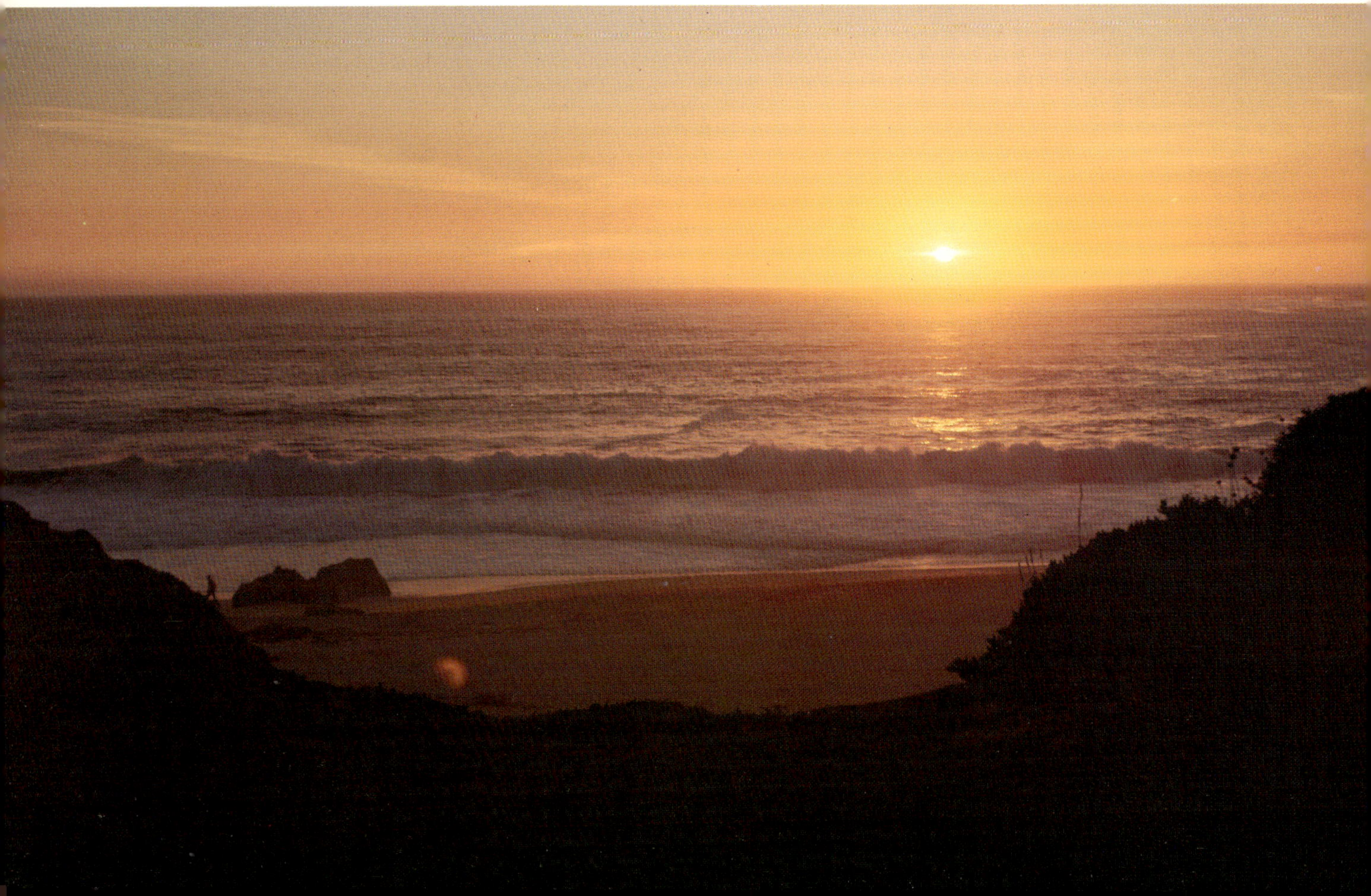

CHAPTER 5

Films and Filters

To now, various aspects of the cameras and photography have been discussed without mentioning the medium on which it all takes place: film. All films have many common characteristics and a few distinct ones. The common characteristics make switching from one film to another relatively easy; their distinct properties make some more suitable to certain situations than others.

It used to be considered good advice (and in some quarters still is), to "choose one film and stick to it." This is less good advice than it once was because films have become more standardized; their overall quality is higher, their results more consistent. More important, though, there are many types of films for many purposes, both black-and-white and color, and it would be foolish to torture one type into use for all situations. Although the latitude of modern film is considerable, it defeats the purpose of many years (and many dollars) of filmmakers' research to extend that latitude unnecessarily. Experiment around; there are dozens of good 35 mm films on the market.

FILM CHARACTERISTICS

All photographic film, black-and-white and color, depends on the same basic reaction: When certain silver halides are struck by light, they become reducible to metallic silver. Granular silver halide particles are suspended in a gelatin emulsion, mounted on an acetate base, and become "film." When certain of the halide grains are hit by light, they change in a not-fully-understood way to contain what is called the "latent image." Later, in a "developer," those same grains are reduced to black silver, and the unexposed particles are removed by a "fixing bath." The result is the photographic image. Black-and-white film has one such emulsion layer; color films contain three, each sensitive to one of the primary colors, with color dyes and developing chemicals as well. The actual differences in films are the result of different sizes of grains, different compounds, different thicknesses of emulsions, and in the case of color films, different color maskings and dye sensitivities.

Film Speed

As with lenses, "speed" in film is a measure of its sensitivity to light. "Fast" films are more sensitive; "slow" films less so. The measurement of film speed has been standardized in this country by the ASA (American Standards Association) exposure index system. The higher the number, the faster the film. (A rule of thumb in estimating an objective value for film speed: The ASA number is the best shutter speed to use with the lens at *f*/16 in noon summer daylight.) Film speed is directly related to granularity (or "graininess," to use the photographic term).

Grain

Grain is the *visible* result of the photographic process. The larger the grains (the little specks in a picture), the faster the film, and the less attractive the picture (except in special cases). Since most film is enlarged, either in printing or in projection, very small grain in the original negative or transparency often becomes objectionable in the print or projected slide. This is the price you pay for increased film speed.

Contrast

Also related to grain size (and to exposure and development), contrast is the difference between lighter and darker portions of an image. The faster, grainier films tend to be less contrasty, therefore they reproduce more of the middle tones of a scene. The more fine-grained, slower films, on the other hand, are contrastier, therefore they tend to reproduce a scene in stark blacks and whites.

Acutance

This dull term means "sharpness." It is the ability of a film to separate light from dark areas and is also a function of grain; the slow, fine-grained films usually have higher acutance.

Color Sensitivity and Balance

Most black-and-white films today are "panchromatic," meaning that they are sensitive to all colors of the spectrum, rendering them as different shades of gray. Older films and some special-purpose films have selective sensitivity.

In color photography, different light sources actually affect the rendition of colors in the subject. Although our minds can compensate for these effects, film cannot; therefore, different color films are "balanced" to produce pleasing, naturalistic effects under daylight or different kinds of artificial light.

Type

Film is classified as "black-and-white" or "color," and as "negative" or "reversal." Negative film produces a negative image, from which prints may be made directly, as may slides. Reversal film (in black-and-white as well as color) starts out negative, but "reverses" itself in processing to produce a positive image directly. This may be used as a projected slide ("transparency"), or it may be used to produce prints. Negative film is *usually* used for prints; reversal film is commonly used for slides.

BLACK-AND-WHITE 35 mm FILMS

Slow, Fine-Grained, Thin-Emulsion

These films are of the "finest" quality for making black-and-white prints. They are high-acutance emulsions, with the finest grain and therefore the lowest film speeds. They tend to render scenes in high contrast, so if the scene is flatly lit, they tend to "pep it up." If, on the other hand, the scene is already contrasty, they exaggerate that effect. Prints from these films can be made at enormous enlargements, as the tiny grain structure is hardly visible even when it is enlarged to 20 or 30 times the original size. One prime drawback to these films, beside their obvious one of low speed (and thus lessened versatility), is their lack of exposure latitude. The scene must be metered "just right," and the films cannot capture details in both highlights and shadows simultaneously.

Film	Manufacturer's ASA/ISO Rating
Adox (Efke) KB 14	20
Adox (Efke) KB 17	40
Agfapan 25	25
Ilford Pan F	50
Kodak Panatomic-X	32

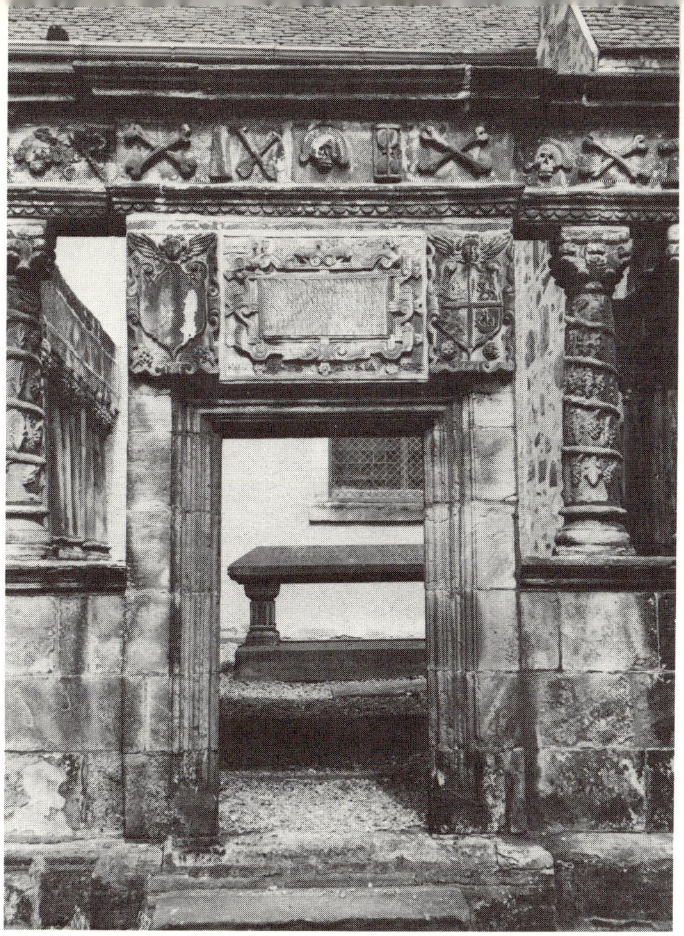

Slow-speed film. This cemetery gate in Inverness, Scotland, was taken on a dull, overcast day on Kodak Panatomic-X (ASA 32). The range of tones is fantastic, the print is sharp, and no grain is visible to the naked eye. Taken with the 50 mm Nikkor, 1/60 sec. at *f*/8.

Medium-speed film. The conditions for the photo below of a horse at the foot of Ben Nevis, in Scotland, were about average in terms of brightness, contrast ratio, and area coverage. Kodak Plus-X Pan (ASA 125) kept a full range of tones in shadowless evening light, allowing for a relatively wide aperture (*f*/5.6) to keep the background soft and a shutter speed of 1/125 sec. in case the horse moved. He didn't. 50 mm Nikkor.

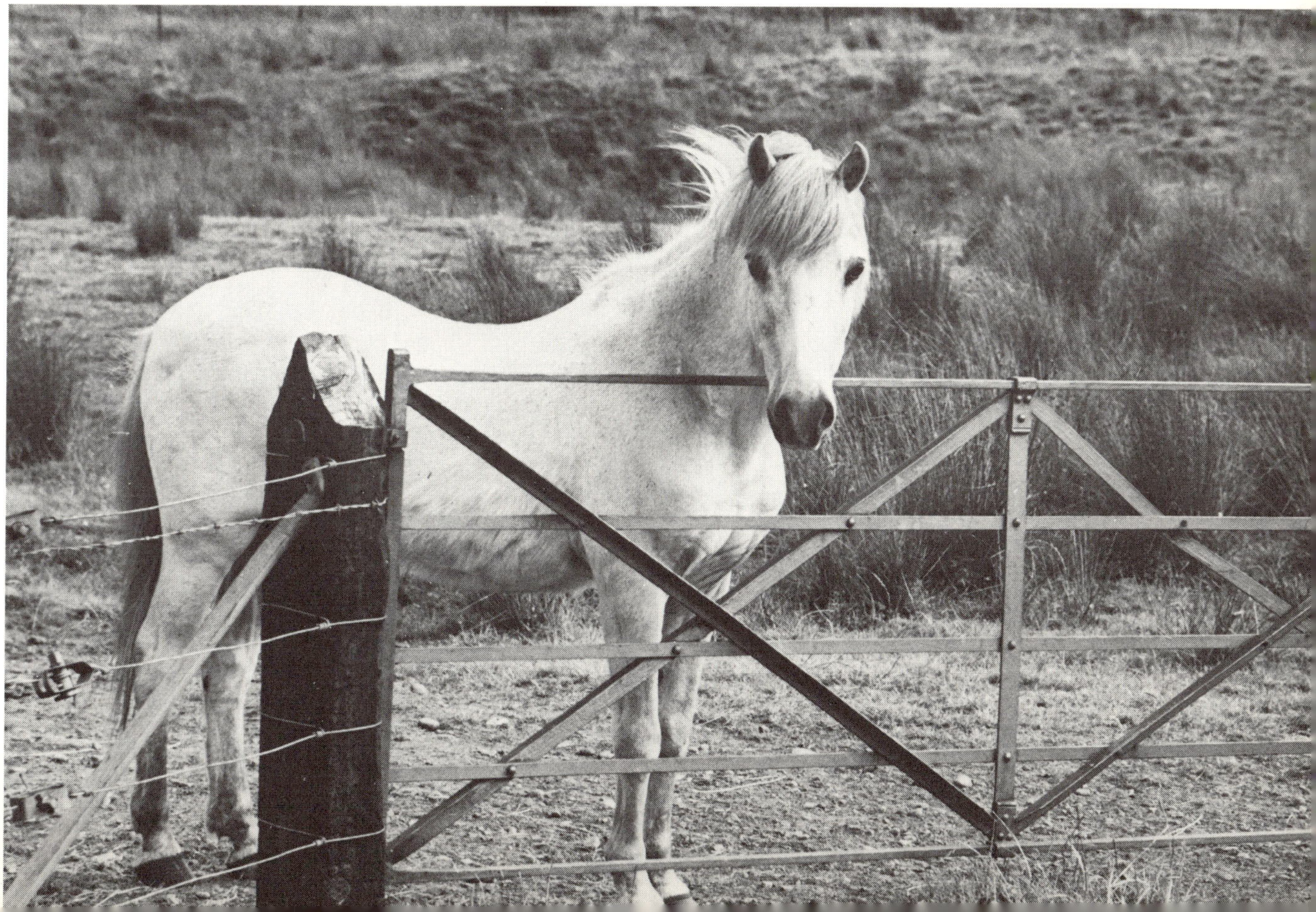

Medium-Speed, Fine-Grain

These very popular black-and-white films combine the best of most worlds. Almost as fine-grained as the slow films, they are considerably faster and therefore considerably more versatile. Not only do they allow the photographer to use faster shutter speeds and smaller apertures (to capture both action and depth), they have far more exposure latitude, resulting from lower contrast. They are "medium" in most important respects—speed, contrast, grain—and "high" in acutance and quality. In this group are found the most versatile all-round black-and-white films.

Film	Manufacturer's ASA/ISO Rating
Adox (Efke) KB 21	100
Agfapan 100	100
Agfapan 200	200
Ilford FP-4	125
Kodak Plus-X Pan	125

High-Speed, Moderate-Grain

This group of films represents the favorite of photojournalists, night and sports photographers, and people who shoot on the move in general. Their very wide exposure latitude favors those who have little time (or patience) to meter carefully and get perfect exposures every shot. From almost any negative, *some* kind of print can be had. They are ideal films for available-light interior shots. The grain, described as "moderate," can be made nearly invisible by careful exposure and development, or conversely, accentuated, for vivid graphic effects. The contrast and acutance in these films are markedly less than in the medium-speed emulsions; highlight areas will usually be gray. These films may be "pushed" to really astounding speeds, when the situation calls for a high shutter speed or a small aperture in adverse lighting conditions.

Film	Manufacturer's ASA/ISO Rating
Agfapan 400	400
Fuji Neopan SSS	200
Ilford HP-5	400
Kodak Tri-X Pan	400

Ultra-High-Speed

As the name implies, these films sacrifice all for speed. They should be used *very* judiciously, and probably not at all if it can be avoided. Their grain is coarse, and in low-contrast situations they flatten tones still further. But their exposure latitude is enormous, and they make possible photographs that could not be taken under any other circumstances.

Film	Manufacturer's ASA/ISO Rating
Kodak 2475 Recording Film	1000-4000

Special Purpose

This category covers a variety of films, not usually encountered by the average photographer, but very helpful when need for them arises. Not detailed here, they encompass high-contrast copy films, infrared, and positive (reversal) films, among others.

COLOR REVERSAL FILMS

These are the most widely-used 35 mm films in America today. "Slides" dominate amateur photography, and they play a vital role in commercial photography as well. Nearly every owner of a 35 mm SLR will want to shoot color reversal film, and most will settle on one brand and type, often to their detriment. Individual color films, in general, are more restricted in their use than black-and-white; they have less latitude and are balanced for particular kinds of light. Thus, it is unwise for a photographer to settle, for example, on a slow-speed, daylight-balanced film for all his color work.

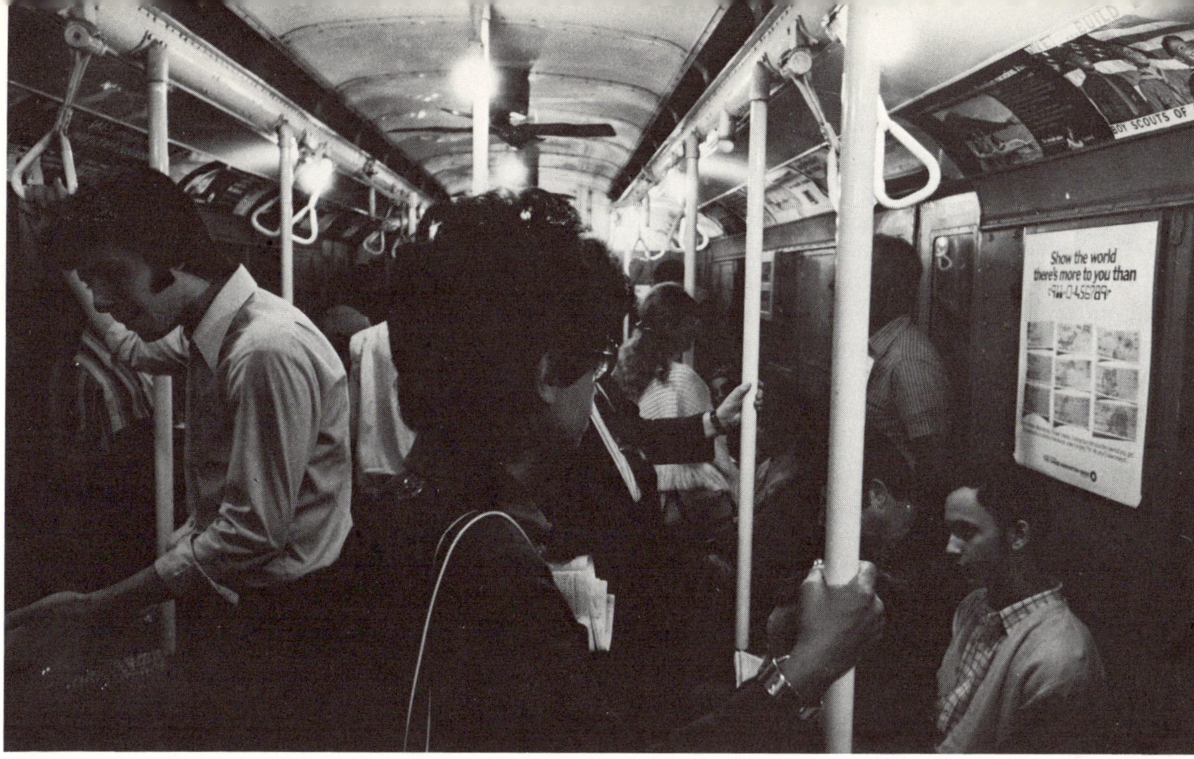

High-speed film. The ideal film for available-light shooting indoors, normally-rated high-speed film permits hand-held shooting at moderate shutter speeds and apertures. There is some grain and loss of contrast, but overall rendition is good, even in poor light, as in this New York subway car. Taken on Kodak Tri-X (ASA 400) with a 28 mm Nikkor, 1/30 sec. at *f*/4.

Ultra-high-speed. When every single photon of light is needed to record an image, either an ultra-fast film, or a fast one "pushed" to a higher exposure index, must be used. This was the case in Madame Tussaud's Waxworks, in London, where the exhibit area was in deepest gloom, and even the figures themselves were dimly lit to increase their lifelike appearance (no, that really *isn't* Sir Winston). Tri-X was rated at 1200, three times its normal speed, for exposures of 1/15 sec. at *f*/2.8 with the 28 mm Nikkor. There is little detail in the shadows, but pushing increases contrast, and the highlights were recorded clearly.

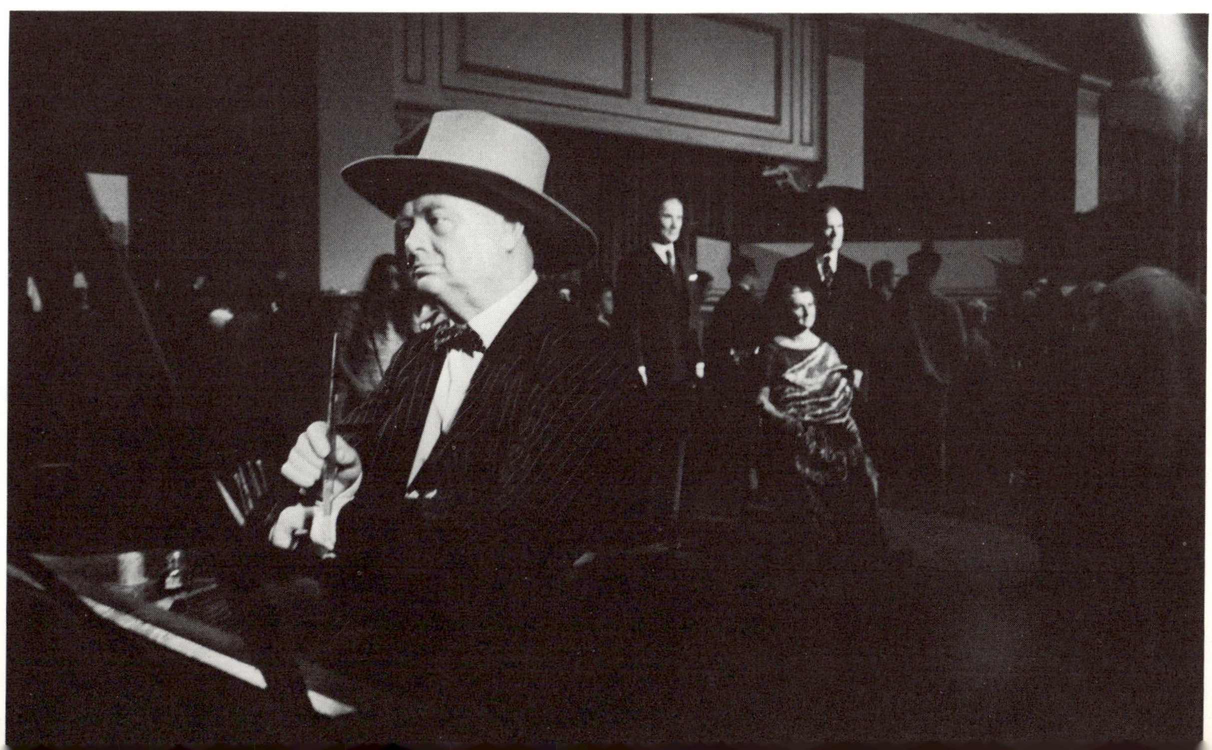

Between brands, color differs markedly. Some types of film aim for, and get very vivid, posterish effects; others strive for softer, more saturated, pastel hues. Film speeds today range as far as with black-and-white films, and generally affect color; the slower films are brighter, the faster films softer. Though not as noticeable in color as in black-and-white, grain is present in all color emulsions and more evident in the faster films, but the recent popularity of faster color films and "push" processing bears evidence of the public's tolerance of grain when it makes possible color pictures where none were thought possible. Acutance and contrast vary as with black-and-white emulsions, with the added dimension of color contrasts that vary from film to film.

The most important technical detail to keep in mind when shooting with color slide film is that the various films are balanced for specific kinds of light. Unlike black-and-white film, where *intensity* of light is all that matters, color film reacts to the *color* of the light as well. The mind compensates for light of different colors; film does not. Therefore, it is imperative that color film be of the proper type, or that the light be filtered to suit the film.

The color of light, also called its *color temperature*, is measured in kelvin units (K)—formerly "degrees Kelvin." It is termed "cooler" (bluer) or "warmer" (redder), with the kelvin scale rising toward the blue end, to the color of clear blue sky. Some representative light sources and their color temperatures are as follows:

Candle—1800 K
100-watt bulb—2900 K
Studio floodlamp—3200 K
Photoflood lamp—3400 K
White fluorescent lamp—4500 K
Noon sunlight—5500 K
Blue flash—6000 K
Electronic flash—5500–7000 K
Skylight—7000–25,000 K

The following films are grouped according to the light sources for which they are balanced.

Daylight Reversal Films

These films, balanced for daylight and *very* similar light (blue flashbulbs and electronic flash), are the "coolest" of the slide films. They may be used in other kinds of light, with filters, at a considerable loss of speed. This will be discussed shortly.

Tungsten Reversal Films

These are films balanced for either professional 3200 K studio floodlamps (Type B films) or regular 3400 K photofloods (Type A). They, too, may be filtered for use with other light sources, and with less loss of speed, as a rule. Although they are in many ways more versatile than daylight films, they are not as popular. They are *not* balanced for ordinary household lightbulbs.

COLOR NEGATIVE FILMS

Color negative films are gradually returning from the realm of the weekend snapshooter, where they have always been popular, to the interest of serious photographers, who avoided them for years. One reason for their unpopularity was the expense or difficulty of getting color prints: It costs more to make prints from a batch of negatives than to process reversal film, and few people are adept at "reading" color negatives. Another reason is both an advantage/disadvantage: Negatives may be printed to almost any color values, regardless of the colors in the original scene. This means that the dedicated color printer can alter his hues delicately; it almost means the drugstore-printer can return the photographer a roll of green faces!

The prints from negative film are nonetheless better than those from transparencies, where an *internegative* must usually be made. Moreover, most negative film sold today is being marketed as "universal"; *i.e.*, suitable for *all* light sources. It really is not, but the control over color in printing makes it nearly so. The principal reason for the color negative's return to grace, however, is the vast improvement in home color-printing equip-

DAYLIGHT COLOR REVERSAL FILMS

Film	Daylight ASA/ISO Rating	3400K ASA/ISO Rating*	3200K ASA/ISO Rating*
Agfachrome 64	64	20	16
Agfachrome 100	100	32	25
Fujichrome 100 (RD)	100	32	25
Fujichrome 400 (RH)	400	125	100
Kodachrome 25 (Daylight)	25	8	6
Kodachrome 64 (Daylight)	64	20	16
Kodak Ektachrome 64 (Daylight)	64	20	16
Kodak Ektachrome 64 Professional (Daylight)	64†	20	16
Kodak Ektachrome 200 (Daylight)	200	64	50
Kodak Ektachrome 200 Professional (Daylight)	200†	64	50
Kodak Ektachrome 400 (Daylight)	400	125	100
Sakura R-100	100	32	25
3M Color Slide 100	100	32	25
3M Color Slide 400	400	125	100

*With proper filtration. See "Filters for Color Film."

†Speed of Kodak Professional Films varies with individual emulsion.

TUNGSTEN COLOR REVERSAL FILMS

Film	Balance	ASA/ISO Rating	Daylight ASA/ISO Rating*
Kodachrome 40 (Type A)	3400 K	40	25
Kodak Ektachrome 50 Professional (Tungsten)	3200 K	50†	40
Kodak Ektachrome 160 (Tungsten)	3200 K	160	100
Kodak Ektachrome 160 Professional (Tungsten)	3200K	160†	100

*With proper filtration. See "Filters for Color Film."

†Speed of Kodak Professional Films varies with individual emulsion.

COLOR NEGATIVE FILMS

Film	Daylight ASA/ISO Rating	3400 K ASA/ISO Rating*	3200 K ASA/ISO Rating*
Agfacolor CNS-2	80	25	20
Fujicolor F-II	100	32	25
Fujicolor 400	400	125	100
Kodacolor II	100	32	25
Kodacolor 400	400	125	100
Kodak Vericolor II Professional, Type S	100	32	25
Sakuracolor II	100	32	25
Sakuracolor 400	400	125	100
3M Color Print Film	100	32	25
3M High-Speed Color Print Film	400	125	100

*With proper filtration. See "Filters for Color Film."

ment and materials in recent years. Both are easier to handle and assure more reliable results. If prints alone are your specialty, or a rare slide or two (which are made with equal facility from negatives), negative film is your best bet.

FILTERS FOR BLACK-AND-WHITE FILM

The black-and-white films in use today are almost all panchromatic; that is, they are balanced to record all colors of the spectrum as varying shades of gray. They do so with different degrees of exactness, but they are capable of making very fine distinctions between shades of the same color. In fact, colors of different hue but the same brightness may register as the same tone of gray; therefore, it is sometimes necessary to change the relationship of the colors striking the film to obtain more vivid photographs. This is done with filters.

Stated very simply, a colored filter will transmit light of its own color and hold back (absorb) light of its complementary color. The complementary color is that color which, when combined with the original color, produces white light. With black-and-white negative film, this means that the filter will *lighten* objects of its own hue but *darken* objects of the complementary color. Thus, the yellow filter (the most common) will lighten yellow on the print (because it has passed more yellow to the negative, which becomes dark) and darken blue (because it has absorbed blue, thus lightening the negative).

Filters absorb some of the total light entering the camera, so exposure must be increased to compensate for the light loss. *Filter factors* are the numbers used to recalculate the exposure. Through-the-lens metering makes this recalculation unnecessary; since the meter measures the light *after* it has been filtered, it gives the correct exposure. You should know the factor anyway, as it reduces the effective film speed. Some common filters, effects on colors, and exposure factors follow:

Designation	Color	Lightens	Darkens	Factor*
No. 6 (K1)	Lt. yellow	Red, Green	Blue	1.5
No. 8 (K2)	Med. yellow	Red, Green	Blue	2
No. 11 (X1)	Lt. green	Green, Blue	Red	4
No. 15 (G)	Orange	Red	Blue, Green	3
No. 25 (A)	Med. red	Red	Blue, Green	8
No. 47 (C5)	Blue	Blue	Red, Green	5

**Effective film speed is found by dividing the ASA number of the film by the factor.*

FILTERS FOR COLOR FILM

Filters for color film serve two main functions: (1) to adjust for *slight* differences in light balance, and (2) to alter the entire balance for the "wrong" film. The filters for the first purpose are called *light-balancing filters* and for the second, *color-conversion filters*. Unlike filters for black-and-white, they are not selective in the colors they affect, nor are they so blatant. Their purpose is to raise or lower the color temperature of the entire scene. Like black-and-white filters, they require some exposure compensation, which the through-the-lens meter can handle automatically.

Light-balancing filters are of two major designations: blue (cooling) and yellow (warming). Without a color-temperature meter—an expensive precision device—their use is determined by trial and error. They are often used in combination with one another, to heighten the effect. The cooling filters are the 82 series (Wratten numbers): 82, 82A, 82B, and 82C, in increasing order of "blueness." The warming filters are the 81 series: 81, 81A, 81B, 81C, 81D, and 81EF, in increasing order of "yellowness."

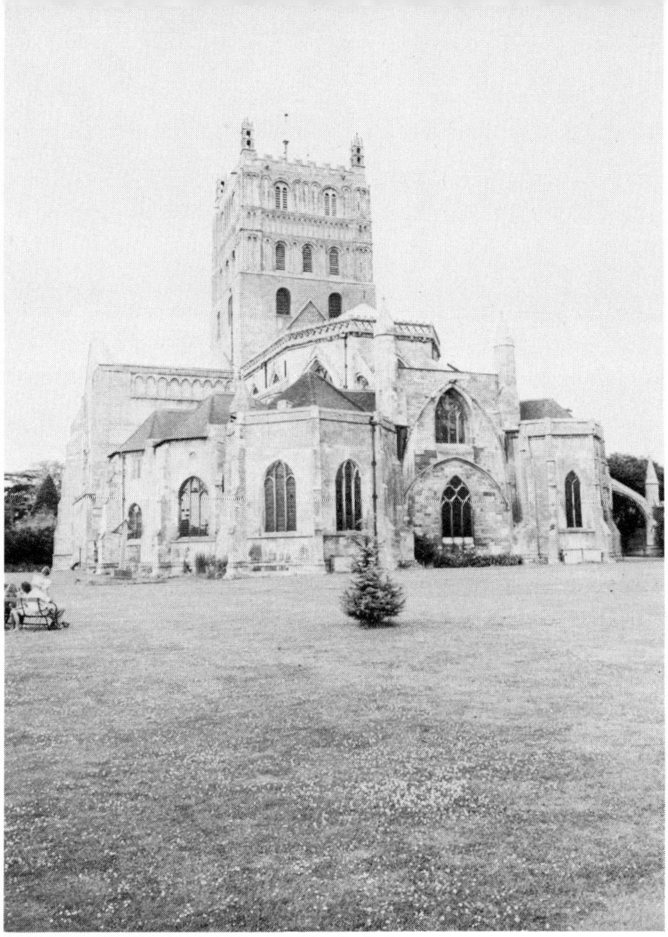

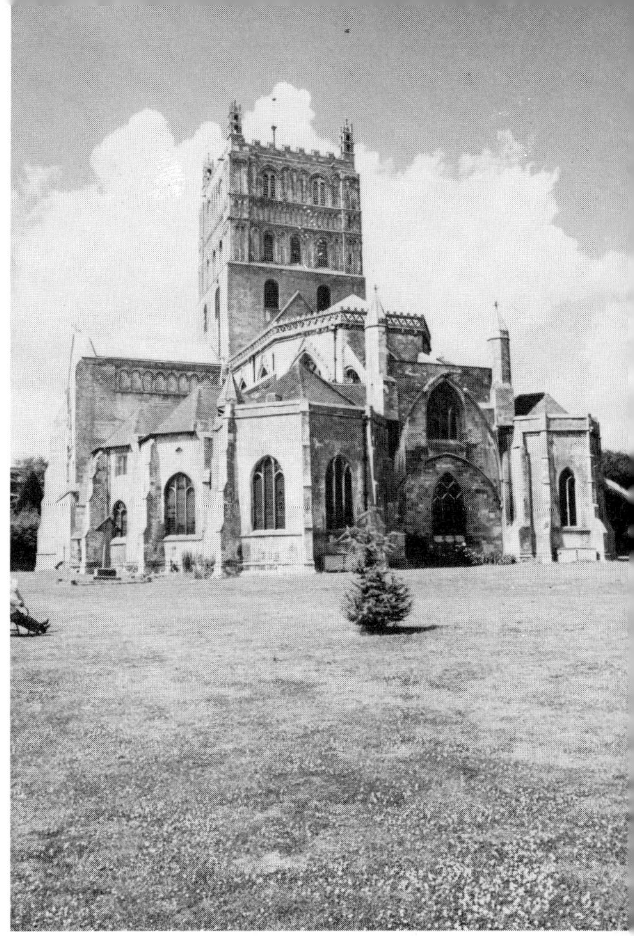

Filters for black-and-white. These scenes of historic Tewkesbury Abbey (where Shakespeare's Richard III lost his kingdom for want of a horse) demonstrate how filters improve the rendition of any outdoor situation. Upper left , no filter resulted in a washed-out sky and lifeless grass the same tone as the building. A medium yellow filter (upper right) darkened the sky, accentuating the clouds, and separated the grass from the abbey. A medium red filter (right) darkened the sky dramatically, and the grass as well. These are the basic black-and-white outdoor filters. All exposures on Ilford FP-4, with the 28 mm Nikkor set at *f*/8. The shutter speeds were 1/500 sec., 1/250 sec., and 1/60 sec.

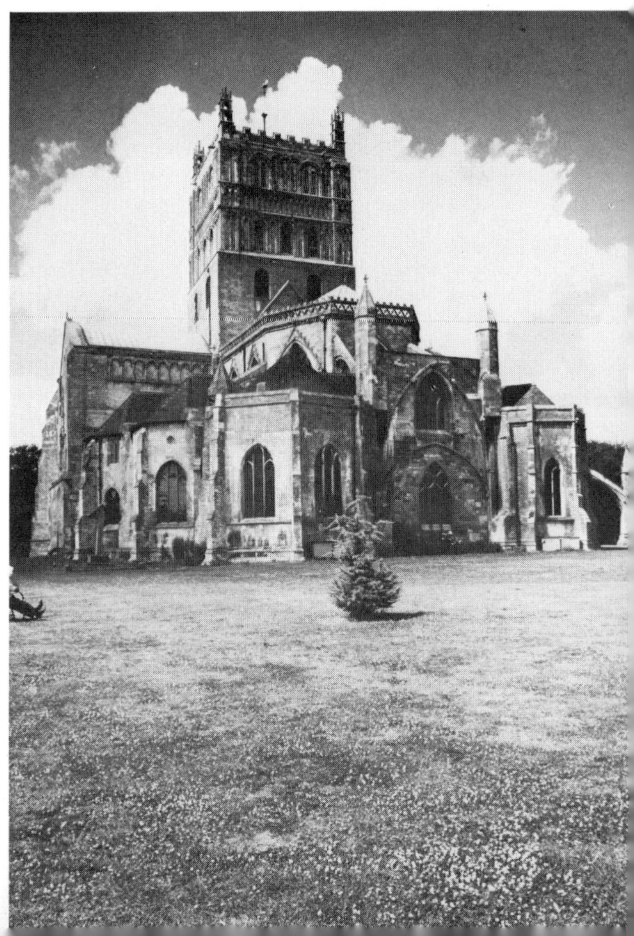

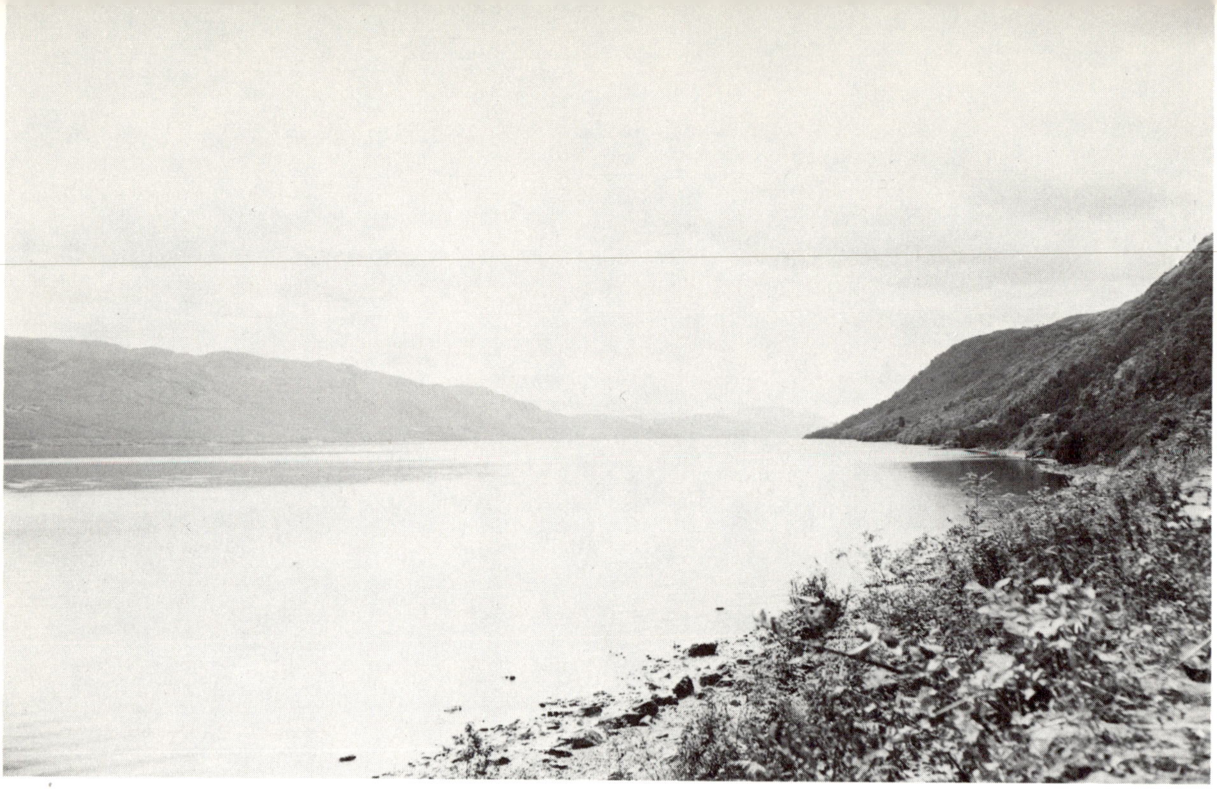

A good example of filtration imparting a mood to a rather ordinary scene. In the first photo, unfiltered, the dead white sky and water, pale foliage, and hazy background make for a very dull landscape. A medium red filter and slight underexposure darken the sky and water, revealing textures in both; penetrate the haze, bringing the background hills in; and give a dark, mysterious air to the shore and foreground at Loch Ness, Scotland. Exposures on Panatomic-X, through the 50 mm Nikkor, were 1/250 sec. at *f*/5.6 (unfiltered) and 1/60 sec. at *f*/5.6.

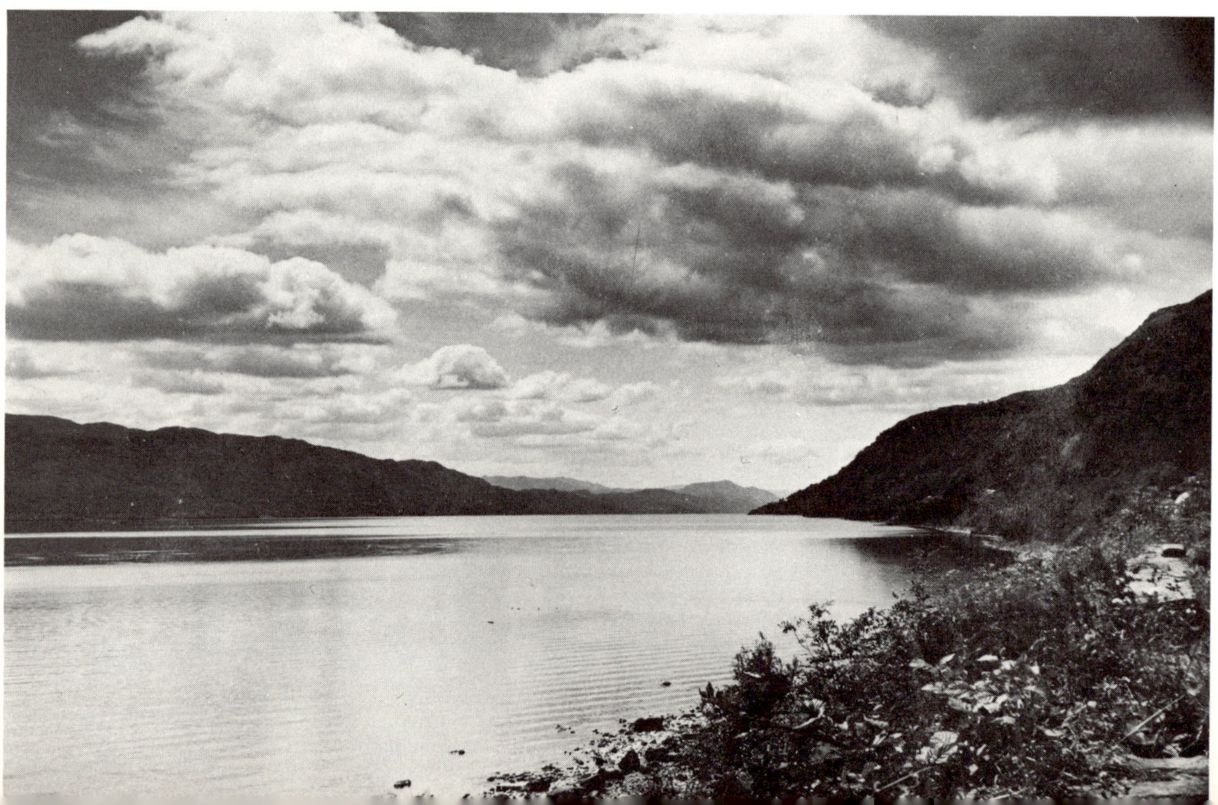

The *color-conversion filters* are more specific. They are used to alter specific light-film combinations. When you encounter floodlamp shooting with daylight film, or vice versa, these filters will bail you out, but with some light loss. They are the bluish (cooling) 80 series and the pinkish (warming) 85 series.

COLOR-CONVERSION FILTERS

Light	Film	Use Filter	Increase Exposure (in Stops)
3200 K	Daylight	80A	2
3400 K	Daylight	80B	1 2/3
3800 K*	Daylight	80C	1
4200 K†	Daylight	80D	1/3
Daylight	3400 K	85	2/3
Daylight	3200 K	85B	2/3

**Aluminum-filled* clear *flashbulbs: M2, 5, 25.*
†*Zirconium-filled* clear *flashbulbs: AG-1, M3, M5.*

There are also *skylight* and *haze* filters, which work the faintest effect in cutting haze and removing excess blue from landscapes and high altitudes. They have no effect at all on exposure. More specialized filters include *color-compensating (CC)* filters, for very dramatic color effects; *fluorescent* filters, to compensate for the "off-color" effects of fluorescent lighting; *neutral-density* filters, which cut down overall light in too-bright situations; and *polarizing* filters, which are used both to reduce reflections from glass or water and to darken blue skylight.

A newer system of filter designation, the *Decamired*, is intended to eliminate the present confusing array of filter names and types by dividing *all* filters into blue and red types, and giving both filters and light sources similar numbers. This system could simplify things considerably, but it is not catching on. Extensive treatments of filtration may be found in *The Filter Guide for Color and Black and White*, by Norman Rothschild and Cora Wright Kennedy, and *The Tiffen Practical Filter Manual* and *Amphoto Guide to Filters*, by Robb Smith, all published by Amphoto.

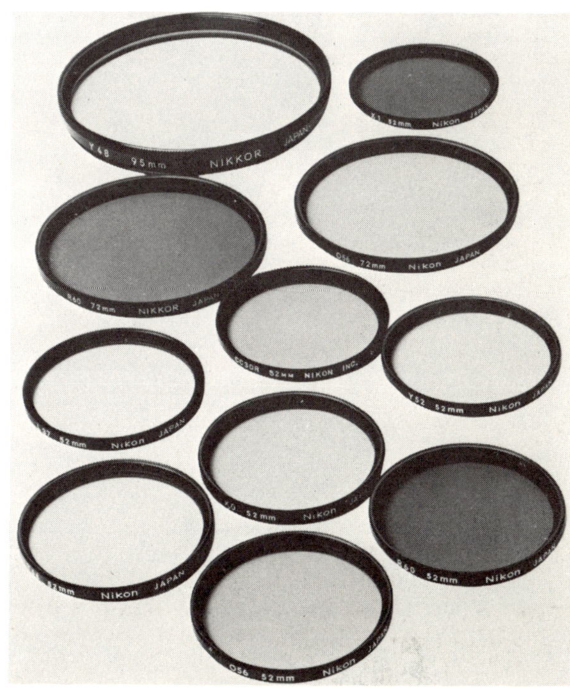

A few of the Nikkor filters, specially made for Nikkor lenses. See the table on the next page for types and sizes available.

NIKKOR FILTERS

As indicated in the previous chapter, Nikon makes a number of the most commonly used filters, for black-and-white and color, especially for Nikkor lenses. These filters are made, as are the lenses, of the finest glass, ground optically flat in Nikon's own factories. They are distortion-free and mounted in metal rings threaded to fit the various Nikkor lenses.

Nikon Filter Factors and Uses

L1B	L1BC	L37	L37C	L39	Y44	Y48	Y52	O56	R60	XO	X1	Polar	ND2X	ND4X	ND8X	A2	A12	B2	B8	B12	Type	Attachment size
●	●	●	●				●	●	●				●	●	●	●	●	●	●	●	Built-in	39 mm
	●	●	●	●	●	●	●	●	●	●	●	●		●	●	●	●	●	●	●	Screw-in	52 mm
	●	●		●		●		●	●			●		●							Screw-in	72 mm
				●		●		●	●												Screw-in	95 mm
			●	●		●		●	●												Screw-in	122 mm
				●	●	●	●	●	●												Drop-in	Series IX

(● = available) * The attachment size of the built-in filter is 34.5 mm.

Available Nikon Filters

Film	Type		Designation	Filter factor	
				Daylight	Tungsten light
Black & white and color	Skylight		L1B	1	1
			L1BC		
	Ultraviolet		L37	1	1
			L37C		
			L39		
Black & white	Yellow	Light	Y44	1.5 (1/2)	1
		Medium	Y48	1.7 (2/3)	1.2 (1/3)
		Deep	Y52	2 (1)	1.4 (1/2)
	Orange		O56	3.5 (1 5/6)	2 (1)
	Red		R60	8 (3)	5 (2 1/3)
	Green	Light	XO	2 (1)	1.7 (2/3)
		Deep	X1	5 (2 1/3)	3.5 (1 5/6)
Black & white and color	Polarizing		Polar	2-4 (1~2)	2-4 (1~2)
	Neutral density		ND2X	2 (1)	2 (1)
			ND4X	4 (2)	4 (2)
			ND8X	8 (3)	8 (3)
Color	Amber	Light	A2	1.2 (1/3)	
		Deep	A12	2 (1)	
	Blue	Light	B2	1.2 (1/3)	
		Medium	B8	1.6 (2/3)	
		Deep	B12	2.2 (1 1/6)	

CHAPTER 6

Basic Photography

EXPOSURE

Aperture, or "*f*-stops," and shutter speeds have been discussed at various times in this book. Now their relationship must be examined, since it is the most fundamental one in making photographs. For any photographic film, a certain amount of light is necessary to expose it and create an image. Depending on the sensitivity of the film (see the previous chapter) it may be more or less, but it must be about the same amount for all of that film. That, in effect, is what shutter speed, aperture, and exposure index are all about: getting the right amount of light to the film.

The shutter speed controls *duration* of light passing through the lens; the diaphragm controls the *volume*. When you have established how much light you need to record the scene, by the exposure meter, you have in fact a wide range of shutter-speed–*f*-stop combinations that will all yield *equivalent exposure*. If the shutter is speeded up (to capture a fast-moving subject, for example), thereby admitting less light, the aperture must be made larger, to admit the necessary amount of light. If the lens diaphragm is stopped down to increase the depth of field, the shutter must be slowed up an equivalent amount. By no accident, each shutter speed admits one-half or twice the light of the adjacent speed; each aperture setting does the same. Thus, when a basic exposure is established, and one setting is adjusted two positions, the other must be reset by two positions also. For example, if, with a film of ASA 125 exposure index, the proper exposure for a scene is 1/60 sec. at *f*/5.6, all the following will be correct too:

Shutter Speed	1/8	1/15	1/30	**1/60**	1/125	1/250	1/500	1/1000
***f*-stop**	16	11	8	**5.6**	4	2.8	2	1.4

Rather than add to your confusion, however, this choice of exposure combinations is your opportunity for creativity. Remembering always that each step in taking pictures is a delicate balance of one quality against another, you have the choice of going for greater (or lesser) depth of field, or greater or lesser "stopping power." In the situation given above, you can shoot with the lens wide open, throwing everything but the main subject out of focus, or stop down the lens all the way to get everything sharp, at the risk of blurring any motion in the picture. In a fast-moving situation, your choice would be dictated by the most suitable shutter speed, but the aperture would follow suit. You cannot compensate for one without affecting the other.

Exposure, Focus, and Depth of Field

How does one take creative advantage of these factors? One way is by using depth of field as a tool rather than a limitation imposed by the light. *Limited* depth may be used to *isolate* a subject; *inclusive* depth may be used to create a pictorial

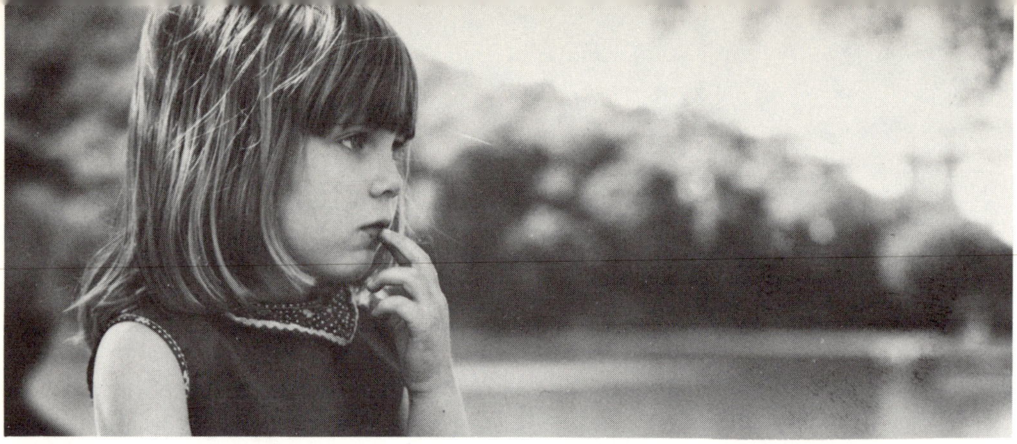

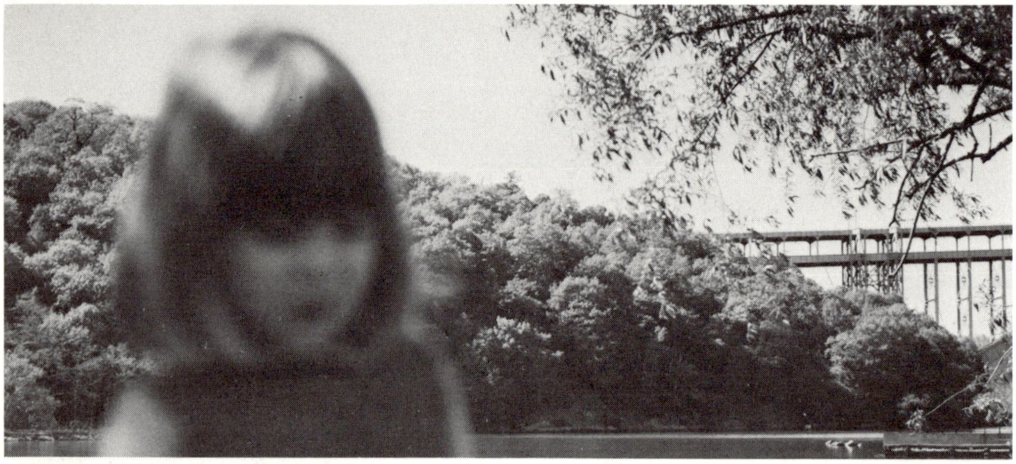

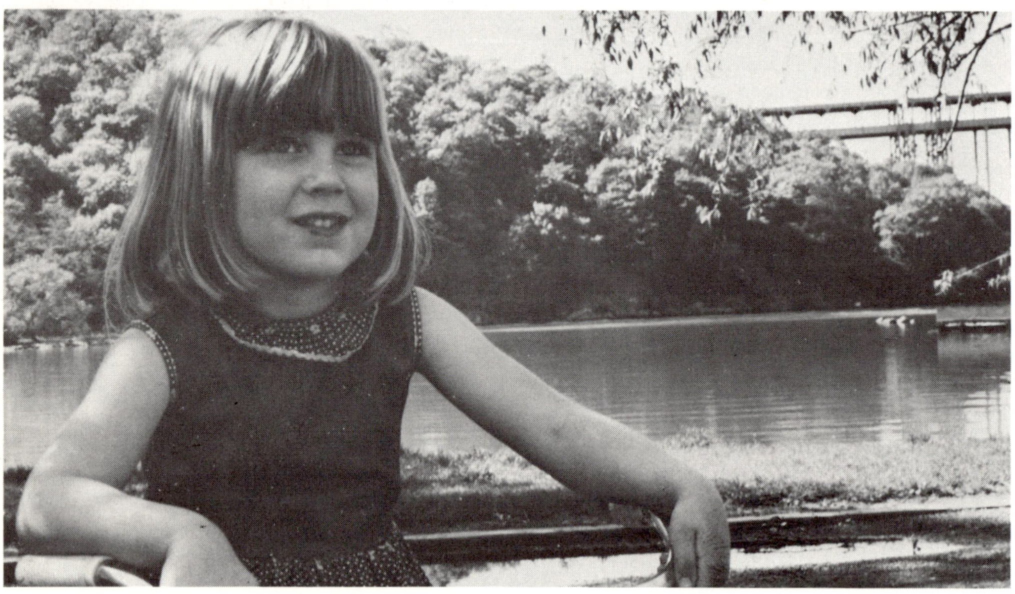

Aperture, focus, and depth. In the first picture, the focus is on the little girl, about 12 feet away, and the 105 mm Nikkor is set at *f*/4; because of limited depth of field, the entire background is out of focus. The second picture is focused at 100 feet, at the same aperture; now the river, trees, and bridge are sharp, but the figure is blurry. By stopping down to *f*/32, however, and focusing at the *hyperfocal distance*—about 30 feet with this lens and *f*-stop—both fore- and background can be brought into focus at the same time.

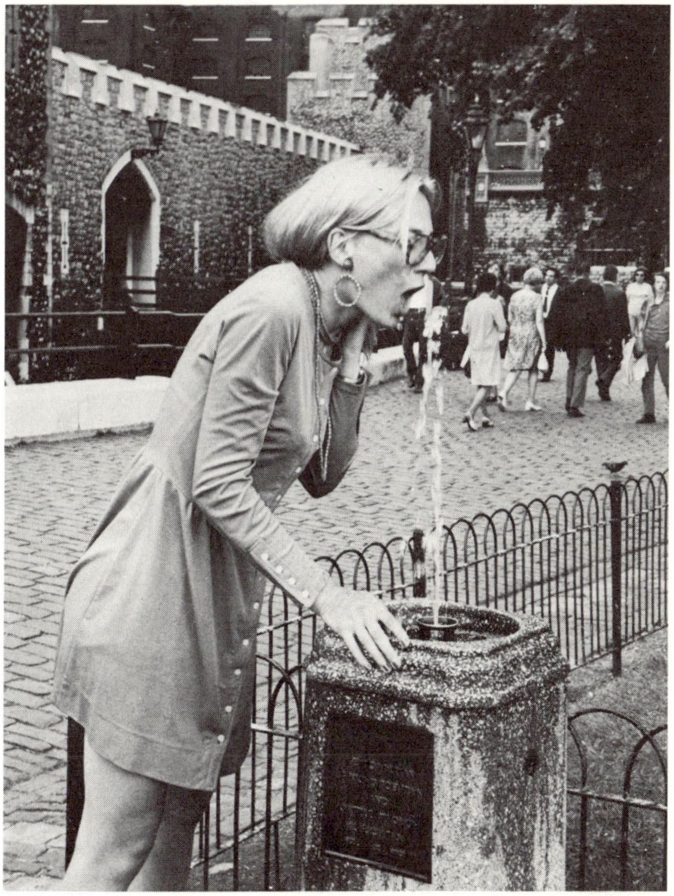

Fast shutter speed. Outside the Tower of London is a water fountain that gives the unwary thirst-slaker a tremendous, high-powered blast of icy water right in the face. With glee, the photographer sat on a bench opposite, and photographed dozens of people—at 1/250 sec.— to freeze the stream of water and the expressions on their faces. Tri-X, with the 50 mm Nikkor at *f*/11.

Slow shutter speed. Night shots, such as this picture of Edinburgh Castle illuminated, require long exposures anyway, so you may as well stop down for better definition and use a tripod and cable release for the really slow shutter speeds that result. Exposure: 4 seconds at *f*/8 with the 105 mm Nikkor on Tri-X.

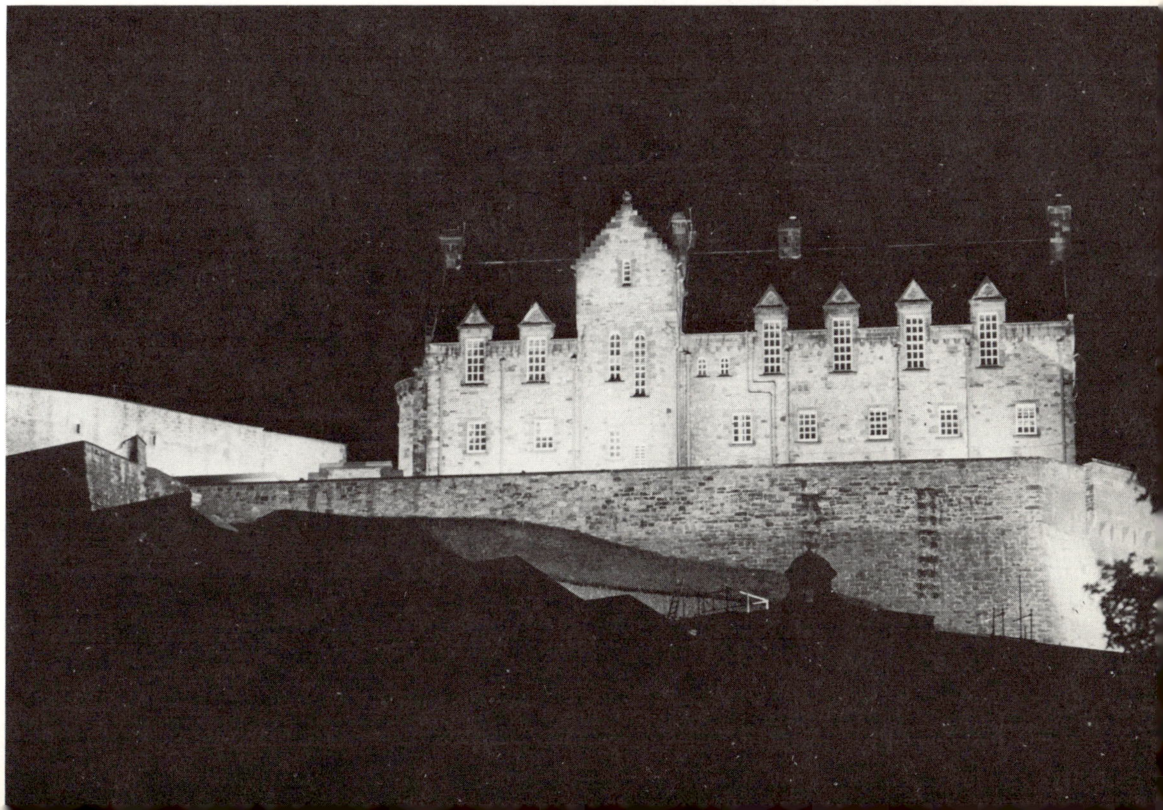

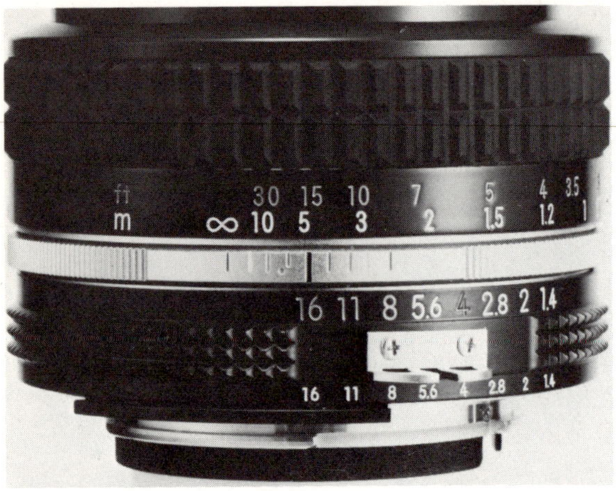

Depth-of-field scale of 50 mm *f*/1.4 Nikkor. Lens is set for *f*/16 and is focused at hyperfocal distance for maximum depth. See text for explanation.

environment. We know that long lenses, close focusing distances, and wide apertures all yield a shallow depth of field. Conversely, short lenses, great distances, and small apertures all increase depth considerably.

Look at your lensbarrel. When you are focused at any particular distance, color-coded lines representing the aperture scale are adjacent to the distance scale. The colored lines, left and right, indicate the near and far limits of depth for each aperture at that focused distance. You can see how dramatically the depth increases as you stop down. By the same token, it decreases sharply as you open the lens. To get useful depth at near distances you *must* stop down; at greater distances, you have more options. In the realm of macro and micro work, there is hardly any depth at all.

Hyperfocal Distance

The maximum depth is *not* obtained by setting the distance scale at "infinity." Looking at the scale will show you that by doing so you are wasting all the "focus" on the far side of the scale. The maximum depth of field for any lens at any *f*-stop is called its hyperfocal setting. It is found by setting the camera at infinity and reading the distance on the *near* limit side of the depth-of-field scale for the *f*-stop selected. If you then focus on that distance, *everything will be in focus from half that distance to "infinity."* In practice, merely set the "∞" mark on the focusing ring opposite the *far* limit of the *f*-stop you have chosen; the lens will then be set for its hyperfocal distance for that stop.

Shutter Speeds

The other side of the exposure/depth coin is shutter speed. In the case of static subjects, any shutter speed that can be conveniently held will do, but with moving objects this is not so. Speeds of 1/60 sec. or faster are required to "stop" even moderate human motion without blur. Speeds of up to 1/500 sec. or 1/1000 sec. are needed when subject motion really speeds up. But is "frozen" motion always desirable? Sometimes a *slightly* blurred subject in an otherwise sharp photograph conveys the *idea* of motion better than "stopping 'em dead." Creative use of shutter speeds may depend on subject motion. If you *pan* (*i.e.*, follow the subject with the camera as you expose), you can keep the subject sharp with a fairly low speed, but blur out everything else.

Above all, control of your shutter speeds depends upon control of camera motion. We stated earlier that camera-shake ruins more pictures than any other fault. With *any* slow speeds (below 1/125 sec.) take great care to steady yourself and the camera. How slow you can shoot handholding the camera, without visible camera-shake, is an individual matter. With most people, it's about 1/30 sec. with the normal lens; with long lenses, it's usually faster. When the light gets bad, or if you want extended depth, *use a tripod*. This is no relic of the past, but a valuable instrument. When you're taking pictures at 1/8 sec. (or two minutes' exposure, for that matter) the tripod and cable release will yield a picture as sharp as one taken at 1/1000 sec.—and you will be able to stop down as far as you like. Excellent books containing complete analyses of the problems of exposure are George Wright and Cora Wright Kennedy's *Guide to Perfect Exposure*, and Fred Picker's *The Zone VI Workshop*, both published by Amphoto.

Alternatives in shooting motion:
In this picture, the shutter was set at 1/500 sec. effectively stopping the motion of the cab.

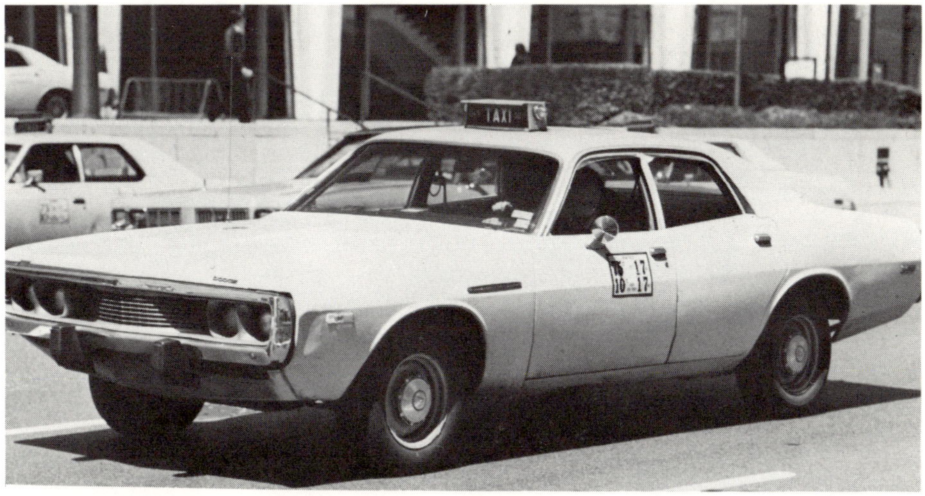

Here, the camera was held motionless, while a slow shutter speed of 1/30 sec. let the cab blur while the background remained sharp.

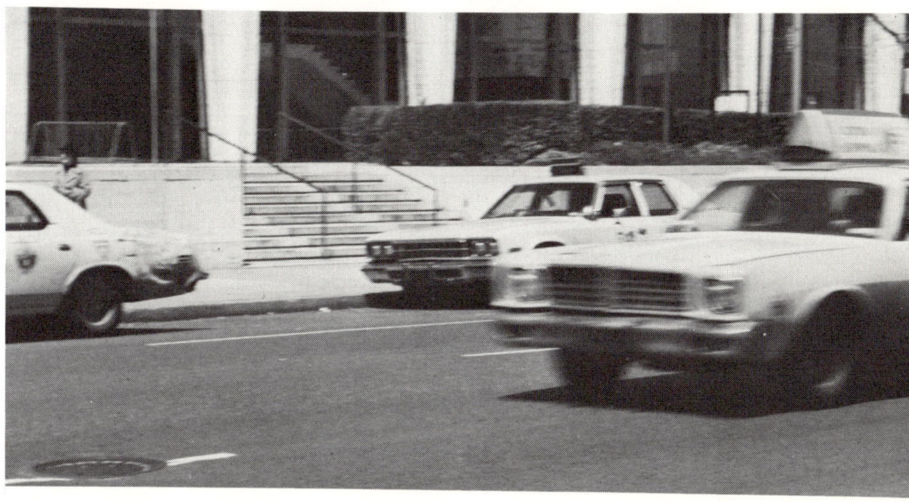

Again, the same slow 1/30 sec. was used, but the camera panned on the cab, keeping it sharp while blurring the background.

All shots were taken with Plus-X and 105 mm Nikkor.

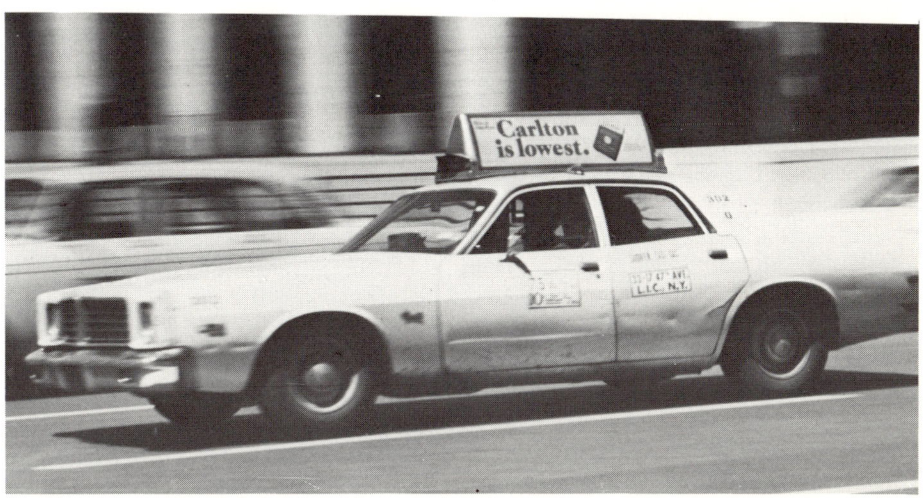

Most photographs are taken in sunlight; but an increasing number are taken by "available light" and by artificial light set up for that purpose. In the space we have here, we cannot discuss in detail the many aspects of light and lighting that make for creative photography. We already know some of the basics—exposure, and its relationship to focus, filtration, lens aperture, and film speed. Here are some of the other highlights.

Direction

Gone are the days (they never were, really) when light "had" to come from over the photographer's shoulder and hit the subject head-on. Today's esthetic frowns on *frontal* lighting, in fact, since it is often flat and uninteresting. *Sidelighting* and even *backlighting* create far more interesting interplays of light and shadow, color and dullness, especially in pictures of people. The "halo" or "hairlight" effect is one of the more attractive results of backlighting, with either sunlight or set-up artificial lights. Strong sidelighting brings out texture details that frontal lighting washes out.

But because you may want details in both highlights and shadows, and because of the limitations of film latitude, you can employ *reflectors* to direct light back onto the subject, thus lightening the shadows. With color film especially, this reduction of contrast makes for a more pleasing effect. Reflectors for this purpose are manufactured in various sizes and shapes, but any moveable reflective surface will do: a large sheet of cardboard or oaktag makes an excellent reflector. An open book, held in a subject's lap, will cast enough overhead light back onto his face to reduce shadows substantially. (Another method of reducing shadows is to use *fill-in light*; this will be discussed shortly.) One warning: do not make a portrait of someone you like with light from beneath. The odd shadows will make him look like a character out of a horror movie! Direct overhead light is to be avoided for similar reasons.

Diffuse light, found indoors in well-lit rooms and outdoors on hazy or cloudy days, is ideal for rendering tones more evenly on black-and-white film, or capturing the full spectrum of colors on color film. Although diffused light is usually less dramatic than strongly directional light, it provides good, even illumination, often as bright as direct sunlight.

Whenever you are photographing in strongly directional light, take the greatest care in metering the subject. Your through-the-lens meter will compensate for most of the inequalities of light and shadow, but you must still think and decide where you wish the accent to be. Especially where the subject is backlit, you must be certain you are metering for the subject and not the background light.

Available vs. **Set-up Light**

"Available light" (or "ambient light," or "existing light") is usually construed to mean indoor artificial light. The term also covers the daylight that comes through windows, poor light outdoors or at night, and any situation, in fact, that might be better called "available darkness." It is the light generally considered to be the most naturalistic for picture-taking, and it has been the main inspiration for the development of modern 35 mm photography, with its present fast lenses and films. Many photographers shoot exclusively by available light and shun any "artificial" lighting, by which they mean set-up lighting.

Actually, the "available-light" effect may be achieved (and often is) by setting up the lights in advance and even using regular photographic lighting equipment, flood or flash. Since a lighting setup should rarely *look* set up (and then, as in portrait or commercial photography, for dramatic purposes only), the distinction between the two "kinds" of lighting becomes blurred. Where the necessity for complete freedom of movement joins the desire to produce pictures with the greatest apparent spontaneity, the available-light approach is the "right" one; load your camera with fast film, open your lens, slow down your shutter, and shoot away. But if the light is bad, and you have the time or means to do so, set up your lighting in advance. You need not pose your subjects to take advantage of better light. On the contrary, merely opening a window shade or attaching a flash unit to your

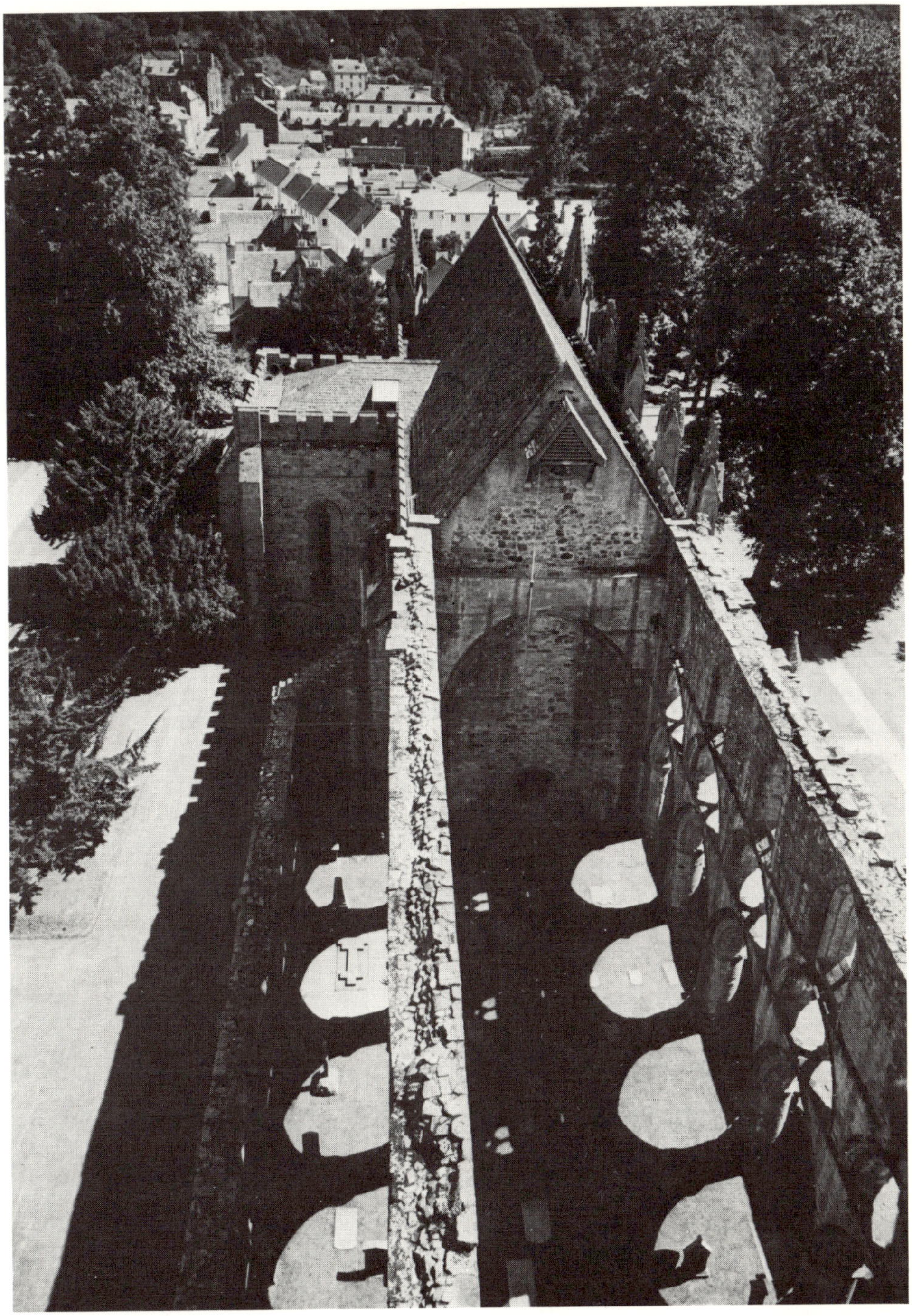

Sidelighting. The "bare ruined choirs" of this 11th-century Scottish cathedral, in the town of Dunkeld, were accentuated by "raking" sidelight, which traced strong shadow patterns of the archways on the ground. This and the vantage point—atop the rickety steeple—made the picture. Taken on Plus-X through a medium yellow filter, 1/125 sec. at *f*/16, with the 28 mm Nikkor.

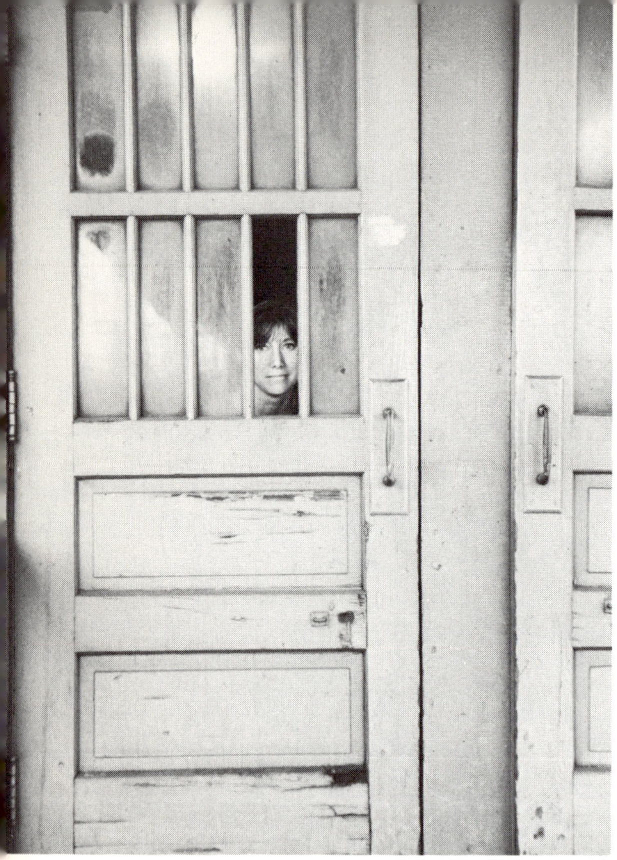

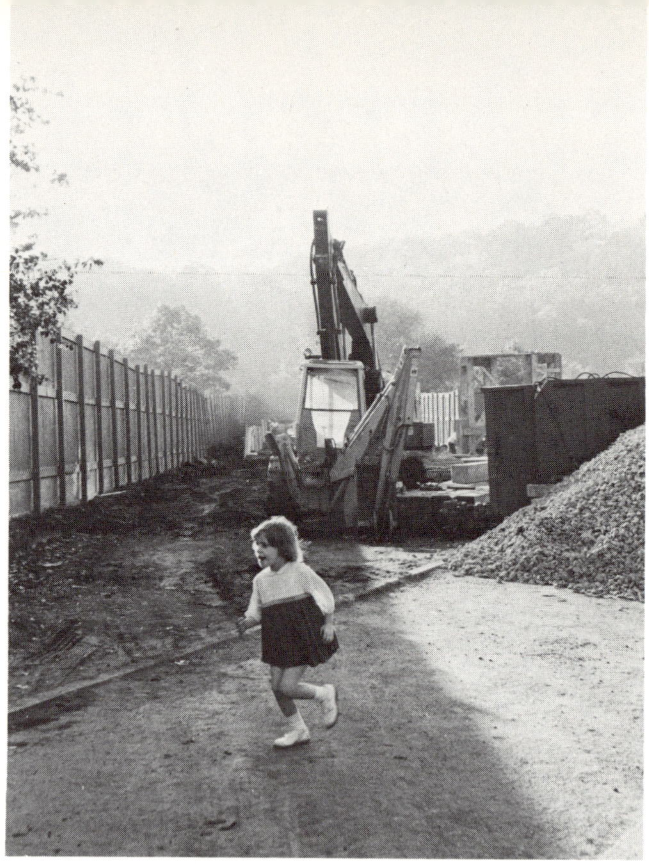

Diffused lighting (top left). The softest light, for greatest tonal variations, especially when three-dimensional detail is *not* wanted. This door in an abandoned railroad station was taken with the 105 mm Nikkor on Plus-X on a very dull day, 1/60 sec. at *f*/8.

Backlighting (top right). A halo of backlight separates the little girl from the construction machinery. Exposure, for the girl, was 1/250 sec. at *f*/5.6 on Plus-X. Normal 50 mm Nikkor.

Toplighting (below). The worst light for people-pictures has some applications for inanimate objects. This Roman sarcophagus at the Metropolitan Museum of Art is lit by floodlights in the ceiling, which bring out the details of the sculpture. Tri-X, 1/30 sec. at *f*/2.8, 50 mm Nikkor.

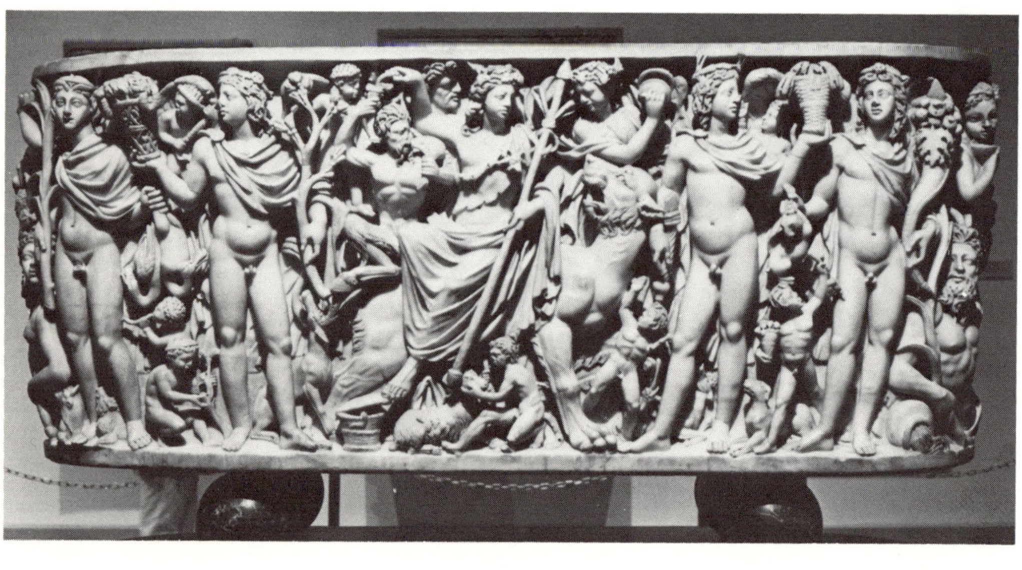

camera gives you the opportunity to get technically better pictures under any circumstances. More elaborate lighting setups, of course, will make exposure even easier, but often at the expense of the informal appearance.

Floodlighting

Photofloods are large, incandescent lamps, which provide a steady stream of light that is easier to set up and work with than any other kind of light. The lamps come in 250- and 500-watt sizes and are brighter than comparable household bulbs. Relatively inexpensive, but cumbersome, they are limited to use where there are electric outlets. They come in color temperatures of 3200 K and 3400 K, and as single-unit reflector floods or bulbs to be placed in separate reflectors.

The principal advantage to using floodlighting is that you are able to see the effect of each light as you set it up, before you take the picture. With a two- or three-light setup this may prevent madness, for the interplay of light and shadow gets quite complex. With flash, you cannot be sure exactly where the shadows will fall until the flash goes off—and often not even then. But with floodlamps, you may study the scene through the viewfinder and adjust the placement of your lights.

Floodlighting is most commonly used to make portraits and still lifes. Either case requires a *main light* and one or more auxiliary lamps. These secondary units are used as *fill-in lights* and *accent lights*. The fill-in lights, like reflectors (which are often used as well), lighten the shadows, to lessen the overall contrast and simplify exposure. They are usually placed farther away from the subject than is the main light, and on the other side. The accent lights (the "rim light," or "hairlight," for example) are used to point up some specific feature. Diffusers, either manufactured or homemade, also soften the harsh effects of direct lighting.

Floodlighting is sometimes used to boost the level of regular indoor lighting. One way is to put flood bulbs in whatever lamps are handy, thus maintaining the normal light balance of the room. A better method is to use *bounce lighting*. Instead of shining the light at the subject, point the flood reflector at the ceiling, at a point midway between subject and lamp. The light will diffuse, and although less of it will reach the subject, you will have eliminated most harsh shadows and restored the appearance of "natural" lighting. Be careful not to bounce the light off brightly colored walls or ceilings if you are shooting with color film; there will be a color cast to all the photos.

There are many excellent books on lighting techniques for photography in general and portraiture in particular. The reader is advised to consult *Light and Lighting in Photography*, by Andreas Feininger, published by Amphoto, for more information on this fascinating aspect of photography.

FLASH AND ELECTRONIC FLASH

All the techniques used with floods may be used with flash, and this accounts to a great extent for the overwhelming popularity of flash photography. Indoors and out, flash units can supply most supplementary lighting needs.

Today, electronic flash (often mis-named "strobe") has displaced flashbulbs for all but the simplest amateur applications. The one advantage to bulb units—initial expense—is illusory: Although a BC (battery/capacitor) bulb unit is inexpensive, the more bulbs or flashcubes you buy, the more expensive it gets. Electronic units use no bulbs, and their batteries are cheap and often rechargeable. In the long run, electronic flash costs less. The units are relatively inexpensive, powerful, portable, and very versatile. The great speed of the flash duration—as little as 1/50,000 sec.—makes it possible to stop action that would be too fast for any shutter. In bright sunlight, flash can be used to fill in shadows to give more pleasing contrast. Bounce flash, multiple-flash setups, and other light-molding techniques have greatly simplified indoor work: they permit smaller apertures to be used and they generate much less heat than floods. Automatic flash units even make exposure calculations unnecessary.

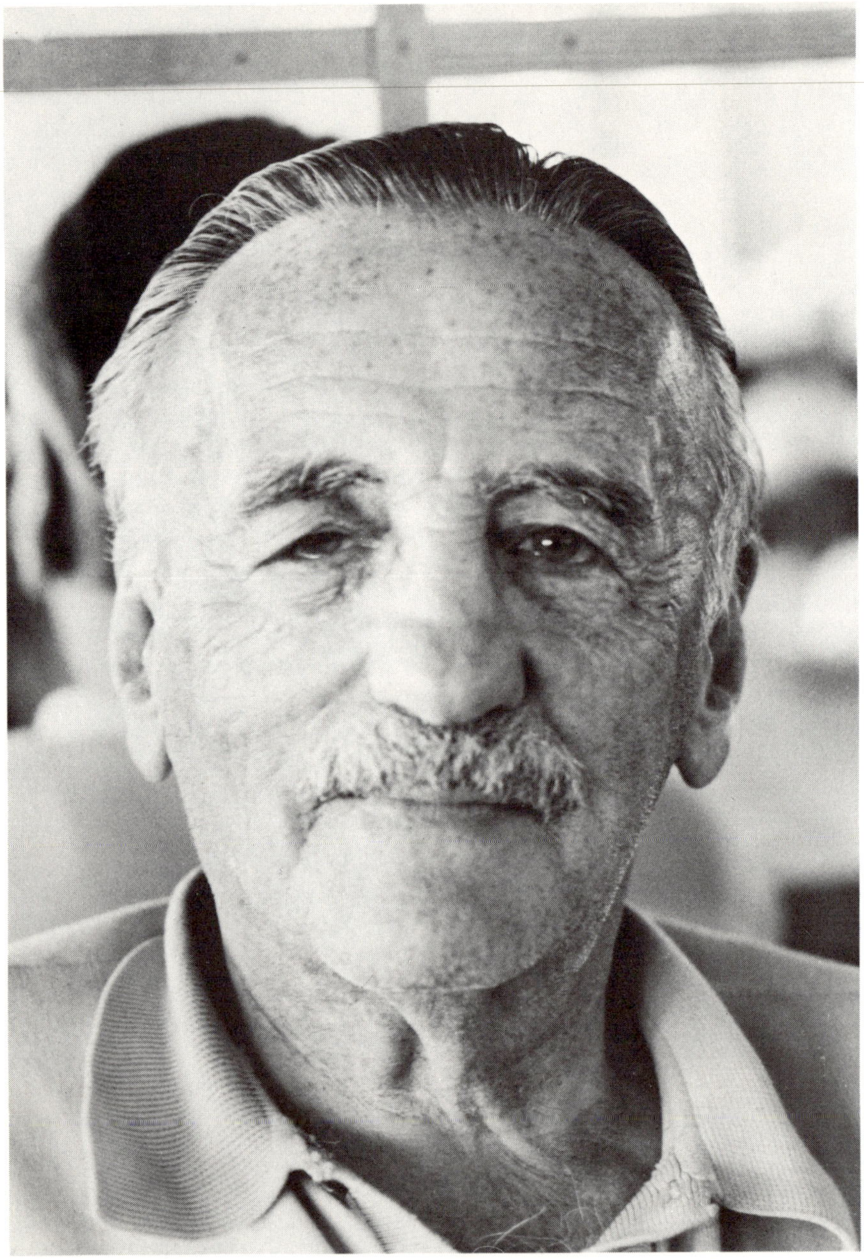

Available-light portrait. Although this picture is not perfectly sharp, the right eye is, and the informal, "natural" look is enhanced by diffused window light and the unposed situation. The 105 mm Nikkor was used up close, wide open at *f*/2.5, 1/60 sec. on Plus-X.

Set-up lighting (opposite). This picture is more "perfect," but has the distinctive, posed look of all formal portraits. Two diffused floodlights were employed to mold the facial shadows for a strong, masculine appearance. The 105 mm Nikkor was stopped down to *f*/8 for greater depth, at 1/30 sec. on Tri-X.

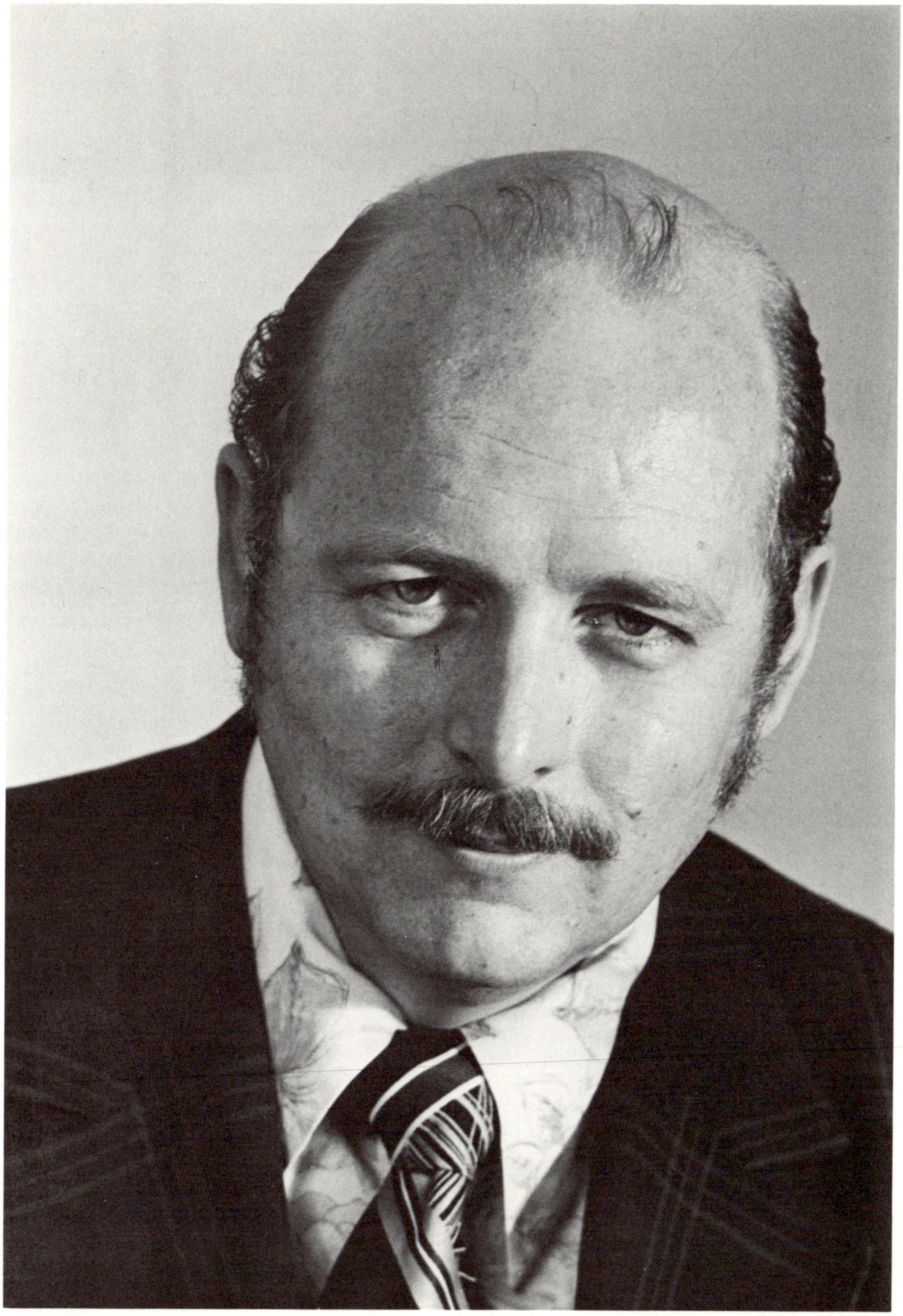

Flash Exposure

Exposure determination with bulb or *manual* electronic flash is quite different from that in ordinary photography. *Guide numbers* are required to determine aperture; they are provided by flashbulb and flash manufacturers for use with their units and various films. Regardless of the shutter speed, the guide number is divided by the distance from flash to subject. Thus, if the GN = 100, and the distance to the subject = 10 feet, then 100 ÷ 10 = 10. Since there is no *f*/10, use *f*/11. (Separate guide numbers are provided for metric distances.) The calculation must be modified if you use *bounced* flash: Compensate for the extra distance the light must travel—from flash *to bounce surface* to subject—as well as light diffusion and absorption. In a room with a light ceiling of average height, take the flash-to-ceiling-to-subject distance, calculate the *f*/stop normally, and open up one or two stops further. If the ceiling is dark, or rather high, open up still more.

The *automatic electronic flash unit* eliminates the necessity for calculating with guide numbers. These units measure the light reflecting back from the subject, by means of a sensor, then quench the flash when sufficient light for the given film speed and aperture is reached. The first such units used only one aperture, but later models permit a range of several *f*-stops, thereby allowing you to select apertures for their depth of field. The compact Nikon SB units are of this type.

The new "dedicated" units simplify the process still further, adjusting the *camera* for proper flash synchronization, as well as themselves. The most sophisticated Nikon units use the camera's through-the-lens metering system to determine the correct light output, even with bounced flash.

Synchronization

All Nikon reflexes are synchronized for use with flashbulbs and electronic flash, but the F3, FM, and EM are fully synchronized for electronic flash only; they use bulbs in a limited range. The latest models provide automatic switchover from "X" (electronic) to "M" (bulb) synch, depending on the shutter speed set. The Nikon F cameras have a multiple flash-synch function, activated by a ring around the shutter-speed dial. Set the color-coded symbol in the window in front of the dial. (If there is a Photomic finder on the camera, you must remove it to get at the ring and change settings.) Since synchronization can take place only at certain shutter speeds with each type of flash unit for each camera, consult the appropriate chart before deciding which to use. For example, electronic flash will only synch with the shutter—even though it is set for "X"—at 1/80 sec. or slower with the Nikon F3 and F2 cameras; at 1/60 sec. with the Nikon F; at 1-125 sec. with the Nikon FM, FE, EL2; and at 1/90 sec. with the Nikon EM. (This is why the dedicated units are so popular.)

Most flash units today make contact with the camera through electrical contacts in the accessory shoe (the "hot" shoe) or, in the case of the Nikon F3's and F2's, around the rewind crank. The flash may also be operated by means of the threaded flash-synch terminal on the camera body (the flash itself may be positioned on the shoe, on a separate bracket, or off the camera entirely). In all cases, firing the shutter activates the flash.

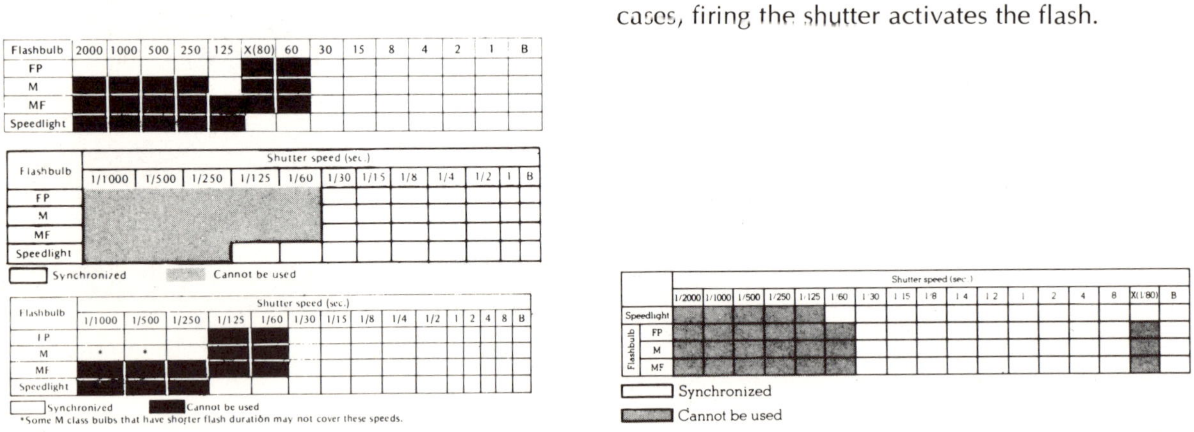

Flash-synch ranges for F2 (top), FM (middle), FE and EL2 (bottom), and Nikon F3 (right).

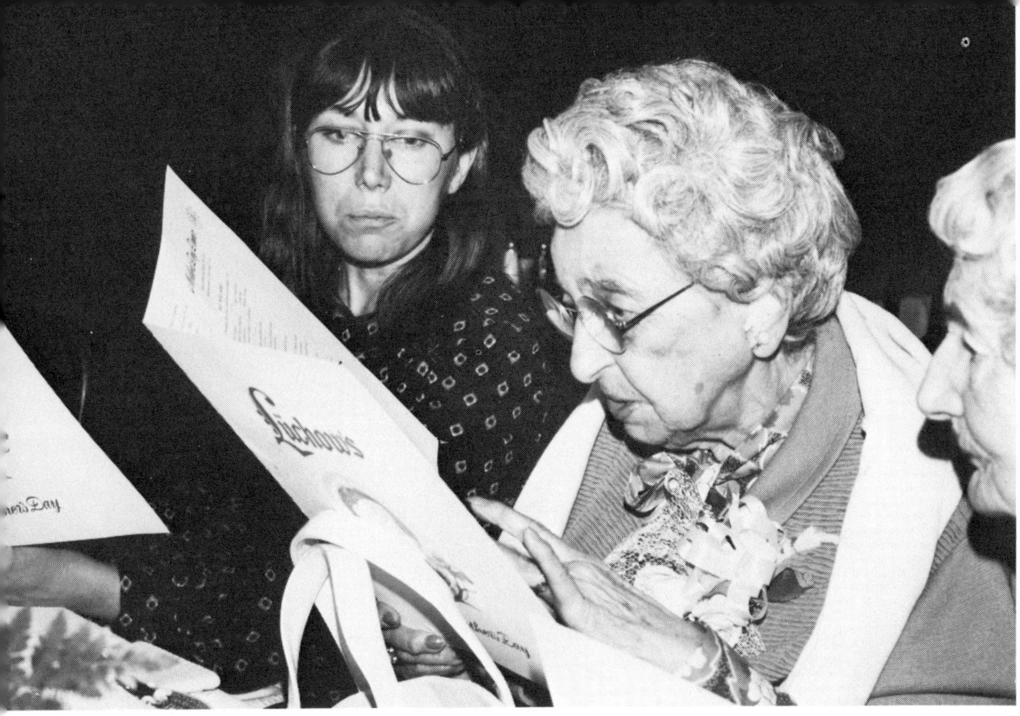

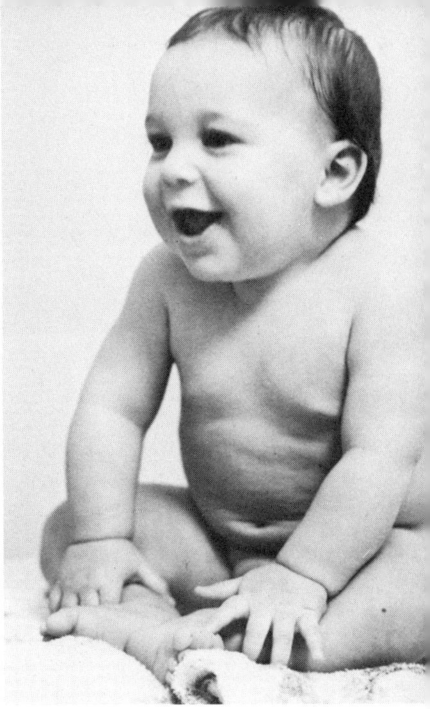

Direct flash (above, left). Characterized by pinpoint sharpness, high contrast, and harsh shadows, direct on-camera flash utilizes the full power of the flash unit. Here, *f*/5.6 could be used for added depth with the 50 mm Nikkor, even in a very dark restaurant with slow film, Ilford Pan F.

Bounce flash (above, right). A much softer, more rounded effect is obtained by bouncing the flash off a wall or, as here, the ceiling. Shadows are minimized, but the larger aperture and lower light level sacrifice some sharpness. Exposure by flash held to the side of the camera, on Tri-X. The 105 mm Nikkor was at *f*/4.

Fill-in flash (below). Flash can be used to reduce excessive contrast by "filling in" shadows. Basic exposure of 1/125 sec. at *f*/16 left most of the girl's face in dark shadow, remainder in glare (left). Asking her to face into the shade, then brightening the shadows with a small flash at 7 feet (but stopping the 105 mm Nikkor to *f*/22 so it wouldn't get *too* light) relieved her squint, lowered the contrast, and kept the background about the same (right). Tri-X, yellow filter.

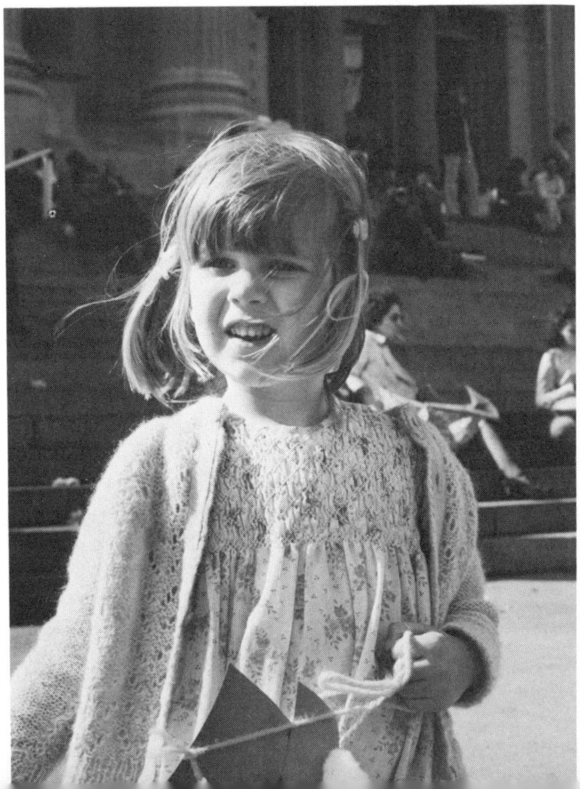

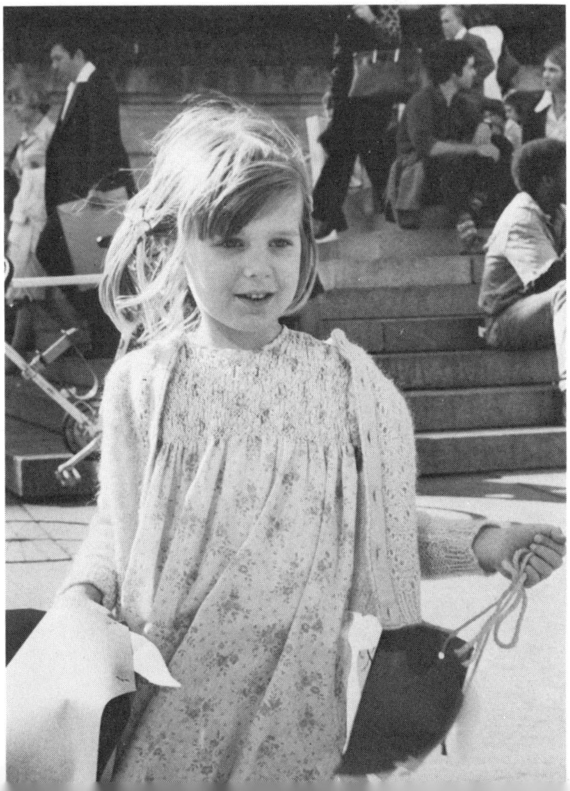

The following are some random thoughts on photographic subjects and a few general pointers on improving your pictures:

People

Close in. That, in two words, will change the average snapshot to a portrait study. Fill the frame with the subject—it doesn't matter whether you pose him or her—but try to avoid stiffness. Here is the best place to use the medium telephoto lens, to eliminate conflicting background matter. On the other hand, your people-pictures may improve by relating the subject to his environment: try wide-angle shots, but use them judiciously. Take pictures of people at work and at play; the SLR was designed for such "grab" shooting. You and your subjects will be pleased with the natural poses and expressions that result. Experiment with different kinds of lighting, and don't be afraid to "push" your camera—it will surprise you.

When you take pictures of children, kneel or crouch; don't stand up and shoot down at them, for the perspective will be distorted. Babies and smaller children present special difficulties; they cannot and should not be posed. Exercise patience, follow them around, learn their pattern of activities, and take as many pictures as you can. Eventually they will ignore you, and you will be able to get fresh, natural pictures.

Groups

Use normal and wide-angle lenses. Wait for interaction among members of the group. One photographer sets up his groups, asks them to pose, snaps the shutter, and tells the subjects the session is over. *Then* he takes his pictures, as they relax. At weddings, family gatherings, and the like, the available-light "grab-shooting" technique gets the least stereotyped results. Flash helps, but usually it ruins any chance of "natural" pictures. A complete study of photographing people singly and in groups is *Picturing People*, by Don Nibbelink, published by Amphoto.

Sports

Use long lenses and fast films. Study the course of action and learn to anticipate breaks in motion (the "peak of action"). Then, snap the shutter as the ball falls or the runner turns. A slightly blurred picture (from *subject* motion, not camera motion) often increases the effect of action. Take pictures of the other spectators, too. At indoor events use tungsten color film for accurate colors, fast daylight color films for action-stopping and special effects. Another Amphoto book, *Focus on Sports: Photographing Action*, by Richard Turner, contains specific tips for photographing many different sports.

Animals

Strangely (or not so strangely), the rules are much the same as for photographing children. Keep low (for small animals), follow the animal until it is used to you, and learn to anticipate its actions. Furred animals require extra exposure. Animals in the wild and birds, fish, and insects require much hard work and special techniques; excellent books in this field are *The Complete Book of Nature Photography*, by Russ Kinne, and *Animal and Pet Photography Simplified*, by Mildred Stagg, both published by Amphoto.

Flowers

The most striking and easiest-to-take color slides are flower shots. Use a normal lens plus various close-up accessories to isolate individual flowers. Paper reflectors outdoors are very useful in throwing light back on flowers for the necessary smaller apertures (close distances = shallow depth of field). They also block the wind, which can make flowers tremble or wave.

Textures

Seek textures in nature (tree bark, rocks) or at home (fabrics, floors). Use sidelighting to emphasize three-dimensionality, and isolate a small part of the object to heighten the abstract effect.

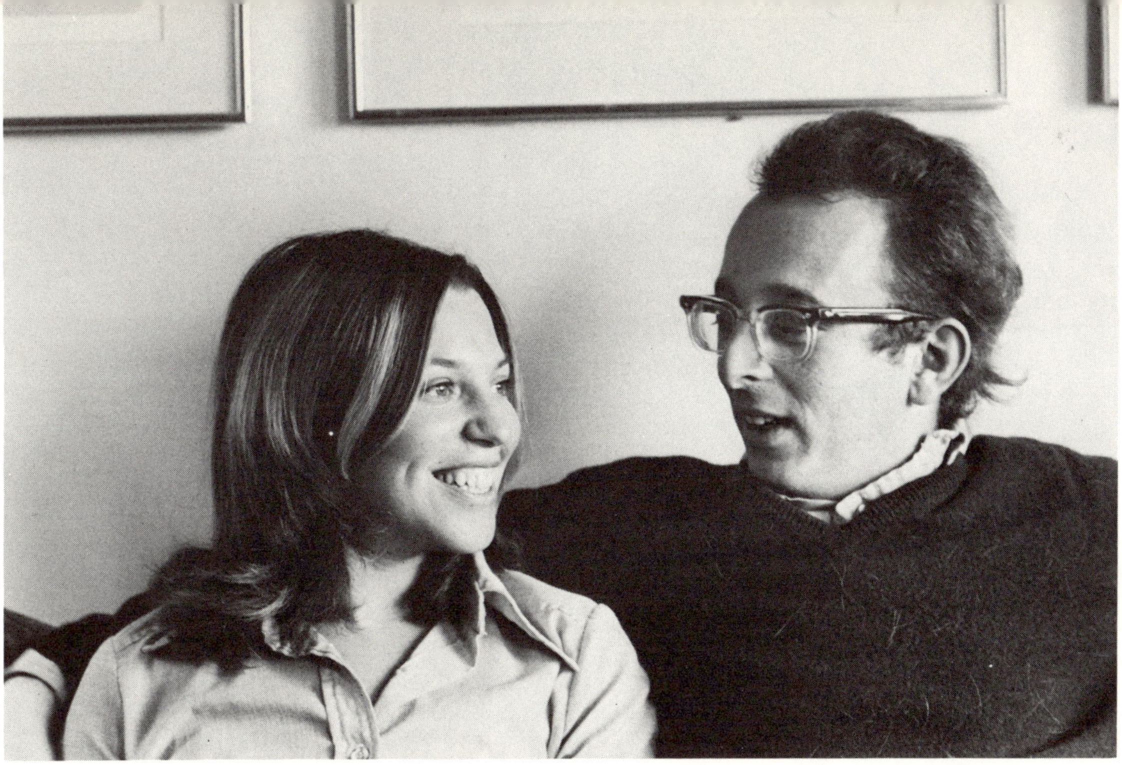

For the informal double portrait above, taken by available light indoors, the camera was placed on a tripod, but after focusing it, the photographer stood next to it and talked with the subjects to relax them. He released the shutter by cable. The 50 mm Nikkor was used to get close while retaining some touches of the home environment. 1/60 sec. at *f*/5.6 on Tri-X.

Is this a rural scene (below) with some children in it or a shot of three kids against a small-town background? No matter; it relates the boys to their environment and vice versa. Grab shot in a small Appalachian town (Neon's the name, not the stuff for sale). Taken from a car with the 50 mm Nikkor on Panatomic-X to retain good contrast on a dark, rainy day. Exposure: 1/30 sec. at *f*/5.6.

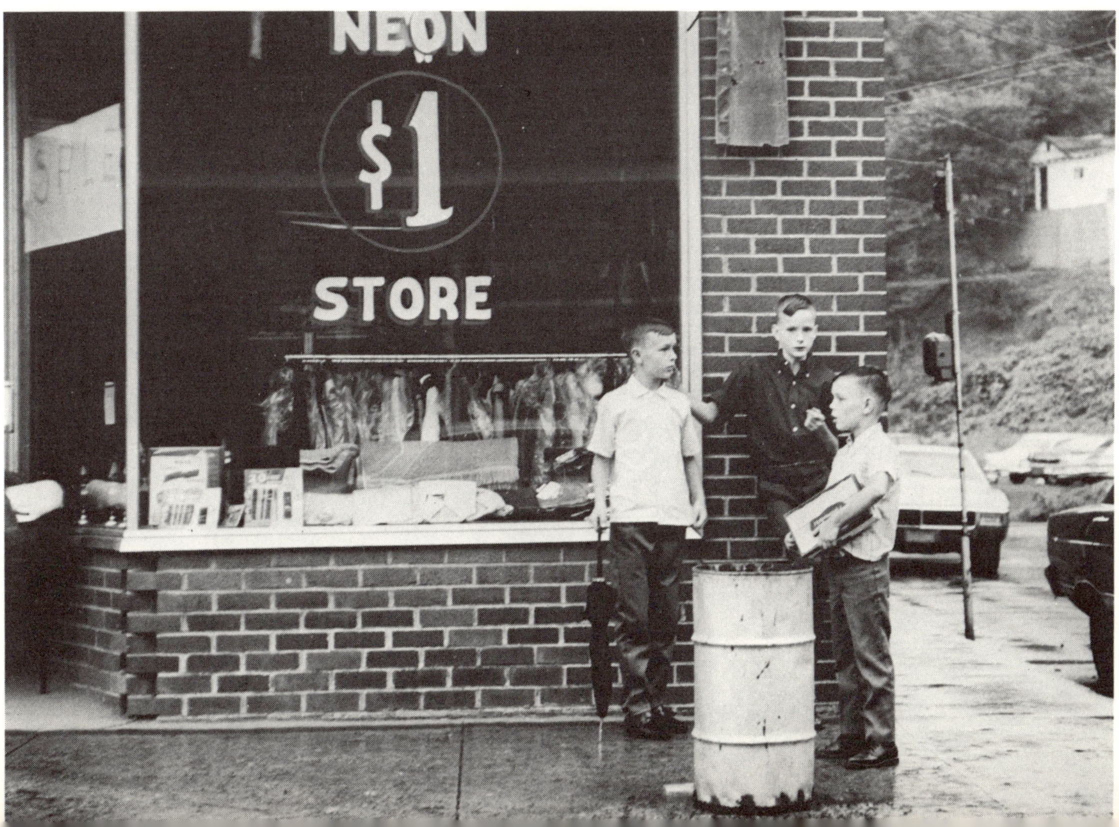

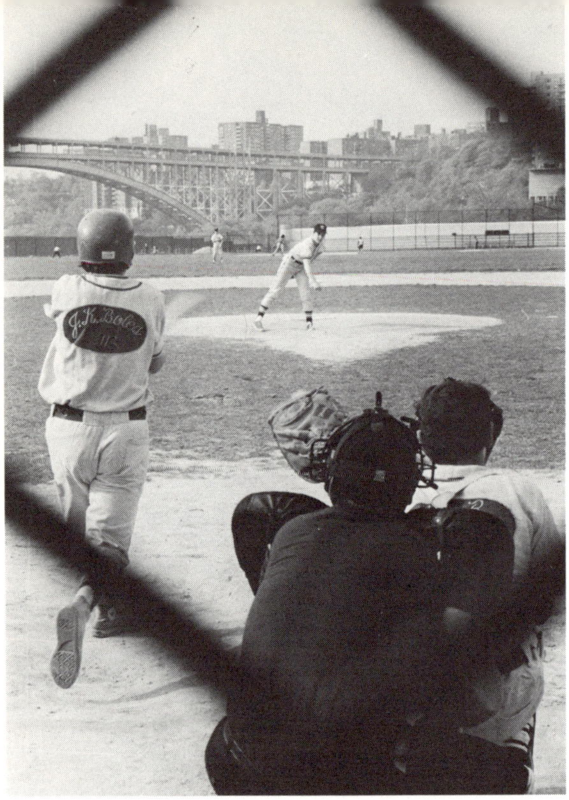

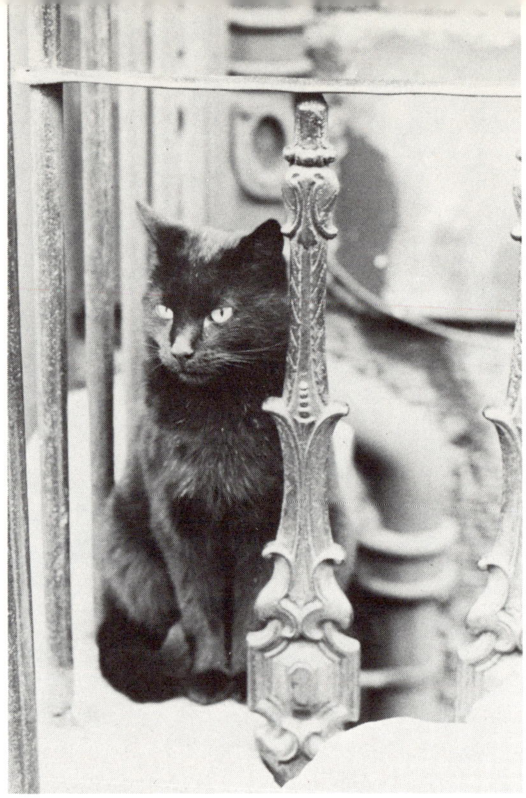

Timing is essential in sports photography, as is a good vantage point. The batter in this Little-League game struck out, but the camera caught the "decisive moment" with a 1/250 sec. exposure that froze all but the swinging bat. Normal 50 mm Nikkor at *f*/16 for great depth, on Tri-X.

The cat was black, the Scottish day was dark. "Normal" exposure on Plus-X would have been 1/125 sec. at *f*/8, but to retain detail in the cat's fur, the photographer gave the equivalent of two stops more, 1/60 sec. at *f*/5.6, with the 50 mm Nikkor.

Good black-and-white pictures of flowers require bright light, contrasty colors, or heavy filtration. These sunflowers were golden yellow and brown, and bathed in light. The 55 mm Micro-Nikkor was used alone at about 1:5 magnification. The exposure on Plus-X was 1/125 sec. at *f*/8.

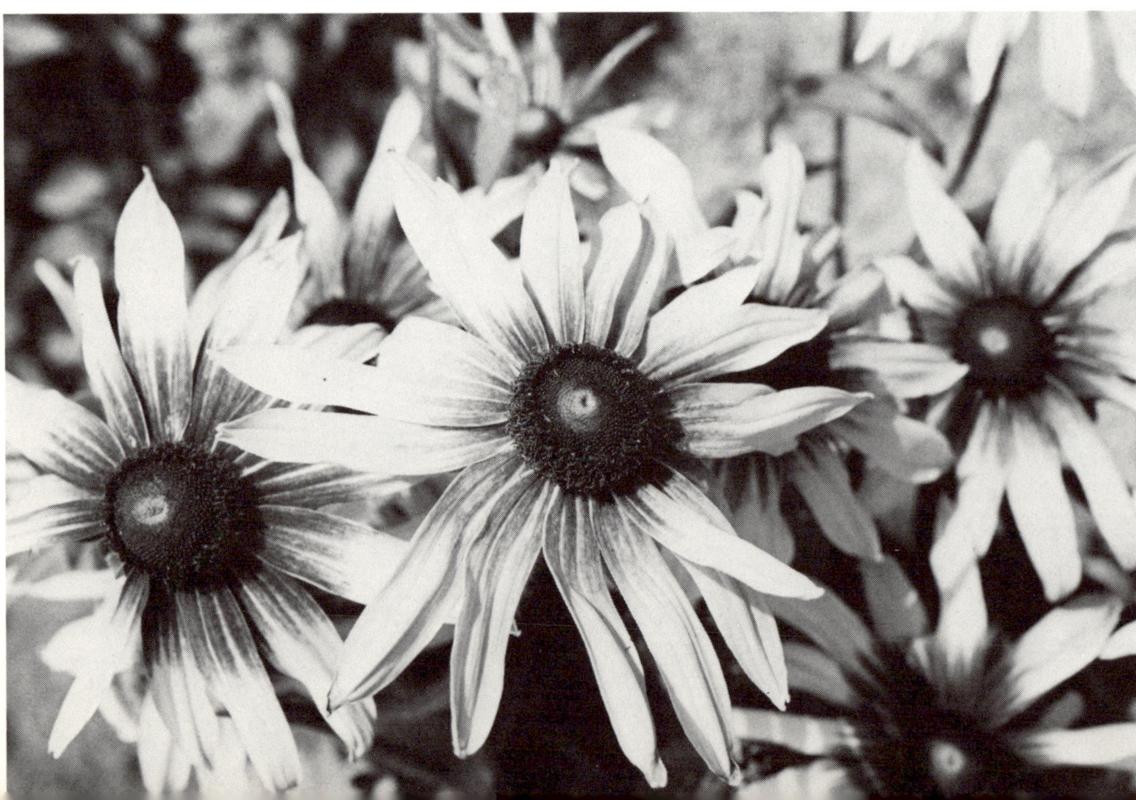

Landscapes

The aspects of light—quality, direction, and quantity—are nowhere more important than in landscape photography. Dramatic shadows give depth and modeling to any scene. The better the overall light, the smaller the apertures you can use and the better your depth of field will be. Color films will capture the seasonal beauties of spring and fall, and even add an extra dimension to winter snow-scenes. Accurate filtration is mandatory for clear landscape photography: a K2 (yellow) filter for black-and-white, and a skylight or UV filter for color films are the absolute minimum.

Architecture

The professional architectural photographer must strive for complete views (called "elevations") of the structure he shoots. The amateur is freer to concentrate on details. Textures in the building materials and designs (stonework and masonry) are accentuated by sidelighting. Wide-angle lenses allow you to get in more of a building without tilting your camera upward, thus preventing the "falling over" effect of converging verticals. Try the slow black-and-white films at small apertures, for depth; and dark filters, for striking sky and cloud effects.

COMPOSITION

More nonsense has been written about composition than about any other aspect of photography. There are few sensible "rules" for composition; perhaps the only one suitable for beginners is: simplify. The more you shoot, the more refined your taste will become and the less likely you are to take a jumble—unless you want to take jumbles!

PROCESSING AND PRINTING

Developing your own films, color or black-and-white, and making your own prints is an area almost every serious photographer wishes to explore. This vast area, often called the "other half" of photography, is outside the scope of this book, but there are many excellent reference works on the photographic darkroom. Some of the most pertinent are: *Lootens on Photographic Enlarging and Print Quality*, by J. Ghislain Lootens, revised by Lester H. Bogen; *Manual of Darkroom Procedures and Techniques*, by Paul Jonas; *The Basic B & W Darkroom Book, The Advanced B & W Darkroom Book,* and *The Color Printing Manual*, all by Bob Nadler; *Darkroom Techniques*, by Andreas Feininger; *The Fine Print*, by Fred Picker; *The Home Darkroom*, by Mark Fineman; and the "bible" of photographic materials and their uses, the compendious *Photographic Lab Handbook*, edited by John S. Carroll. All are published by Amphoto.

CAMERA MAINTENANCE

General

Keep your camera clean, dry, and unbumped to insure its long life. Keep it in its case when you are not using it, and do not store it in a small confined space—like the glove compartment of your car—where it might get hot or damp. Never leave it lying in the sun. Before putting it away, release the shutter, set the lens to infinity and cap it, and open up the diaphragm to maximum aperture, to relax spring tension. If you are storing it for a long time, remove the batteries and place some dessicant, such as silica gel, with the camera to absorb moisture. If *anything* jams, binds, or creaks, take your camera to the store where you bought it or to a reliable camera repairman. The modern SLR is a very complex device; a little tinkering on your part can turn out to be very expensive.

Cleaning

Before loading the camera, lightly dust off the front lens element and the camera interior with a rubber blower-brush (ear syringe), while holding the part to be dusted down, so the dust falls away. This should be *all* the cleaning normally necessary. If grease spots or fingerprints get on your lens, though, you must remove them immediately. Use lens tissue and a standard liquid lens cleaner, but use them very sparingly. The coatings and optical glass are soft; excessive rubbing will damage them, excessive amounts of cleaner will loosen the lens elements. Never use silicone-treated eyeglass tissue on your lens. The chrome and leather parts of the camera should normally require no cleaning.

Disasters

There are three major disasters that may befall your camera: dropping it, getting sand in it, and immersing it in water. In the first two cases, do nothing to the camera, but take it immediately to your repairman. In the last instance, if the camera has been dropped in water, keep it immersed, in a bucket or tank (flush it with fresh water first if it has fallen into salt water), then take it in for repairs. A few drops of rain will do no harm, but don't let it get soaked.

Your Nikon is a sturdy, rugged instrument. With a minimum of care and a little good sense, it will serve you for years and years.

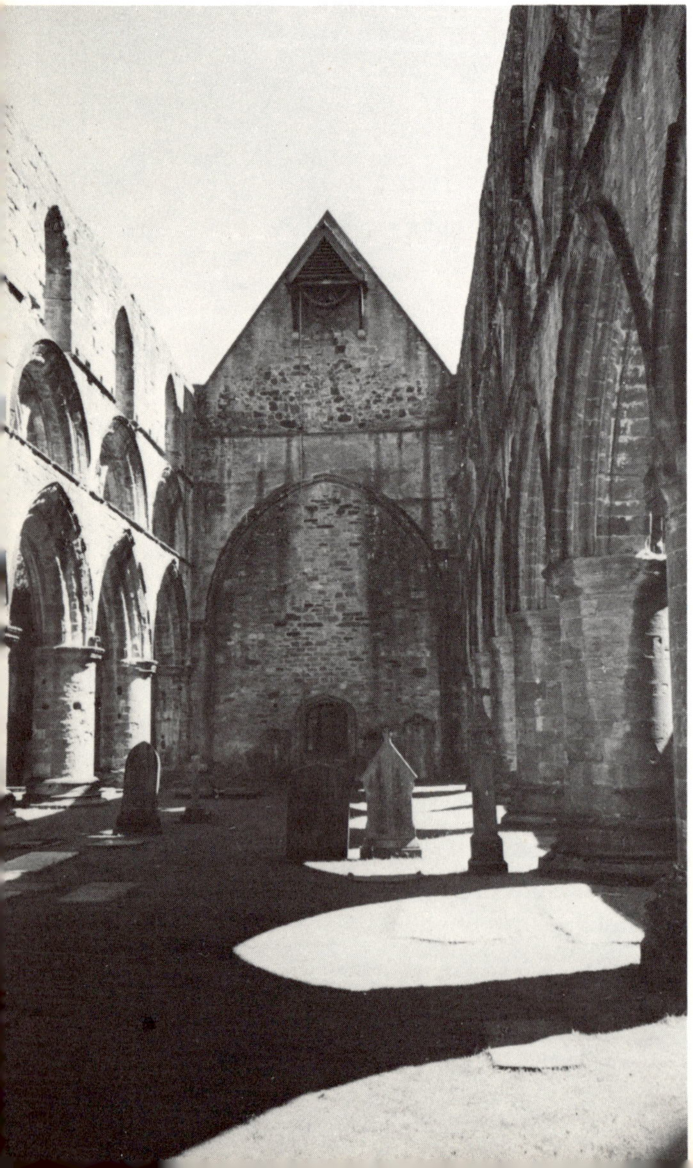

An architectural detail. Part of the cathedral at Dunkeld shown earlier. Again the 28 mm Nikkor allowed the photographer to record a substantial part of the exposed interior, as sidelighting brought out details of the stonework and the graves set into the overgrown floor. 1/60 sec. at *f*/16 on Plus-X with a yellow filter.

INDEX